Negotiating Gendered Identities at Work

Other books by the authors

GENDER, POWER AND ORGANISATIONS
Susan Halford and Pauline Leonard

GENDER, CAREERS AND ORGANISATIONS
Susan Halford, Mike Savage and Ann Witz

Negotiating Gendered Identities at Work

Place, Space and Time

Susan Halford and Pauline Leonard
University of Southampton

First published 2006 by
PALGRAVE MACMILLAN
Houndmills, Basingstoke, Hampshire RG21 6XS and
175 Fifth Avenue, New York, N.Y. 10010
Companies and representatives throughout the world

PALGRAVE MACMILLAN is the global academic imprint of the Palgrave Macmillan division of St. Martin's Press, LLC and of Palgrave Macmillan Ltd. Macmillan® is a registered trademark in the United States, United Kingdom and other countries. Palgrave is a registered trademark in the European Union and other countries.

ISBN 13: 978–1–4039–4112–1   hardback
ISBN 10: 1–4039–4112–2   hardback

This book is printed on paper suitable for recycling and made from fully managed and sustained forest sources.

A catalogue record for this book is available from the British Library.

Library of Congress Cataloging-in-Publication Data
Halford, Susan.
    Negotiating gendered identities at work : place, space, and time / Susan Halford and Pauline Leonard.
        p. cm.
    Based on an empirical study of identity making by doctors and nurses working in British National Health Service hospitals.
    Includes bibliographical references and index.
    ISBN 1–4039–4112–2
        1. Sex role in the work environment–Case studies. 2. Gender identity–Case studies. 3. Spatial behavior–Case studies. 4. Time–Social aspects–Case studies. 5. Identity (Psychology)–Social aspects–Case studies. 6. Hospitals–Staff–Case studies. I. Leonard, Pauline, 1957– II. Title.
    HD6060.6.H353 2006
    306.3'615–dc22   2005058982

10 9 8 7 6 5 4 3 2 1
15 14 13 12 11 10 09 08 07 06

Printed and bound in Great Britain by
Antony Rowe Ltd, Chippenham and Eastbourne

To Jon Clark: a friend and inspiration,
To John Holden: a father who always believed I could.

Contents

Preface

Issues of identity and change are at present of deep concern to many of us, both at work and in our non-working lives. Questions as to who we are, or who we might be, enter our daily lives at many different levels. As individuals, and media consumers, we are constantly encouraged to think about and perhaps work upon our personal identities, as social and cultural processes emphasize constant self-evaluation and change. As citizens, many of us have argued for recognition and acceptance of our different identities in terms of our rights and ability to live our lives in different ways. As workers, many of us have been subjected to dramatic redefinitions of our professional and working identities in recent years, such that what it means to be, for example, a teacher, doctor, bank clerk, shop assistant or engineer has changed in both performance and perception. In academia, of course, there has been sustained and sometimes heated debate in the arts and social sciences on issues of personal identity: what it is, where it comes from, and whether or not, or how, it changes. It would appear that identity, in this period of late modernity in which we all live, is both of real personal and practical interest, as well intellectual and theoretical concern.

This book is about identity at all of these levels of interest, through the prism of gender identities at work. At one level, it tells personal stories about a very particular group of people working in two organizations in the South of England with whom we did some research. They are some 50 doctors and nurses working in hospitals that are both involved in substantial organizational and professional changes. Through a detailed ethnographic exploration of the doctors' and nurses' daily working lives, and the hospitals in which they work, we examine the ways in which the various members of each organization make and perform their personal identities at work, and in the interplay with home. We look at the pressures on them to construct certain types of identities as a result of the ongoing cultural and discursive changes in their organizations and professions. We examine closely the distinctive and multiple ways in which each person responds to these, how they carve themselves out in particular ways in their different and distinctive organizational situations.

In particular this is a book about gendered identities. In the stories of our doctors and nurses, it was clear that gender is (still) ever present: explicitly drawn upon as a resource in the construction of people's identities or implicit behind the talk about their organization, profession and domestic arrangements, and the consequent opportunities and constraints they felt in their lives. It clearly mattered whether we were talking to a man or a woman – gender was no mere backdrop to their lives and the ways they saw themselves. It was an intrinsic part of the broad social and organizational landscape, which they had to negotiate on a daily basis. But these landscapes were complex, differentiated and unequal: and as such gender was interwoven with other constraints and opportunities in the making of selves and lives. Our book is, then, about negotiating gendered identities at work in a double sense: as women and men negotiate the gendered pressures on them to be certain types of people, they must also, negotiate individual identities for themselves.

Tracing the dynamics of identity from this perspective requires close attention to the intricacies of these every day working lives. But, the detail of these stories and biographies is not only interesting from the micro-processual insight it gives us into gender and identity-making, and the personal lessons that we may learn from looking at the lives of others. We also develop theoretical understanding of identity at a more abstract level. The stories we tell indicate the complexities of the processes of identity-making at work, the subtlety of the interplay of identity-resources which are drawn upon in this process, the diversity between people, as well as of the intricacy of the power relationships between organization and employee.

The book is about personal identity in another sense too. As its researchers and writers, our identities have, of course, been very much involved in the process at every stage. The research originated, quite a few years ago, from personal and academic concerns with the fact that 'identity' was a highly contested concept in theoretical terms, but very little empirical research existed to explore these rather abstract understandings. We wanted to start to redress this imbalance by designing a research project that focussed quite directly on processes of identity making and performance.

This book is about the research study, but at the same time of course, it is also more than this. It is about our identities as researchers doing the research. We want at all times to acknowledge our own presence in both the ethnographic study we undertook in the hospitals and in the ideas we discuss in this book. As a result, we have not kept ourselves out of the text, or attempted to write in an impersonal or 'objective' style. Throughout the book, we make use of our observations and feelings, and each chapter contains 'vignettes' which acknowledge and record the ways in which we were embedded in the practical process of doing research, and the differing experiences we each had. At many times, our professional work identities were questioned too, by either the doctors or nurses we were talking to, or by us as we negotiated ourselves through the research. Sometimes we found the research – and our role as academics – quite difficult to justify: here was someone breaking off from heart surgery to talk to us, there was someone asking us to move out of the way so that they could manoeuvre the crash-paddle machine around us. Whilst at times we felt belittled by what we were doing, at other times we found ourselves treated as important 'management consultants' who were going to sort out the pressures on the nursing staff – something that also made us feel as if we had been got 'slightly wrong'! Further, as two women researchers, we were also often reminded of our gender as an aspect of the research process, and the subsequent negotiation of our identities and interpersonal relations that this involved. Some of the male consultants and senior registrars treated us in a similar way to the female nurses they worked with – at times we too felt slightly patronized and sexualized. Female nurses and sisters regularly responded to us as confidantes, sharing mutual experiences and understandings about such aspects as combining childcare responsibilities, pregnancy and birth, or some of the difficulties of working with 'bitchy bosses'. This only served to reinforce our awareness of the ever-present aspect of gender in hospital and organizational life. In spite of these juxtapositions of our identities, we each became totally involved in what was starting to feel like a new set of workplaces. The quite different spatial and temporal experiences that the research sites offered added to these new performances of ourselves. Whilst the windswept South coast was battering Susan, Pauline might be negotiating through the manicured landscapes of business park-land. The architecture of each hospital started to feel welcoming and familiar. We came to enjoy meeting in 'Daphne's', the sixties-style café in one of our hospitals for coffee and a chat with the head cook. Night shifts too were an eye-opener: at 3a.m. in the morning, one of us was having tea, biscuits and a cosy gossip with the night staff of a geriatric ward, the other was sharing sausage sandwiches and a joke-swapping session with the doctors in A and E. Our working lives at Southampton often felt a long way away.

Getting to know the places, spaces and times of our doctors' and snurses' lives was crucial to understanding their worlds of work and how they were in them. We needed not only to *talk* to them about their work but to see them in it – *being* doctors and nurses. What were they like at 2 o'clock in the morning and was that any different from 2 o'clock in the afternoon? The participants in our research were all doctors and nurses: but how much did it matter whether they were in one town or another? One hospital or another? One ward or another? Or on a night shift or a day shift?

This book will reveal that it did and does matter, and that a knowledge of place, space and time enables a distinctive approach to analysing and understanding processes of identity-making in work organizations. This is at once about both the personal and the particular, for it is through a focus on the mundane, everyday routines of lives, set as they are in the particular landscapes of work organizations, that broader theoretical questions of identity may be addressed.

Acknowledgements

Creating this book has been a challenging process: exciting, exhilarating and exasperating. Not to mention taking a long time. Ultimately we are responsible for its flaws and imperfections, and we are only too aware of these. But we are indebted to many people and organizations, in many different ways for their support. Without ESRC funding, the research which underpins this book could not have begun. We are grateful too for ESRC support through maternity leave for both of us, despite the incredulity of some in academia that such a thing should be allowed! But without the help and enthusiasm of the managers, doctors and nurses in each of our two hospitals nothing could have happened next. We were amazed, invigorated and touched by the interest that was shown in our research – at least by enough people at each hospital – and by the resources that they made available to us. We are grateful too to the British Medical Association for their interest in our research, and for the fascinating, if truncated, study of race and racism in medicine that began from our shared interests. The encouragement of the Royal College of Nursing Institute at Oxford was heartwarming. Earlier versions of the work in this book have been presented at meetings of the International Sociology Association, The Institute of British Geographers, The Association of American Geographers, the British Sociological Association, and at the Gender, Work and Organization conferences and we are grateful to members of these audiences for their feedback and suggestions, many of which have made their way into this book in one form or another. We would also like to thank our colleagues at Southampton for providing an interesting, lively and dynamic context for our research.

Finally, Susan would like thank Dave Laflin, for his unwavering belief, Alice and Esme for their healthy perspective on life and colleagues at NORUT Social Science in Tromsø, Norway, especially Ann Therese Lotherington, for providing a welcoming home in the last stages of writing this book. Pauline would like to thank Guy for his real interest and continuous support, and William, Frances, Edward and Emily for their patience when 'mum is in her study' – and their ability to get her out of it. Badger and Molly have also provided amazing stress counseling.

1
Introduction

The starting point for this book was a desire to open up our understanding of the relations between gendered organizations and personal identities: to explore the effects of gendered organizational life on our sense of who we are and how we live our lives. This book is at once, then, a book about both the large and the small, about the social and the individual and about the relationships between the two. Indeed, to be interested in identity is to take on one of the central preoccupations of social science, the nature of the relationship between people and their social world. It was changing ways of thinking about this relationship that launched us, quite a few years ago, on the theoretical and empirical enquiries that underpin this book. At that time, the notion that individual identity could simply be read off from social-structural location was being replaced by the concept of subjectivity within which it was argued that multiple and competing discursive constructions of who we could be would play themselves out between and within individuals. Work in this area was suggestive of the complexities involved in the construction of identity and highlighted the potential for differences *between* individuals in previously accepted social structural categories, such as man/woman or black/ white, as well as *within* individuals themselves as they encountered a range of discursive possibilities. These theoretical developments around gender, as well as race and sexuality, stressed the fragmentary and fluid nature of subjectivities as we move through time and space, insisting that identities are constructed by, and embedded in, the different places, spaces and times of particular lives.

This book picks up these theoretical debates through a new study of gender identities at work. Throughout, our aim is to extend our understanding of the relations between gendered organizations and working selves. We approach this by drawing on a range of theoretical materials, from within and beyond organizational sociology, and engaging these theories and concepts with a new empirical study of identity-making by doctors and nurses working in British National Health Service hospitals. In this book we trace the configurations of gender that position women and men in our organizations: the gendered discursive, textual and material contexts of our doctors and nurses working lives. At the same time, we endeavour to explore how these women and men position themselves in relation to these configurations and – precisely in the practices of doing so – contribute to the making and remaking of gendered organizations, in repetitive as well as changing ways. Our aim is to explore these processes in fine detail. Through this study we open up the complexity and diversity of women's and men's working identities as they are negotiated in particular spatial and temporal contexts. We hope to bring these contexts and the identities that are negotiated within them to life: to present a richly textured account of the places, spaces and times within which complex and dynamic gendered working identities are negotiated. First however, this chapter clears some theoretical ground, taking an overview of contemporary approaches to gender, identity and organization; raising the questions that arise from this; and outlining the theoretical framework that we use to approach these throughout the remainder of the book.

Approaches to gender, identity and organization

It has now been well established that gender has an integral relationship with work and organizations: that the social practices generally understood to constitute work organizations in the modern Western world rest on gendered discourses and assumptions (Acker 1990; Savage and Witz 1992; Alvesson and due Billing 1997; Halford and Leonard 2001). Gender is embedded in organizational structures, through the design of work organizations, for instance in job-grading, career ladders and methods of recruitment and selection, which have been shown to privilege those skills and work histories that are typically associated with male workers (Halford and Leonard 2001).

Gender is also central to both the rationale of organization and to lived organizational cultures. As Pringle (1988) amongst others has noted, the bureaucratic form of organization that is virtually synonymous with work organization in the modern Western world should be read as a commentary on a particular form of masculinity, based on an instrumental rationality which excludes the personal, sexual and feminine. Whilst this is an ideal-type construction of how organizations work, and widely refuted, it nonetheless presents a powerful discourse of how 'efficient' and 'effective' work organizations should operate. In empirical studies of gender and work we see a raft of other ways in which the everyday life of organizations is gendered. Amongst other channels, gendered hierarchies and understandings operate through communication and language, imagery, the deliberate construction of cultural values and representations of the organization through 'mission statements' (Halford and Leonard 2001). In sum, bureaucratic organization is a socially situated practice that draws on gendered assumptions and practices in its design and operation – it operates with a gendered substructure (Acker 1992).

In the National Health Service, this picture of the gendered bureaucratic organization is further complicated by the presence of powerful professional groups. (See Chapter 2 for an extended discussion of the following summary). Indeed, much of the debate about the organization and running of the National Health Service over the past 20 years has concerned the relative power of bureaucratic and professional frameworks and decision makers. Throughout their historical development both medicine and nursing have been interwoven with particular understandings of gender, indeed of the gendering of each profession. Simply put, the origins of the modern medical profession is closely tied to a scientific, detached and emotionally cool masculinity whilst nursing is closely tied to a caring, other-orientated femininity. Of course, the gendering of both professions is historically dynamic, and has been contested *within* the professions in a variety of ways but, nonetheless, gender remains a central feature in the construction of both professions today. Over the past 20 years, the medical and nursing professions have also faced a significant challenge from *outside* of their ranks as new forms of managerialism have become ascendant in the National Health Service. Whilst once healthcare was run according to professional discourse, the introduction of a thorough system of general management has privileged bureaucratic systems and discourse (Exworthy and Halford 1999) which, as we have seen above, has been strongly associated with particular accounts of masculinity. So, in the case of medicine and nursing in the National Health Service, gender is embedded in everyday organizational life in multiple and competing ways, through diverse mechanisms. Our question is: what are the effects of these gendered configurations on women's and men's sense of self as they go about their work?

The sociology of gender and organizations offers us an historical archive of answers, embedded in the frameworks of their ancestry and in their particular temporal contexts. Tracing these debates over time explains the context in which we developed our approach to gender, identity and organization. In early accounts of gender and organization the question of identity remained largely implicit, although firm assumptions were made. For writers influenced by liberal feminism, an essentially un-gendered self was distorted by the unequal treatment of women and men at work, such that they might internalize these gendered attributes and articulate them as their sense of self (Kanter 1977). Meanwhile, for those more influenced by radical feminist thinking, deeply gendered selves (perhaps even essentially gendered selves) were either affirmed – for men – or denied – for women, in work organizations that were made in the image of masculinity (Ferguson 1984; Marshall 1984). Put simply then these accounts rested on a liberal-humanist conceptualization of the self, in which relatively fixed and coherent selves were seen to stand in particular relations to gendered organizations.

From the late 1980s onwards this conceptualization of identity in work on gender and organizations became increasingly untenable. Debates in feminist theory more widely questioned the univeralism that was inherent in this type of account, pointing to the profound differences between women and between men, generated – at least – by class, sexuality and race. No longer was it possible to speak of 'woman' and 'man' as if we knew what that meant in terms of an individuals' identity. At the very least, we would need multiple categories that took class, sexuality and race into account. Beyond this, however, the more through-going critique that poststructuralist-influenced accounts made of earlier renditions of relations between gender, identity and organization provoked a more fundamental re-think. Following Foucault, poststructuralism denies an essential human and/or gender identity, turning instead to the concept of subjectivity. Rather than focussing on women's and men's working lives, the attention is to constructions of gender in organizational discourse. Here, the theoretical argument is made that organizational discourse operates as a powerful set of ideas and frameworks which draw the boundaries for the working self. Particular categories of person and criteria for their identity (Rorty 1988) are presented in organizational discourse. Through processes of self-surveillance and self-discipline the working subject is produced (Rose 1989; du Gay and Salaman 1992; Casey 1995). Workers are literally subjected – made subject – through these discourses. Tracing the gendered dynamics of these processes, it has been widely argued that the bureau-cratic and managerial discourses which dominate organizational life privilege a particular masculine subject position (Kerfoot and Knights 1993; Collinson and Hearn 1996; Kerfoot and Knights 1996; Halford, Savage and Witz 1997; McDowell 1997). Here the masculine subject is characterized as 'carving up the social and organizational world into a series of projects' (Kerfoot and Knights 1996: 92) with an underpinning orientation of control and the instrumental use of others. In general terms, this is understood as 'disembodied, self-estranged and socially disengaged' (Kerfoot and Knights 1996: 92). In more specific terms, it has been shown that this masculine subject is historically dynamic, shifting in recent times from the sober, authoritarian patriarch to the risk-taking, go-getting entrepreneur (Kerfoot and Knights 1996; Halford, Savage and Witz 1997; McDowell 1997). Conversely, femininity has been excluded from the most privileged organizational constructions of the working self. Instead, discourses of the feminine working self – as 'other' orientated, caring, and more motivated by family than career offer a ubiquitous and clearly subordinate alternative, as do representa-tions of career-orientated women as bitchy, bossy and unfeminine (Pringle 1988).

This poststructural approach marked a significant step forward in thinking about the gendered self at work. Critically, it insists that we move beyond essentialism and universalism. Subjectivities are multi-ple, competing, and in an uncertain relation to actual selves, to the sense(s) of self that individual women and men may have in any given place, space or time. However, initially this approach left open the question of how these gendered representations of the working self are related to the selves of women and men working in gendered organiza-tions. As Hall (2000) explains, more generally, whilst this approach offers us 'a formal account of the construction of subject positions within discourse' it reveals rather little about how 'certain individuals occupy some subject positions rather than others' (Hall 2000: 23). At a theoretical level the answer to this hinges on the question of power. Sometimes it was argued that organizational discourses are so powerful that gender identities are '...written onto living bodies much like com-memorations on the gravestones of the dead' (Kerfoot and Knights 1996: 85). However, this type of approach has been criticized for down-playing the agential subject (Benhabib 1992) and failing to address the ways that people resist, manoeuvre and play with discursive practices (Iedema and Wodak 1999; Newton 1999). Endorsing this precisely, in other formulations of the theoretical argument about gender and organizations it was suggested that women and men were active in positioning themselves between competing discourses, rather than simply being subjected by them.

Following this, recent empirical work in organizational sociology is suggestive. In particular, there has been a raft of recent studies which show that individuals are active agents in their responses to gendered organizational discourses (Halford and Savage 1997; Leonard 1998; Strangleman and Roberts 1999; Whitehead 2001; Thomas and Davies 2002). Specifically, in response to managerially imposed discourses of the entrepreneurial self it has been shown that individuals, both women and men, use competing discourses, from within and beyond organizational life, to take up distinctive positions along an axis from acceptance, via modification, to resistance. Whitehead (2001), for example, found that women managers in his study of managerial change in Further Education draw on representations of femininity to challenge newly emergent subject positions based on discourses of effectiveness and efficiency, closely tied to masculinity. Their responses were diverse. Whilst some established competing identities based on feminized notions of being 'relational' and 'inclusive' in their managerial style, others were effectively able to draw on masculine-style performances at work as a direct contrast to the identities they were expected to perform in other aspects of their life. Clearly the imposition of this particular discursive identity of entrepreneurialism did not run smoothly and nor did it operate in isolation but rather in articulation with other competing discursive constructions of subjectivity, that were used in creative ways.

Similarly, Linda McDowell's (1997) study of merchant banking showed the care with which women and men positioned themselves at work. Women and men working in merchant banking were clearly constrained by particular constructions of masculinity in this type of work in the performance of their work identities. On the trading floor, the supreme trader is male, young, and aggressively heterosexual. Indeed, the job of trading involves an exaggerated performance of this hegemonic masculinity, including boasting of sexual exploits, harassing women traders 'for a laugh' (as has been the subject of recent press interest) and even booking female strippers to perform on the trading floor. Their language reinforces this performance, with heavily sexualized metaphors being used to describe both the work and those successful at it: 'big swinging dick' is one such term. McDowell suggests that individuals do not simply acquire the identity they are required to perform in the workplace, but are active agents in the orchestration and presentation of these performances. This is illustrated by the performances of older women, who found that they could mobilize parodic versions of femininity, including the stage-managed use of clothes and make up as well as body language and behaviour, to confer career advantages.

These studies of the gendered self at work clearly tell us that people *respond* to particular gendered organizational discourses, that they accept, modify and resist. The trajectory of debates about gender, identity and organization has moved from an essentialized identity, where women and men were simply assumed to bear particular identities by virtue of their sex; to subjectivity, which concentrated on reading textual and discursive representations of feminine and masculine subject positions; and on to a new concern with identities, in which individuals are active agents who negotiate their selves from a range of available textual, discursive and material resources. It is here that we enter the debate. We argue that gender is still an important aspect of this negotiation process, and that we must be careful not to lose sight of the broad persistence of inequities that women continue to face. Penetrating the *range* and *limits* of 'available textual, discursive and material resources' is crucial to our understanding of how gender, organization and identity work in practice. We need to understand therefore more fully the constraints on the availability of resources which each and every individual may draw upon. Are these different for women and men, and if so, how? Are opportunities to exercise agency within and against these equally available? In order to develop this sort of full and nuanced picture, we need to get particular. We need to look closely at the places, spaces and times of work in which these actual processes of identity-negotiation take place. In the following sections therefore we outline our framework for exploring these processes in organizations. To do this, we argue, we must cast our net wider, and borrow from debates beyond the specific study of gender and organization.

Negotiating gendered identities

In this book we understand that our identities and our own sense of ourselves are continually emerging through what we feel and do and say. Unlike earlier accounts of identity, there is no 'real' self, outside of this. But through our repeated and continual doing of identity, 'the active, productive and continual weaving of bits and pieces' (Harrison 2000: 502), a *contingent* sense of self emerges. Re-phrasing this specifically in relation to *gender*, it is through the continual inscription and re-iteration of symbolic norms of gender in everyday life that a 'gender identity effect' (Campbell and Harbord 1999: 229) is created. Thus, whilst we are subjected to the possibilities of how we can be as gendered individuals; our constant doing of gendered subjectivities generates a sense of self, which can be used to exercise the agency to negotiate between subjectivities. As Thrift and Dewsbury (2000) claim 'the very same process of inscription enables the formation of a subject' (Thrift and Dewsbury 2000: 412) that is capable of exercising agency: '[t]he subject is formed in submission then but cannot be reduced to that submission' (Thrift and Dewsbury 2000: 412). Certainly, we cannot stand outside of the discursive, structural and material forces that determine the parameters and possibilities of agency, but the articulation of these discourses at the level of the subject requires a certain degree of individual agency, the *negotiation* of identities from the available discourses. As Weedon (1997) writes of the gendered subject s/he

> exists as a thinking, feeling subject and social agent, capable of resistance and innovations produced out of the clash between contradictory subject positions and practices (1997: 6)

This draws our attention to the *ongoing* nature of negotiation. As Jenkins (2004) argues,

> Too much contemporary writing about identity treats it as some-*thing* that simply *is*. This pays insufficient attention to how identity 'works' or 'is worked', to process and reflexivity, to the social construction of identity in interaction and institutionally. Indeed, identity can only be understood as process, as 'being' or 'becoming'. One's identity – one's identities indeed, for who we are is always singular and plural – is never a final and settled matter (Jenkins 2004: 5).

Gender identities have to be constantly 'reaffirmed and publicly displayed by repeatedly performing particular acts in accordance with cultural norms...which define masculinity and femininity' (Cameron 1997: 49). The performances may be repetitive or disjointed, identities may appear stable or be fragmented but, whatever, the negotiation of identity is ceaseless, it never stops. The process of 'identity-making' is a continually ongoing one, for identity can never be fixed and finished, once and for all. We are always still becoming.

Where does this general proposition lead us in thinking specifically about gender and organizations? As we come to work, and go about our work, we have always already engaged in the production of an identity and sense of self (Odih 1999). This comes from our own biographies, our previous negotiations with gender, class, race, sexuality as well less social-structural resources for the self, ideas of personality for example as fun or reliable or grumpy. As we enter work organizations we encounter a further (and related) range of textual, discursive and material possibilities for the negotiation of self. Whilst many of these can be read as gendered, we cannot expect that all will have gender at their core. Gender identities are negotiated in a 'web' of social practices, which are not necessarily gendered (McNay 1999). If we are concerned with identities empirically, it is difficult, perhaps pointless, to seek to isolate gender from other practices of identity (Alvesson and due Billing 1997). In the making of identities, gender may not be at the forefront of our awareness all the time (Bradley 1996) but is woven in and out of both the fabric of working selves and the agentic process of making the self. This is not to downplay gender. Not at all. But it is to recognize the way that gender identities are lived and to take this seriously in theoretical terms. Gender is a key resource, which people *may* or may *not* make relevant in their articulation of their own and others' identities. Gender is fluid, dynamic, complex and subtle: sometimes of importance, sometimes not. In the ways in which it intersects with other aspects of identity, including race, class, ethnicity, age, sexuality and physical ability it is able to produce multiple differences between women and men's identities.

Thus, the negotiation of our identities is an everyday process created and recreated through the routines, activities and practices of our daily lives (Crossley 1994). Identities are negotiated in the 'homeward trudge of daily existence', 'the dull routine, the on-going, go-to-work, pay the bills' routine and ordinariness of the everyday (Lefebvre 1994) as well as the big events of our lives. To talk of 'negotiating the self' is thus to convey the broad interpretation of these processes that we take – negotiating here is not only about what people *say* but also what they *do*. It is also about *where* they do it and *when* they do it. Identities are done in a variety of ways: through speech, talk and narrative, through body and performance, dress and appearance, as well as through thought and memory. Identities can be displayed and performed in many ways. We thus need not only to listen to people's talk, but also to capture the complexity of the contexts within which they live of their working lives: how they move their bodies through the places, spaces and times of their work;

where they go, when and why. We are not talking here in merely abstract terms: negotiation takes place in the very active details of the places, spaces and times in which our lives are lived, which mean that we are produced, and produce ourselves in particular ways. Individuals exercise agency in their negotiation of identities, but the capacity of a person to be active and creative *depends* upon the resources, 'habitus' in Bourdieu's terms, which he or she has. Identities are actively negotiated in fluid and unpredictable ways, but they are also situationally contingent (Barth 1981). The context provides the resources through which identities can be negotiated.

We argue then that it is only through attention to these contexts that we can fully explore the relations between gender, identity and organization. The multiplicity of these contexts and the resources they offer enable women and men to position themselves, and be positioned in multiple ways – but that is not of course to say that they are *equivalently* positioned, or that they have equivalent opportunity to position themselves. We must not lose sight of the importance of power, and the presence of unequal power relations in these negotiation processes. The pervasiveness of discourses and resources constructed through and built upon gender differentiation means that despite 'breakthrough moments of resistance and empowerment' (Baxter 2003) or even instances where gender is felt to be invisible, an imbalance of power and opportunity is likely to be ever present.

Identities in place, space and time

In this book, we approach the analysis of context through the concepts of 'place', 'space' and 'time'. We want to develop these categories, to situate both individual women and men and particular work organizations in context: to explore the gendering of individuals and organizations in place, space and time. As individuals engage in the negotiation of identities, they do so in the contexts of their everyday lives: as they move between the spaces of their work, between the places of work and home and through different times of the day and night. These shifting contexts provide a range of resources through which gendered selves may be negotiated. Similarly, the organizational context is shaped by both time and space. It is not simply that organizational discourses may change over time or that one organization may be different from another. Rather, as we explain below, organizations are complex formations of different spatial and temporal relations. The implication of this is that the places, spaces and times of organizational life offer multiple and competing resources which are negotiated by individuals as they construct and perform their working identities. In the ways that not only organizational spaces, but also places and times are invested with particular meanings, they interplay with the discursive and material conditions in which we are situated. Whilst this complexity means that place, space and time are integrally interwoven with one another, we now consider each in turn in order to develop our discussion more fully.

Place and space

> Class, gender and race have so often been treated as if they happen on the head of a pin. Well they don't – they happen in space and place (Cresswell 2004: 27)

Gendered organizations and working selves are constituted in particular places and spaces and, themselves, contribute to the construction of those places and spaces. Even in the days of globalization and cyberspace, organizations are (usually) situated somewhere and these 'local attachments' remain significant (McDowell 1999). Similarly, organizations themselves are complex combinations of different and distinctive spaces, from the boardroom to the cloakroom, offices, to corridors and receptions. It is our argument in this book that identities are not simply negotiated *in* these places and spaces. Place and space do not merely provide a backdrop for the negotiation of individual identities but are both central resources in the construction of working selves (Lefebvre 1991; Keith and Pile 1993; Soja 1996) *and* are made and re-made through these on-going negotiations of self. In short, people make places and spaces, and these places and spaces make people.

Contemporary Geographical understandings of 'place' stress that the grounded locales of everyday life are produced by a range of social, economic and cultural processes from the very local to the global (Massey 1994; Cresswell 2004). It is the on-going and dynamic articulation of these processes in particular locales, the 'constellation of processes' (Massey 2005: 141) that produces 'place'. Thus to think of work organizations as work *places* is to make links to the range of spatial relationships that constitute them: to connect organizations with their locale and with the national and international relations that contribute to making them. What then is the significance of this for constructions and negotiations of gendered selves at work? It is to recognize that the gendering of organizational workplaces is the ongoing and complex interplay of relations operating at a range of spatial scales. It is to bring together gendering dynamics operating at the general as well as the particular level and to recognize the complexity of the gender constellations that come together in place. It is – in part – through our engagement with these places that gender identities are negotiated, and it is – in part – through this negotiation that places are made and re-made. Whilst on the one hand, we have to negotiate places in order to live our daily lives, the given aspects of 'the walls, doors, windows, and spaces of flow....' (Cresswell 2004: 35), at the same time places are never fixed and finished, but always ongoing through processes and practices. Thus although we live and work in places that come pre-structured – embedded with particular interests in the context of unequal power relations – these places are not operational without practice in them (Creswell 2004; De Certeau 1984). Place is thus interesting in terms of the macro processes of structure and discourse through which it may subject people, as well as at the micro level of the individual biographies of the people negotiating it. At both levels however, it has to be constituted and reconstituted through reiterative social practice: made and re-made on a daily basis (Cresswell 2004). This is then a non-essentialist and dynamic understanding of place, (rather than a notion of 'preconstructed' space (cf. Bourdieu)) in which places 'take shape only in their passing' (Thrift 1999: 310). To think of it in this way is also to see place as part of an agentic identity-making process: 'the raw material for the creative production of identity', and one which 'provides the conditions of possibility for creative social practice', 'marked by openness and change rather than bounded-ness and permanence' (Cresswell 2004: 39). It follows, therefore, that we would not expect to find singular presentations of particular places in empirical accounts of the relations between workplace and self. Rather we fully expect to find multiple meanings, and hope to trace these as they are used in the negotiation of working selves.

Connected to this, we cannot see workplaces as homogenous spaces. We must recognize that organizations are not only places but are also made up of complex configurations of multiple, distinctive and differentiated spaces, each offering different potentials for the negotiation of gender identities. Like workplaces, these organizational spaces 'embody gender attributes' (McDowell 1999: 144), bearing the weight of past associations with particular genderings, as masculine spaces/feminine spaces or associated with particular gender performances. In the course of our daily working lives, we journey continuously through this organizational patchwork of spaces. Some of these organizational spaces are appropriated by management for particular purposes, as architecture and décor are used to communicate messages about status or service. These may make workers feel more or less uncomfortable facilitating or constraining the performance of certain identities (Crang 1994). Spaces are thus often physical representations of discursive constructions, enabling semiotic readings of phases in the life of an organization. However, as with place, there is no envelope or pre-given context of space (Glucksmann 2000), into which people are fitted. Rather it is the ongoing arrangement of spaces and relations within them which are important. People interact with and in space and as such it is always productive. In this formulation, drawing on the work of Lefebvre, space both creates *and* is created by human agency (Knowles 2000). Following Lefebvre, Massey (1994) has shown that spatial organization makes a real difference to how a society works and changes. It has 'causal effectivity' (Massey 1994: 255) in the intersection of configured social relations and processes of identity-making. As such, it deserves our full attention.

Time

Attention to the temporal context of working lives immediately insists that we recognize the multiplicity of times implicated in negotiations of the working self. Certainly clock time dominates our understandings of time in the West, and especially in work organizations, and in this domination it is enormously significant not least for the gendering of organizations. For clock time has been strongly tied to dominant accounts of masculinity as rational, controlled and linear (Odih 1999): this construction of time contributes centrally to constructions of 'organizational man' and vice versa. Conversely, feminine time has been represented in terms of caring, other-oriented time, not bound by clock watching, mechanistic time but process-driven and on-going (Odih 1999). Exploring the implication of organizational temporalities for the negotiation of gender identities means investigating the significance of these binary gendered conceptualizations of time, as well as other notions of time, such as lifetimes, body time, and timing and rhythm. Within particular organizations, these temporalities are constructed in potentially distinctive and iterative ways across our understandings of the past, the present and the future (Adam 1995). Gendered organizations are constructed through these multiple and simultaneous times through their pasts and their projections of the future, as well as their presents. In the organization of work, organizations organize, and are subjected to, temporal demands and routines, which can create multiple timescales and differing dimensions for employees. The differing ways in which personal shift-work and time-sheets, production and delivery times, seasonal rhythms and global market demands are constructed may create very differing, and unequal, experiences within which working identities may be made and performed. (Whipp, Adam and Sabelis 2002). The reorganization of time is often central to the organizational change, whether in changes to working practices or timescales for organizational goals and personal careers. This may impact on women and men in different ways.

Changes may also occur over time, within the life course of an individual, and these too are gendered. Adam's (1995) ideas on the multiplicity of time are particularly relevant here. She explains how different aspects and conceptual understandings of time can be *simultaneously* experienced and constituted. The clock time of work schedules, for example, are constantly challenged and undermined by other, non-commodified times. Responsibilities at different stages of life may mean that time is also to be spent in caring activities, for young, old, or relatives with needs. Many men and women also give time to expressive and creative purposes: sports, hobbies and interests. Simultaneous with all of these aspects is the presence of memory, and memories of the past may include yet another, different relationship to time, and impact on our relation to the present and future. Future plans or ambitions may indeed also compete with or even overshadow present relationships to time (Adam 1995). Time too is thus a multiple and complex resource, which may be performed, used and understood in different ways: and often simultaneously.

Negotiating identities in gendered organizations

This book is about the gendering of organizations and identities in place, space and time. It is an exploration of the gendered resources of organizational landscapes and timescapes (Keenoy and Oswick 2003) and the negotiations of self that women and men make with these. We want to explore the ways that identities are made from particular resources as they are continually constituted in space and time (Pile and Thrift 1995: 29). Different places, spaces and times offer distinctive opportunities and constraints in the making of different kinds of lives and subjectivities (Hacking 1986). This book then is about social structures and the exercise of agency: the discursive power of organizations to change us, the very ways in which we may think, act and understand ourselves and others; and the power of employees to resist such organizational attempts at our identities. It is about the texture of our working lives, and how we negotiate our selves through the gender configurations of which we are a part. Through our empirical work we aim to add detail to our understanding of these processes. However, this is not to claim that we should merely explore the 'playing out' of discursive subjectivities in the workplace. Rather we aim to show that that in the tracing of these negotiations our understanding of these gendered organizations is transformed. Gendered organizations and gendered identities are continuously made and re-made, but how this is done is in the particular context, in its places, spaces and times. Therefore this context does not simply offer an illustration of already constituted processes or identities. It is *integral to* these processes and identities. In this we are arguing that our theoretical as well as our empirical understanding of gendered organizations, gendered identities and the relations between them *must* acknowledge the centrality of particular spatialities and temporalities. These cannot be an illustration of abstract theoretical accounts, but must be central to the very conceptualization of these accounts.

In the rest of this book we explore these arguments further, using both theoretical and empirical resources. Following our insistence on situating research in the particularities of specific organizations, Chapter 2 begins this task with an extended account of the specific constructions of gender within medicine, nursing and the National Health Service. Chapter 3 offers a detailed methodological account of our approach to researching identities, beginning with an explanation of comparative methodology and an introduction to the specific hospitals where we conducted our research. This chapter also explores contemporary debates about how to research identities and explains our methods in more detail, linked to our concern with both the said and the unsaid, what people do, how they do it, where and when, as well as what they say about this in interviews.

Following this extended introduction, each of Chapters 4 to 7 presents the substantive empirical material from our research. Each chapter is led by the exploration of a key concept: place, space, everyday time and lifetime respectively. Each chapter begins with an overview of contemporary theoretical thinking about this key concept, explaining what it offers our understanding of gender, identity and organization and how we use the concept to approach the empirical material from our study. The empirical sections that follow use these theoretical insights to analyse negotiations of gendered selves at work made by the doctors and nurses working at our two case study hospitals.

In more detail then, Chapter 4 draws on geographical debates about place, to explore individual constructions of workplaces and the ways that these are used in the negotiation of selves at work. This shows how the *where* impacts on organizational configurations of gender, as well as on individual agency in the negotiation of gendered selves. This notion of workplace extends accounts of 'organizational culture' more commonly used in studies of gender, identity and organization, placing it in a wider theoretical and empirical framework. Chapter 5, turns to focus on the highly differentiated spaces within work organizations and the ways that these are conceived, perceived and lived (Lefebvre 1991). In particular we focus on embodied practice – spatial patterns and styles of comportment – in these organizational spaces of everyday life: how people use spatial resources in the construction and performance of identities and, furthermore, that identities may shift and slip as individuals move between the spaces of everyday life. This suggests that far more care must be taken in thinking about 'organization', which exists not as a abstract homogenous set of relations or processes, but is produced through embodied action in highly differentiated organizational spaces.

Chapters 6 and 7 shift our attention from space to time. Chapter 6 explores the gendering of everyday times at work, showing that conceptions of time are central to the gendering of medicine, nursing and management and the distinctions between them. However, we also argue, constructions of time are also contested within medicine, within nursing and within management, offering diversity in the opportunities and constraints for negotiating gendered selves at work. Chapter 7 shifts the focus away from everyday time to explore how women and men negotiate gendered working identities through narratives of their lifetimes. Here, in particular, are clear connections between the everyday and the broader social political and cultural contexts that shape lives and identities. Through close attention to the narratives that were presented to us, we see lifetimes as both resource and constraint in the negotiation and performance of gendered working identities.

Finally, Chapter 8 begins with an overview of the arguments that we make in this book about relations between gender, identity and organization. Specifically, we draw together the claims that are made about the continued importance of gender – in all its complexity and diversity – in the negotiation of working identities. But Chapter 8 also turns attention to one final piece of unfinished business, rarely considered in academic studies of identity: how do individuals talk about the *concept* of identity? Here we show that the different accounts of identity that are offered are *themselves* underpinned by gender, as gendered resources and constraints are used to produce distinctively gendered accounts not only of 'what I am like' but also of 'what I am'.

2
Situating Identities

Introduction

In the last chapter, we argued that identities are derived in practice: through our engagement with the resources that are available to us as we move through the times and spaces of our everyday lives. These resources may connect backwards and forward through time and space, but it is through their embodied enactment that they are brought into and taken out of use as the materials from which identities are fashioned and re-fashioned. Within this framework, this chapter begins our exploration of the working identities of doctors and nurses in the British National Health Service with an overview of the most obvious 'raw materials' on offer: professional and organizational resources. This is a key part of our research methodology: what are the available discourses for the construction of medical and nursing identities? What are doctors and nurses 'like' in abstract terms? And how/is this gendered? Understanding this was critical to our new empirical research on working identities, enabling us to be informed about the broad contexts of medical and nursing work and offering an initial framework for interpreting individual accounts of working identities.

Situating identities

In this chapter, we outline the professional and organizational resources through which doctor's and nurse's working identities may be constructed and performed. Specifically, we examine the professional resources offered by nursing and medicine and the organizational resources of the British National Health Service . Here we draw on an impressive body of previous research, which has unpicked the discursive nature of these resources and emphasized the subjective implications for doctors and nurses. This is not the place to replicate the detailed historical and textual work that has been done in these accounts and for which we are immensely grateful. Rather our intention here is to offer an overview of this literature as a step towards our central concern which is to explore the effects and the uses made of these discourses in everyday working lives. However, in doing so, we wish to highlight two important aspects that are more or less implicit in previous accounts and which we will develop further in our own empirical research. First, it is important to recognize the dynamic and uneven nature of professional and organizational resources, specifically over time and space. Whilst we can summarize existing accounts of historically-rooted professional and organizational discourses, we wish to draw particular attention to the inter-textual nature of these discourses. As new iterations of medical and organizational discourse emerge they do not simply erase and replace earlier discourses. Rather new meanings exist *through* and *alongside* older ones: building on earlier meanings or defined in contrast to them with multiple meanings jostling and competing for attention. Similarly, both professional and organizational discourses may be spatially constituted, working out distinctly in particular locales and organizations. Second, we want to draw some attention to the importance of the *material* as well as the discursive, to recognize the importance of material working practices – the tasks that doctors and nurses actually do – and the physical artifacts connected to medical, nursing and managerial work. Amongst other things buildings, uniforms, high technology equipment, bed linen or drug trolleys may all feature on the construction of 'medicine', 'nursing' and 'management, or what it means to be a doctor, a nurse or a manager. As Latour (1994) says 'objects are never just objective or neutral, they contain and reproduce … congealed labour' (p. 40): they store and activate past actions, as well as symbols and meanings and may come to carry these from their origin to other times and spaces beyond. The significance of both discursive and the material remain to be explored in our own research, but here we highlight some key points of enquiry.

Professional resources

Research into the construction of medical and nursing discourse has been strongly influenced by feminist interventions, exposing the gendered dynamics at the heart of each. It has been effectively shown that both the professions of nursing and medicine are articulated through strongly gendered discourses, with profound implications for the construction of nursing and medical work and careers. Put simply, we cannot understand nursing without also knowing that it is feminized or medicine without also knowing its masculinized history. Furthermore, we gain greater insight into the construction and meanings of nursing and medical discourse once we recognize that these have developed in relation to each other: they are partly responsible for making each other, as we will show below. At an abstracted level, these professional resources offer gendered subject positions, though attention to historical changes reveals their complexity. However, subject positions are not only gendered, but classed and raced too (Hallam 2000). The interplay of these dynamics is complex and defies neat historical chronologies. Whilst there have clearly been historical shifts, medicine and nursing do not offer monolithic or static resources of identity, but multiple and even competing resources within their own professional boundaries and in relations between the professions.

Nursing

Contemporary nursing carries with it, in discursive and material forms, tensions that have pervaded the nursing for at least 150 years. Images of mother, whore, angel, harridan and professional are woven together across the three centuries offering complex and competing representations of what it means to be a nurse – of nursing identities. The Victorian tension between the 'harpies' of Dickens' novels – hard, cruel and morally dubious – and the selfless and virginal angels associated with Nightingale's vision of nurses persists today, in competing representations of nurses operating in the popular imagination and the mass media. At the same time, long-standing debates about whether nursing can, or indeed should, be regarded as a profession continue, unresolved in many ways, despite the professionalizing strategies of registration in the 19th century, the development of an independent 'nursing process' in the 1970s and the increasingly credentialized approaches of the 1990s and onwards (Jolley 1995; Davies 1995; Davies 2003).

These tensions have been played out in heavily gendered terms. Historically, most nurses were women. Indeed in the UK men were not permitted to register as nurses until 1949, and not actively recruited until the late 1960s. But more than this, nursing has always been linked to femininity. Hunter (1988) explains this through the domestic placing of nursing work, as women's work, tied to feminized attributes of caring, altruism and concern with bodily matters. These translate into practical and routine work tasks linked by an intimate engagement with the body and emotional concern for the mind. Jolley (1995) cites a Hospital Magazine from 1905: 'nursing is mothering' and a London Matron from 1888: 'a nurse must "never ask why", and as seldom as possible "how": be content to bear unmerited blame ... not to be surprised to find herself vehemently repressed if she ventures on the faintest suggestion, and especially if she is at all forward or clever' (Jolley 1995: 93). This echoes Victorian constructions of the binary opposition between masculinity and femininity in the household (Davies 2003), a gendered relation that was carried over into the relationship between nursing and medicine. Indeed, it has been widely argued that the submissiveness associated with nursing is central to the marking of professional boundaries with medicine and to the routine enactment of the superior status of both the medical discipline and individual doctors (Palmer 1983; Stein 1967; Porter 1995). Thus, historically, nursing work supports medical work (Davies 2003), it is not autonomous and this works thorough a profoundly gendered dynamic.

Whilst the construction of nursing is clearly gendered, Hallam (2000) shows that it is also and simultaneously classed and raced. Certainly, Nightingale's Victorian vision of nursing was centrally about re-classing nursing, shifting it away from association with working class and towards 'respectable' middle class femininity. By the 1950s, nursing represented a feminine middle class aspiration both in terms of the work and its associated identities but also in its links with medicine and the potential route that nursing offered into successful middle class marriage to a doctor (Hallam 2000). The racialization of nursing has worked historically through the channelling of non-white women into auxiliary roles, subservient not only to doctors but to more senior, white, nurses. This drew on racially specific ideologies that mark ethnic minority women as suitable only for the lowest paid and lowest status work, considered to be unskilled and, notably, the work which white women would not do (Hill-Collins 1990; Essed 1991). Thus, although the British actively recruited Caribbean women as nurses, they were explicitly restricted to State Enrolled Nurse training, not the more prestigious State Registered Nurse training. This meant that they could never expect to build hierarchical careers within the but were structurally contained in the lowest level of nursing (Bryan, Dadzie and Scafe 1985). In the 21st century, whilst black and Asian nurses account for 25% of nurses of 55 years old, they account for less than 3% of nurses under 25, leaving Christine Hancock (ex-General Secretary of the Royal College of Nursing to conclude that '[t]he younger generation has listened to the older generation's experience of racism and harassment and decided that they don't want to go through the same thing' (EOR 2000: 24). It seems that in the contemporary period, the racialization of nursing is whiter than it has been for half a century.

The feminization of nursing has meant that men entering nursing work have been treated with suspicion, centred on both their masculinity and sexuality, and regarded as either Casanovas or as homosexual (Jolley 1995; Naish 1990). Although male nurses display comparatively very high levels of career mobility (EOR 1998), overall numbers remain small, at 10% in 2002 (Nursing and Midwifery Council 2002). This is despite gender-specific recruitment campaigns offering a more masculine representation of the profession. Hallam's (2000) analysis of recruitment literature aimed specifically at men during the 1960s reveals an emphasis on technology, not caring: '[n]ever is there a suggestion that the "tender loving care" traditionally rendered at the bedside by young female nurses could also be done by men' (Hallam 2000: 115). Thus, masculinity in nursing became linked to specific forms of work, often less closely engaged with the emotional needs of patients – dealing for example with sedated patients in Theatres or life and death encounters in Emergency Departments – and frequently mediated through high technology equipment, the displacement of people with machines. By contrast, the work tasks associated with feminized nursing retain a high emotional content and a high level of routine caring tasks such as changing and bathing. The objects involved here are mundane: bed sheets, a thermometer, a bath or a dressing. Whilst, as Davies (1995) points out, these tasks and the mundane objects with which they are associated are conducive to professional nursing practice – assessing wounds, psychiatric care, and so on – both are regarded as low status and relatively unimportant.

However, from the 1970s nursing in the UK has been subject to a round of significant 'professionalizing' projects, which have attempted to carve-out an autonomous sphere for nursing that can be placed *on a par* with medicine, as part of multi-disciplinary team work rather than within a hierarchy of professions (Porter 1995). The concept of the 'nursing process' was imported from the US to refer to nursing as a therapeutic profession in its own right, rather than a system of maintenance work for doctors (Harrison and Pollit 1994). This strategy built on the relational and interpersonal aspects of nursing, re-naming these in overtly professional terms, such that the 'holistic' and 'patient-centred' contribution made by nursing came to be represented as a parallel process to medicine, making a distinctive, valuable and above all independent contribution to patient care. Alongside this, professional nursing organizations in the UK have developed credentiallizing strategies building intellectual capital and nursing theory (Porter 1995) in pursuit of a 'unique body of nursing knowledge' (Jolley 1995: 105). In 1987 the UK Central Council for Nursing, Midwifery and Health Visiting proposed Project 2000: a new system of nurse education that emphasized academic knowledge, and took early nurse training away from the wards and into University lecture theatres. In an extension of this, all nurses were required to maintain on-going portfolios of postgraduate training (Salvage 1992) and even publication. Project 2000 and the ideas associated with it represented a major shift in representations of nursing and in nursing work, to overtly include abstraction, thought, intellect and an independent contribution to medical work. Alongside this, and connected to pressure on the government to reduce junior doctors hours, nurses have increased their range of clinical competence and responsibility by taking on tasks that could formerly only be discharged by a doctor. This has expanded the objects that nurses use in their work, objects that carry the weight of medical expertise and bodily intervention, including the prescription of drugs (government targets are that 50% of nurses should be able to do this by 2004) and carrying out intravenous drugs and fluid administrations (Walby et al 1994). Lastly, nursing work has also been altered substantially by the restructuring of hospital management. (See Organizational Resources, below, for further details). The devolution of many managerial responsibilities to ward level has had consequences for the workload, skills and responsibilities of nurses, involving them in extensive paperwork and/or computerized record-keeping as well as personnel management, performance monitoring, budgeting and ordering.

In these professionalizing strategies we see the emergence of a new discourse of nursing, as credentialised and managerial, alongside the intensification of a more traditional nursing discourse – centred on patient care – re-invented for the 21st century. These constructions of gendered nursing identities may be traced through readings of the uniforms worn by nurses and the politics that they have mobilized. Nursing uniforms convey complex and gendered meanings, linked to servants' uniforms of the Victorian era (Jolley 1995) and modern 'servants' such as chambermaids and waitresses (Savage 1987); to sexual fantasy and (for male nurses and nurses in high technology specialities) to androgynous professional ideals. Certainly the nursing uniform has changed over time, reflecting historical changes to nursing discourse, but the rate of change has been uneven. Uniforms but are a matter for local decision. Whilst some hospitals have adopted new styles, others have maintained more traditional versions and even *between specialities* and *within* hospitals, we see significant variations. In this sense, nursing uniforms bear the weight of competing interpretations of nursing discourse as it shifts and sticks over time and space. They are used of symbols of meaning linked to both historical interpretations and future projections; and linked to the identities of particular places and spaces of nursing practice. But more than simply reflecting meaning, uniforms may also have a subjective effect on the wearer. Savage (1987) argues that the nursing uniform casts the wearer as a blank slate, on which the nursing identity can be inscribed, whilst Hallam (2000) argues that

> The nurse's uniform bears the traces of ... changing virtues and resistances, inscribing on the bodies of those who wear it the ghosts of nursing foremothers (p. 51).

These values are re-articulated through '... the transforming process of putting on the uniform' (Hallam 2000: 52).

In this brief account we have shown that nursing discourse operates through multiple layers of meaning and that these meanings are interwoven with material tasks and artefacts. This offers the broad terrain for the construction and performance of nursing identities, naming the dispositions through which nursing identities may be fashioned: what nursing identities are and can be like. Whilst we see that some resilience to meanings over time, these meanings may be subject to challenge and reinvention in a continual and dynamic process over both time and space.

Medicine

Like nursing, the history of professional discourse in medicine reveals persistent central claims about the 'kind of person' who could and should be allowed to become a doctor. At heart this has been a masculine subject, as well as a white and middle class one, although of course we now see increasing numbers of women and ethnic minority doctors in the UK medicine. Despite this, these historical representations of the gendered, raced and classed medical subject have not disappeared but find echoes and re-articulations in contemporary discourses and debates.

In the UK, the Medical Act of 1858 established clear requirements for entry and registration to the medical profession. Although women were not formally excluded even this stage, Pringle (1998) concludes that they might as well have been as '...[t]he field of professional medicine was defined as masculine territory' (p. 25). The first woman registered as a doctor in 1849, but despite this – and the opening of the London School of Medicine for Women in 1874 – the construction of professional discourse continued to represent 'the doctor' in masculine terms. This had a number of strands. In part, it concerned vocation and time. The 'good' doctor immersed himself in medicine 24 hours a day, placing medicine above all other callings and was able to work beyond the normal boundaries of physical and mental exhaustion (Pringle 1998). This sits uncomfortably, of course, with discursive representations of woman as mother and the material demands of actual motherhood (to be elsewhere and to carry out other quite different tasks). It also carries a sense of physical stamina which, whatever the reality, did not concur with ideals of Victorian womanhood. The construction of a medical disposition was also critical to the gendering, racialization and class specificity of professional medical discourse. Pringle (1998) cites William Osler, a key figure in UK medical training in the late 19th century, who defined the professional ideal as the ability to '...remain cool, precise and confident in all situations' (Pringle 1998: 28). The gendered sub-text to this hardly needs unpicking! Nearly a century later Young (1981) recalls continuation of this ideal, stressing rationality, aggression, competitiveness, emotional coolness and unquestioning self-confidence as key qualities represented in medical training and hospital sub-culture as emblematic of the medical identity. Nearly two decades on from this, Wear (1997) describes how 'the inscribed body of the physician ... is marked as decisive, objective, rational and above all composed' practicing a 'forthright gaze, handshake and stride' (p. 105). These remarkably consistent elements of the medical disposition might all be coded as generically masculine, although this takes specific forms within medicine. Rationality finds its roots in the construction of medicine as a natural science, within a scientific epistemology that privileges observable fact and laws. Aggression and competitiveness are linked specifically to career motivations. Senior doctors are represented as people with 'killer ambitions', 'god-like creatures' and 'not very nice people' (Allen 1994: 245). Emotional coolness, 'detached concern' (Wear 1997: 104) and the principle 'don't get involved' (Young 1981: 150) all effectively mark medicine out from nursing. Of course doctors deal with bodies – an engagement strongly coded as feminine – but this is not the *intimate* engagement so central to nursing practice. All these characteristics comprise the unquestioning self confidence demanded by the medical disposition.

Yet the acquisition of this rational, aggressive, detached and confident subjectivity is itself a paradox. Contrary to its representation as certain and controlled, medical practice is fraught with uncertainty, risk and the ever present threat of failure. Rather than face or accept this, Stein (1967) argues, doctors cultivate an aura of omnipotence, 'pretence' of absolute knowledge and power (Porter 1995). Different mechanisms may be deployed to achieve this: for instance, protecting knowledge and tasks within the medical profession or couching knowledge/practice in specialized technical language (Young 1981). Doctors control interactions with their patients, and with their colleagues, though use of time and space, marking professional and social hierarchies: practicing power and privileging their knowledge and status over others. But they cannot do this alone. The reactions of others are key to the maintenance of professional superiority and nurses, as doctors' closest colleagues, play a key role with their subservience. Observing this in practice Stein (1967) refers to the 'doctor nurse game'. In this game, both doctors and nurses know that the input of nurses is critical to doctors' knowledge of the patient. However, the nurses must defer to the doctors and only make recommendations in a passive register. This gives the doctors the information they need without threatening their superiority. Over time, Porter (1995) argues, the rules of the game may have shifted slightly – with some watering down of the authoritarian omnipotent and the compliant subservient. Porter (1995) describes four ideal-typical constructions of the doctor-nurse relation: unmitigated subordination, informal covert decision making by nurses, information overt decision making by nurses and formal overt decision making by nurses. However, Porter (1995) concludes that all four forms of inter-professional relations are alive and kicking, articulated in complex and dynamic combinations.

Of course, the medical disposition is not only gendered, but simultaneously classed and racialized. Medicine is perhaps the quintessential profession and, despite the credentialized nature of state sanctioned professions, it is well documented that the movement into and through the professional ranks is closely tied to class, race and gender. Entrants to the medical profession have historically been overwhelmingly from the middle classes, and doctors are particularly effective in securing inter-generational stability, with doctors' children disproportionately likely to enter into medicine themselves. But more than this, the medical disposition reproduces key aspects of middle class affect:

detachment, intellect and cool arrogance. Coolness and distance also contrast with representations of black masculinity as uncontrolled and over-emotional (Segal 1990); whilst the arrogance and macho masculinity associated with medical professional discourse stand in opposition to representations of Asian masculinity as quiet, gentle and unassuming (Cheng 1997). Nonetheless, by 2003 as many as 35% of National Health Service hospital doctors identified themselves as belonging to an ethnic minority (Cook et al 2003). Within medicine today racial difference is mobilized through discourses of language and cultural competence (Cook et al 2003), validating white British doctors as the 'best' doctors, with major appointment decisions often determined, in practice, by the foolishly blunt instrument of 'foreign sounding names' (Esmail and Everington 1993; 1997).

However, it is important to point out that both race and gender are constituted unevenly across medicine. The apotheosis of a masculine medical disposition is still to be found in surgery, where there is (still) an emphasis on physical strength, hardening to suffering and the embodied authority and decisiveness that lie at core of medical tradition. When we think of surgical identities 'we think of domineering, confident, decisive, practical people, rugged individuals, doers rather than thinkers' (Pringle 1998). This contrasts directly with physicians, who are represented as '... tentative, unable to make quick decisions ... introverted and intellectual, even effeminate' (Pringle 1998: 78). This latter representation is perhaps most exaggerated in the representation of General Practitioners, cast as failed hospital doctors and opposed as 'dumb' in contrast to the 'bright' doctors who stay in hospital medicine (Pringle 1998) ideally – perhaps – moving into surgery. Similarly, we see gender and race differences across the hierarchy in medicine. Whilst women comprised almost 50% of medical graduates in 1991, only one in four had achieved consultant status by 2001 (EOR 2001). Senior clinical and managerial status is still largely the privilege of male doctors. Similarly, whilst ethnic minorities comprise 35% of all hospital doctors they make up only 20% of consultant posts but as many as 65% of the staff grade posts (Cook et al 2003), widely recognized as a career dead-end.

However, none of this is immutable. Despite surviving for the best part of 150 years, there are some recent challenges to the central tenets of professional medical discourse. One very practical challenge in the UK context comes from the Government's agreement in 1991 to tackle the 'long hours' culture of hospital medicine in which 100 hour weeks had become routine. The 'new deal' with the British

Medical Association promised a reduction in junior doctors' hours to 56 per week by 2004, bringing this down to 48 by 2009 in line with the EU working time directive. This intervention clashes sharply with the way that time is represented in earlier constructions of professional medical discourse and has provoked strong reactions from some senior doctors who resent the way that professional inculcation through total immersion has been undermined, de-valuing their own working histories but also bureaucratizing professional practice and, they claim, making it impossible to train doctors effectively.

These events link to broader sociological arguments about deprofessionalization. From the 1970s onwards there have been claims and counter-claims about the loss of professional authority and status, amongst medics and other professionals (Friedson 1994). In general this reflects the popularization of critiques that have re-cast the professions as essentially self-serving and mechanisms of social control rather than altruistic and unambiguously 'good' (Elston 1991). More specifically, recent years have seen an increase in public alternative sources of public knowledge through campaign groups, the internet and the mass media, for example, and the public naming and shaming of medical failings. Linked to this, there has been a growth in litigation, as patients and relatives challenge the decisions made by doctors. Associated with these changes Lupton (1997) identifies new discourses of professionalism that avoid 'authoritarian and coercive approaches' (p. 492) and emphasize instead communication and empathy. Lupton (1997) argues that doctors are 'expected to be "reflexive" in the medical encounter' and to 'exercise self-surveillance and know themselves better so they might better relate to patients' (p. 492).

Like nursing then, medical professional discourse carries a range of more or less explicit subjectivities offering opportunities and constraints for the construction of medical identities. These are clearly differentiated over time, but also spatially, for instance within the different fields of medical practice. From Surgery to General Practice, doctors are constructed through distinct tasks and dispositions: from knives, saws and the confidence it takes to use them, to coughs and colds and sympathy. Distinctive meanings are embedded in the material tasks and spaces of different medical practice. How these are taken up at the level of embodied identities, in particular times and places is the focus of the following chapter in this book. However, in our focus on the working identities of doctors and nurses working in the UK public sector we must first consider the discursive frameworks and materials offered at the organizational level.

Organizational resources

In 1948 the British government brought doctors and nurses into a centralized system of nursing for the first time. However, the implications of this change for the construction of medical and nursing subjectivities appears to have been minimal, until the early 1980s, as the professions retained autonomy within the health service, facing few challenges to the dominance of professional discourse. Since 1982, the National Health Service has been subject to continuous forms of organizational change that directly confront professional autonomy and promote alternatives to traditional professional subjectivities. Indeed, the transformation of working subjectivities has been central to the achievement of these reforms, as we will explain below. In what follows we describe this in two main phases, from 1982–1997 when successive Conservative governments pursued policies to introduce competition in the health service as a means to greater efficiency; and from 1997–2004 when the Labour governments largely replaced competition with an emphasis on quality, similarly designed to introduce substantial changes to the organization and practice of medical and nursing work in the National Health Service.

Until 1982 the organizational framework appears to have offered little in the way of alternatives to the professional construction of working subjectivities in medicine and nursing. This was for two main reasons. First, the professions were left to manage themselves with little external interference. Each profession maintained its own hierarchy and was responsible for its own internal management. Indeed, the Salmon reforms of 1966 extended the nursing hierarchy beyond the level of Matron, such that it became parallel and equal in status to the medical and financial administrative hierarchies within the overall management of the National Health Service (Bolton 2004). Each hierarchy was autonomous and the system was expected to work through consensus. However, whilst the Salmon reforms put nursing on a par with medicine, and gave the profession greater authority, there was some concern that it represented a shift in the nursing career towards general management and would facilitate a male takeover of the nursing hierarchy and indeed, by the early 1980s over half of the senior management posts in nursing were held by men, who comprised just 10% of the profession overall (Davies and Rosser 1986). Thus, although nursing – like medicine – remained responsible for its own management the Salmon reforms introduced opportunities for new nursing subjectivities based, for the first time, in managerial dispositions rather than those of patient care. The second limit on the significance of organizational resources to nursing and medical subjectivities was that the professions remained the primary actors in the National Health Service. Doctors and nurses were given complete clinical freedom such that 'the shape of the total service provided by the National Health Service was the aggregate outcome of individual doctors' clinical decisions, rather than the result of decisions made by politicians, policy makers, planners or managers' (Harrison and Pollit 1994: 35). The managerial role was reactive, dealing with the problems originating elsewhere in the system – from doctors, nurses or trade unions. Describing this era LeGrand (2002) refers to the organizational structure in the National Health Service as a 'clan culture' that 'relied upon politicians and civil servants to allocate the resources at the macro level and gave medical professionals the freedom to make ground level decisions as to what patients should receive what treatments' (p. 144). Thus, up until 1982 the organization of the National Health Service largely confirmed the status and hierarchies of medicine and nursing, underpinning the professional resources on offer in the construction and performance of working identities.

Since this time, the National Health Service has been subject to major organizational changes with profound implications for the construction of medical and nursing subjectivities. The changes were heralded by the setting up of the Griffiths Committee to report into the management of the National Health Service. In his report Roy Griffiths (then the Chief Executive of Sainsburys) was scathingly critical of the lack of overall managerial control on the health service and recommended the establishment of a new system of *general* management. In place of the parallel hierarchies and consensus management the Griffiths report recommended the introduction of a cadre of general managers who would take overall responsibility throughout the National Health Service. These managers would be proactive, goal setting and directive (Packwood 1997) drawing explicitly on generic managerial skills and values quite distinct from professional skills and values. However, the nature of healthcare meant that it was not possible for managers to take direct control throughout the hierarchy. Medical and nursing work still relies crucially upon professional judgement and doctors, as well as nurses, inevitably retained some authority through their clinical decision making. At this level, managerial control was implemented in a different way: by devolving managerial roles to doctors and nurse and making *them* responsible for managerial decisions. Explicitly managerial tasks were added to senior professional roles. As Ackroyd (1996) puts it 'it is through the actions of senior doctors that the aims of management can be realised' (p. 613) and so attempts were made to incorporate doctors into the process of change (Harrison and Pollit 1994; Dent 2003). The 'vehicle for control' became the incorporation of professionals themselves into managerial roles 'subject to managerial parameters' (Harrison and Pollit 1994: 93) doctors work re-configured – getting them to do it themselves.

In structural terms, the key mechanism to achieve this involvement was the establishment of clinical directorates within hospital medicine, loosely based on individual services. Each service, surgery or maternity unit for example, became responsible for its day-to-day running and was headed by a senior professional in charge, assisted by other professionals in auxiliary managerial roles, for instance as Business Manager. Whilst Clinical Directors were initially overwhelmingly doctors, Business Manager posts were frequently taken by nurses. Indeed, despite fears that the introduction of general management would top-slice the nursing career above ward level there is evidence that increasing numbers of nurses are moving into these new posts. Each directorate became the fund-holder for the service, making the professionals in charge responsible for their own budgets. But these changes were more than structural. The generation of new subjectivities was central to the change. As the culture of the professionals tangled with the emergent culture of the organization (Packwood 1997) new competencies and skills are demanded and new personal qualities required. As Doolin (2002) remarks (on New Zealand, but it could as well be the UK) '...hospital clinicians [were constituted] as enterprising subjects, aligning their clinical behaviour with the broader goals of the governmental programme' (Doolin 2002: 369) encouraging '...autonomous, productive, self-regulating entrepreneurial behaviour' (Doolin 2002: 3).

More than 20 years after Griffiths, and following the successive election of two Labour governments, much of the organizational and managerial structure *at hospital level* is still in place. However, the internal market that drove the broader National Health Service system has been largely abolished and there has been a shift in discursive framework for managing the National Health Service and in the goals that are expressed. Under the banner of 'modernization' the Labour governments have announced substantially increased funding to be 'accompanied by reform' (HMSO 2000) of the National Health Service which is represented as '...a 1940s system operating in a 21st century world' (HMSO 2000: 2). These changes are to be achieved through a focus on 'quality'. Every trust is required to 'embrace the concept' (HMSO 1997: 6:12) which is articulated through a set of *principles* – quality improvement, leadership skills at clinical team level and clinical risk reduction programmes – but *not structures*, underlining that individual Chief Executives alone were responsible for ensuring 'appropriate local arrangements' (HMSO 1997: 6:14). In 1999 a legal duty of quality was 'imposed for the first time' (HMSO 1997). This was enabled through a new and extensive framework of clinical governance, designed to monitor, evaluate and improve levels of service and accountability through both internal and external mechanisms. Once again, doctors are key players in the implementation of these changes. In each hospital a senior clinician is responsible to the Chief Executive for clinical governance, and clinicians are central to the system of external inspection. However, the medical profession is not autonomous in the system of clinical governance, which involves both managers and 'the community' in making evaluations, and as such it is represented by some as unwelcome interference and as a further demise in traditional medical autonomy (Starey 2001).

Since this time, the Labour governments have continued to move forward with their programme of modernization, introducing new quality inspection mechanisms and offering hospitals that are most successful in these terms 'foundation' status, allowing even more managerial independence at unit level. Some degree of competition has also been re-introduced, allowing Primary Care Trusts (the purchasers of hospital services) to switch providers under certain circumstances and allowing hospitals to earn extra money through elective surgery activity, rather than being bound solely by block bookings from their PCTs (HMSO 2002). Within nursing, a new grade of 'modern matron' has been established, and senior nurses are now seen as a vital link between operational and strategic management and as important agents for cultural change (Bolton 2004).

These changes to the organization and management of the National Health Service present doctors and nurses with new work tasks, and a new framework within which their work is set. Alongside these specific changes closely linked to professional tasks, skills and subjectivities, the introduction of general management tied status and income to management success, initially though the star rating system and more recently through the introduction of Foundation Hospitals. Associated with this there has been the development of corporate branding and organizational promotion: the deliberate construction of organizational identities, positioning hospitals within the local area and within the National Health Service. The move to Trust status opened up new sources of funding for hospitals and this enabled a wave of new build and refurbishment linked to hospital promotion and identity. These broader changes are a significant context within which professional activities are performed and working identities constructed.

The changes in organizational resources outlined above have of course been accompanied by broader social and cultural changes in the gender structures of workplaces as well as in discourses of management. In the last 20 years or so, women have increasingly appeared as managers and leaders in most professions and organizations in industrialized countries, and management discourses have shifted to include women as managers and potential managers. Indeed, women have been increasingly positioned as having a crucial role to play as leaders in organizations, with claims that they bring a different 'relation-centered style' to management that is particularly beneficial to public sector organizations (Hegelson 1990, Rosener 1990). The NHS has been an important sector in which this gendered shift has been played out. It employs a greater proportion of women at senior levels than the private sector: 58% of managers and senior managers are female, and three-quarters of entrants onto the National Health Service management training scheme over the past five years were women (National Health Service Confederation 2004: 3). Equality issues have been important in the cultural agendas of the NHS as an employer, as well as for the professional institutions such as the Royal College of Nursing and the British Medical Association. Targets have been set to increase the number of women in senior positions across the board, from Chief Executives to senior clinicians and nurse-leaders. Women-only courses are funded to enable women to address some of the hurdles which may prevent them from considering senior management positions, whilst men are encouraged to embrace equal opportunities and diversity in recruitment and selection procedures. Incidents of senior women leaving top positions in the Health Service are regularly scrutinized by the media, and questions are asked as to whether a glass ceiling still exists, and what can be done about it.

The climate has thus shifted considerably from the early days of the Health Service, when women were solely regarded as nurses, whilst men were their doctors and leaders. With equal opportunities and diversity being buzz words within management discourses, women are able to construct working identities as managers, and many come into the profession and/or organization with this aim. At the same time however, the health service has been long established according to a masculine career model which demands long hours and 'decades of immersion' (Pringle 1998). Although management discourses may have shifted to include women, the subject positions which they offer are only recently recognizing the importance of flexibility and alternatives to the full-time norm. Women who attempt to combine a senior career with the demands of bringing up a family are still as unusual in health service organizations as they are elsewhere.

Conclusion

The gendered professional and organizational resources which have been outlined in this chapter may all be drawn upon in the construction of medical and nursing identities: the interpretation of how to be when doing the job. However, whilst it is essential that we are knowledgeable about these gendered resources, they are only part of the puzzle and a highly abstracted part at that. How individual doctors and nurses, women and men, respond to and engage with these resources is another matter. Whilst the nature of the professions and of the organizations within which they are embedded may be important in the construction and performance of individual working identities, we must not assume that the former tells us all we need to know about the latter. Indeed, a central aim of this book is to open up the relationship between abstract resources of identity on the one hand, and the embodied and enacted use of these resources on the other.

In order to accomplish identities, these *generic* resources and discourses must be interpreted within *specific* contexts – the actual places, spaces and times within which people operate in their everyday working lives. It is these contexts, that are already constituted and ever being re-constituted, which are our focus of attention. How are the multiple and generic discourses described here constituted on the ground? What are the opportunities and constraints for the negotiation of gendered selves in these times and places? How do lived material practices, actual objects and artifacts contribute to the making of gendered organizations and gendered selves? People negotiate their identities within these very particular temporal, spatial and material contexts, and what they may desire in terms of the varied resources that are available to them must be accomplished in everyday practices and routines. At the same time, other people's agendas may jostle in competition, such that outcomes can in no way be pre-determined, but may remain subtle and ambiguous. It is only through attention to this complexity that we can fully explore the relations between the available discursive resources and working selves. It is to the question of how this might be researched in practice that we now turn.

3
Researching Identities

Introduction

In the previous chapter, we described the ways in which medical and nursing subjectivities are constructed through professional, organizational and gendered discourses. We argued that it is important that we have an understanding of these in order to appreciate the broad cultural frames within which working identities are articulated. However, we have also noted that these are highly general and abstracted accounts of professional and organizational subjectivities – they show us the subjective terrain on which working identities are constructed and performed, but they do not inform us about what people actually *do* on this terrain and the ways that these subjectivities are *lived* by doctors and nurses working in the National Health Service. In Chapter 1 we outlined three key ways in which we can look beyond the general discursive construction of medical and nursing identities. First, we should recognize the importance of *context*. How nursing and medical identities are constructed is contextually situated: both in time and space. As Allen (2001) claims '[n]ursing jurisdiction is highly situated, that is, the way that it is "done" varies in different locales' (p. xi). The same is true of medicine of course (Lupton 1997). Yet our knowledge of the ways that practice is '... shaped and experienced in different spatial, geographic, economic, political and cultural contexts' (Lupton 1997: 493–4) is very limited. Second, we need to recognize that professional and organizational discourses, and the ways in which these are gendered, are not the only resources of working identities. Work and organizational life is not sealed-off from other times, spaces and sources of the self. Whilst the importance of these resources *may* diminish in working times and spaces, they may not do so, and the links between different resources in the construction and performance of working identities is – for us at this stage – an empirical question rather than a theoretical one. Third, and critically, we have argued that *agency* operates to negotiate identities from the available subjective resources: this is complex, subtle and ambiguous. Identities may be both stable and fluid, and again this is a contingent question, as identities are accomplished through practice in everyday life.

These claims lead us to ask specific research questions: How do the doctors and nurses actually construct and perform their working identities? What is the place of professional and organizational resources in this? How important is gender here? Are other resources important in the construction and performance of these working identities? How do place, space and time impact on these processes? Clearly, researching these questions required us to develop a methodology that is both sensitive to context, as well as giving attention to individual accounts.

Comparative methodology

Our claim from the start has been that context matters. To this end, a comparative methodology was important, allowing us to pursue this claim empirically. In order to explore how medical and nursing identities are constructed in place and time we conducted case studies of doctors and nurse working in two markedly different hospitals. Our selection of case studies was based on the criterion of difference: difference in relation to organizational type, organizational change, and difference in relation to medical and nursing practice. We sought to find very different hospitals, as these would enable us to explore our theoretical claims about the importance of context in the construction and performance of working identities. We 'found' a number of potential candidates and evaluated this short-list through interviews with key informants in each Trust. Against our expectations we found considerable enthusiasm for our research! Framed in terms of organizational and professional change, questions of identity and agency appeared to be of great interest to senior managers who readily approved the access that we requested. Following this process of evaluation we selected two case studies: Seaside and Lakeside.

'Seaside Memorial Hospital' is a small (60 bed) Community Hospital situated on the periphery of a fading holiday resort on the South coast of England. It is mainly concerned with the rehabilitation and medium term care of the elderly, although it has a small 'minor injuries unit' and has seen the development of a number of specialist outpatient services for the local community over the last few years. 'Lakeside', is a large (700 bed) District General Trust Hospital on the edge of London, widely recognized for its leading specialties, particularly in surgery and emergency medicine. At Seaside, nurses and auxiliaries provide patient care in the hospital. With the exception of one consultant, the doctors are all employed on 'staff grades' by the hospital and consultants from a nearby District General Hospital provide much of the medical input on a clinic or ward round basis. The hospital had a general manager, although this was a relatively new initiative and staff frequently recounted the previous and more long-standing management of the hospital by a matron, who controlled everything from nursing rotas to cleaning arrangements. Staff still describe Seaside as small and friendly or, more critically, as *'a substantial piece of National Health Service property run like a cottage hospital from the 1950s'* (Douglas, one of the nurses). By contrast, Lakeside has a complex managerial and clinical matrix structure. Several of the senior doctors and nurses have international standing and the hospital has a reputation as a 'trailblazer' and for cutting-edge management, following its early attainment of Trust status in 1997. It was awarded the maximum of three stars in the 2002/3 National Health Service Performance Ratings and expects to become an National Health Service Foundation Trust in October 2004. This places Lakeside in a select band of hospitals which lie in the tier just below the most prestigious London teaching hospitals. In order to exaggerate the comparison further, whilst we include all the nursing and medical activities at Seaside, we concentrated on three of the most prestigious specialties at Lakeside: surgery, orthopaedics and accident and emergency.

Knowing context

Our initial interviews with key informants during the selection process had already offered some insight to each of our hospitals, but it was an essential part of our methodology that we should acquire further knowledge of Lakeside and Seaside, and their locales, before communicating directly with doctors and nurses about their working lives. We needed to know more about the context of these: about the contextual resources within which professional and organizational subjectivities were experienced and from which – or against which – working identities were fashioned. To achieve a better working knowledge of the hospitals we conducted further interviews with key informants drawn from the following: the Chief Executive, the Unit General Manager, the Director of Nursing, the Director of Clinical Services, the Director of Human Resources and the Director of Surgery. It was not possible or appropriate to interview every post-holder in each Trust. Rather, our aim was to hear a wide range of management views about the organization and to learn from this about the context for working identities. Of course, these key informants represent the senior management in each case. As such they offer an important overview of the context as they see it and, since they are responsible for designing and managing the organization they have power to *set* significant aspects of the organizational context for the doctors and nurses working there.

However we were also concerned to establish a sense of the context in everyday practice. This is not captured from a solely managerial perspective, and we were concerned not to place undue reliance on key informants (Bryman 2001). To achieve further knowledge we began our first round of what we thought would be *non-participant* observation in the hospitals. Our goal here was to get more of a 'feel' for the organization, as it is accomplished, across its different times and spaces. To this end, our observations took place over a 24-hour period, and were conducted in different spaces across each hospital. We were given authority to move freely within the practical boundaries of patient confidentiality and hygiene. Initially, we followed structured observation sheets, to make maps of the spaces under observation, to record who was present, activities and conversations. But these were immediately supplemented with more ad hoc observations, which soon came to be far more detailed and provocative than anything we had structured in advance. Indeed, we came to appreciate that whilst we were non-participants in the sense that we were not working as doctors or nurses, and nor were we patients, we were of course taking part in the places, spaces and times of hospital life. Whilst were not, then, strictly 'observing' nor, in social scientific terms, strictly 'participating', are activity was one of *engagement* with the sights, sounds and smells of our hospitals, and with the differentiated time and space routines within the hospitals. Seeing our method in this way, as engagement, opened up our reflections on organization, embodiment, identity and performance in productive ways, and was an approach that we applied more fully in our second round of observations. (See below). This initial engagement proved valuable in two important ways. First, as we had intended, they gave us some first hand knowledge of the context of doctors and nurses' working lives. Second, our engagement offered an important resource in later interviews. Our knowledge appeared to offer us some credibility with doctors and nurses and enabling us to ask detailed and informed questions. More than this, we were able to understand specific points made by doctors and nurses about particular spaces, times and practices and pursue the significance of these in a very precise and grounded ways.

In addition to the hospital, we attempted some engagement with the local areas. In each case, our intention was to get a feel for place in terms of the wider locale that the hospitals were in. At Seaside, we walked the streets between the hospital and the seafront on a cold September Friday morning, stopping off for coffee in windswept cafes. In contrast, Lakeside is situated amidst business parks and out of town shopping malls, and much of our 'getting to know the area' involved negotiating the roundabouts and flyovers connecting a variety of satellite towns.

The contextual work that we carried out in selecting our case studies and developing our knowledge of them was key in our approach to researching identities. This was slow, deliberate and painstaking work. Our argument is that context matters: the when and the where make a difference to how working identities can be constructed and performed. But, now we have to address our other main argument: that identities cannot be read-off from the subjectivities on offer through organizational and professional discourses or through context. It is what people *do* with these that matter. As well as getting to know the places and spaces of our organizations therefore, we also needed to get to know the people that worked there.

Knowing people

Two main methods were used in order to research the identities of the people working in these contexts – interviews and observations. These two methods operated in dialogue, with one informing the other throughout. Our contextual observations informed our interview questions, whilst these interviews informed later observations: where we went, who we looked at, and what we looked for.

Interviews

Across a range of sociological perspectives, interviews have been a preferred method for those of us interested in researching identities empirically (Cohen and Taylor 1976; Willis 1977; Sharpe 1976; Shotter and Gergen 1989; Freeman 1993; Leidner 1993; Casey 1995; Josselson and Leiblich 1995, 1999; Antaki and Widdicombe 1998). Verbal accounts of individuals' lives are 'a key source of social knowing' (Knowles 2000:

11) and a critical resource for those of us interested in the work of constructing identity (Cameron 2001). We too endorse the interview method as a rich and unique source of material: it offers us information and insights that we cannot gain in any other way. This is how we can explore our interests of lived experiences: these are best told by the people who have those experiences (Denzin 1989). In the first part of this section we describe our practical arrangements for interviewing and offer an overview of sample and our interviewing techniques. However, the interview method, and the material that it produces, is far from straightforward when we are concerned with identities. Indeed, the method raises some profound questions: first about the production of information; second, about the status of the material that is generated; and third, about the position of researchers to read and name identities from individual narratives. We deal with these in the second part of this section.

Sampling and interview method

Our original aim was to carry out the same number of interviews in each hospital. This was a manageable number in relation to our resources, both as interviewers and in analysing the material. (See below). In the event, it became more realistic to implement a 17/33 split between the smaller and larger hospital. In each case, we sampled potential interviewees from the full staff lists for our case studies (this was confined to Surgery, Orthopedics and Accident and Emergency at Lakeside) taking seniority and sex into account. Sampling in relation to ethnicity was more difficult. We were not provided with this information about individuals and we had to resort to the use of names to make guesses about this. We fully recognize that this practice has dubious value but believe that it was better than making no effort to include ethnic minority doctors and nurses in our research. Interviews were carried out during the doctors' and nurses' working hours (day and night) and on hospital premises. Sometimes this meant management offices or even the personal offices of senior staff, other times a side room or sluice room. Often interviews were disrupted by bleeps, by patients or by other staff.

The interviews followed a loose structure. At the beginning of each interview we outlined our research and explained that all material would remain anonymous outside the research team. We outlined the structure of the interview and made it clear that interviewees were free to decline to answer any questions and to terminate the interview at any time should they wish. We aimed to speak as little as possible and to allow interviewees to address these themes freely. Our intention throughout was to generate biographical narratives: stories of working lives which would tell us where people had worked and lived, how they felt about the different places and times of work, how they felt about changes in their professional and organizational identities. Within the interview, therefore, we were obviously keen that people would talk in relation to our key concepts: of gender, as well as space, place and time. This could obviously be done obliquely, but on occasion we would also ask more direct questions. Interviews thus commenced in very broad terms, starting with participants' current jobs and, moving from this, to asking how they had come to be in this particular here and now, to encourage their personal and professional life stories. We prompted them to think about gender at different life stages here: to what extent did the fact that they were a boy or a girl, a young man or woman, or perhaps now, an older woman or man, frame their life choices and decisions? Did they feel gender was an important factor in any way, either personally or professionally? In order to develop our interest in agency, and relationships to the discursive constructions of identity, we also invited them to think about change in terms of their professional and organizational lives. How did they feel about these? Had these impacted on the way they felt about their jobs, and themselves?

We also asked them more directly about the hospital in which they were now working. Here we probed according to our themes of space, place and time, as well as that of gender. We asked them, for example, why they had chosen to work at this particular hospital, and what they liked or disliked about it. Was it a 'gendered' place: for example, in terms of its organizational culture, or its attraction to women or men to work there? Did they feel they worked well here: did they 'fit in'? We asked them about the different spaces of the hospital: were their places, for instance, where they liked being or going to more than others? How did they feel about the different spaces they visited or spent time in, and, crucially, how did these *make them feel*? Were there any gendered spaces – where, and how? Time was a concept that needed rather less probing: it spilled over into the talk of the nurses and doctors, as a constant pressure point in their lives. All talked of the pressures of work routines and demands, as well as their attempts to combine work with the other aspects of their lives and identities.

Towards the end of each interview, we asked questions which were more explicitly about 'identity'. We described the broad differences between modern and post-foundational approaches to identity and asked for the doctors' and nurses' views on this, and in relation to how they saw themselves. It may be the case, as Chase (1995) has argued, that people will not respond well to such directly sociological questions if they do not relate to them. In our experience, however, as they were placed at the end of an interview that had invited reflection on individual experience and identities, these questions provoked engaged and thoughtful responses. Many really enjoyed this question, whilst for others it sparked off some almost sad reflections on their lives. These responses also pushed us to see the theoretical questions from doctors' and nurses' points of view rather than only imposing our interpretations.

Clearly, our interview material can in no way be seen as unmediated, transparent or straightforward accounts of either lives or identities. Interviews are no more than an opportunity to speak according to particular expectations and observations are obviously framed through the eye of the beholder: what is seen is mediated through that person's own knowledge, experiences and agendas. In terms of the interviews we held in our research, the invitation came directly from ourselves: researchers unknown to the interviewees, and they followed more or less an agenda set by us. As we have argued throughout this book so far, context matters to the construction and performance of identities and the interview is a particularly critical example of this. Interviews carry a weight of expectation and appropriate performance, both on the part of the interviewer and the interviewed. Interviews offer some particular opportunities and constraints in the construction and performance of identities. In many cases people expressed hesitancy, even nervousness, at the start of the encounter. The narratives that they offered have to be seen in this context. They represent the situated production of knowledge in which we, as researchers, also played a part. Identities are expressed through social interaction, in this case interaction between the interviewer and interviewee, in which both are constructing and performing identities, not least in relation to each other. We cannot of course be precise about the impact of the interview, or the researcher, on the narratives that are produced this way. Were it even possible to replicate the interview with another interviewer, to examine reliability, we could not know whether similarities and differences were to do with the interviewer, or something else. We could not know what respondents might say to a third, fourth or fifth interviewer or to their family, friends or strangers in a different context. These are inherent features of the interview method, whether they are recognized or not. And they are features that have become all the more recognizable through post-foundational theorizing about identities, which – of course – claims precisely that identities are indexical and occasioned (Collins 1998). This raises important questions about the status of interview material in relation to identities. Is this material *only* a product of the interview, with no relation to any other times or spaces of individual lives? Or are there connections, such that the material produced is more than an artefact of the interview alone?

A second key issue about the use of interviews as a method for researching identities concerns the extent to which individuals are *willing* or even necessarily *able* to articulate their identities in the ways that would answer our research questions. There are questions here about memory: what can people remember and what do they select to pass on (Plummer 2001)? There are also questions of privacy: we cannot expect people to recount personal matters to strangers or to relive difficult or painful times, although sometimes they do in practice. Further, there are questions about accuracy and fantasy: what checks do we have that what people are telling us is a credible account of their lives? How reliable is the material that we are offered, whether through the interviewees' conscious or unconscious mediation of the stories that they tell? Or indeed, does this matter?

What interviews do offer, however, is a 'window' onto lives lived (Denzin 1989). It is probable that this is not the only window from which lives might be seen: it has a restricted view and only from one aspect: the context of the interview on that day and in that place. But there will be some connection. Interview narratives are not free-floating, constructed 'any old way' (Cameron 2001: 174); they cannot be completely fabricated at will (Somers and Gibson 1994). Rather, they are '...cut from the same kinds of cloth as the lives they tell about' (Denzin 1989: 26). There may be no absolute truth to the interpretations offered '...only multiple images and traces of what has been, what could have been and what is now' (Denzin 1989: 86) but these are important to the person telling the story (Portelli 1998), in this context, and we cannot expect any more than this.

A third issue therefore, and one which is relevant to both interviews and observations, concerns the position of the researcher in knowing and telling the identities of others. In our use of analytical methods, which we discuss more fully below, we have the power to make interpretations and links, to include and exclude pieces of talk or interactions: all of which the subjects might contest. This is inevitable. However, at no point are we claiming to know people better than they know themselves or to offer definitive accounts of their identities.

Observing/Engaging

Following the interviews, we carried out a second phase of engagement across the times and spaces of our hospitals. This time, our purpose was to move beyond the contextual and observe *identity performances*. We should be clear: we were observing the actions of doctors and nurses, their context and their effects but these observations were made through *our engagement* with the places, spaces, times and people we encountered. *We* read identities in the performances of doctors and nurses. Our interpretations are not (necessarily) the same as the interpretations that individuals would make of their own performances. Unlike the verbal narratives, we have no account from the individuals that we observed of the meanings and intentions orchestrating their performances. But both *despite* and *because* of this, this method offers a valuable addition to our repertoire.

Despite the differences between observations and interviews, we would not want to overstate these. Interviews offer individual accounts, but these are framed by the fact that they *are* interviews and in listening and interpreting these accounts we, as researchers, obviously draw on a range of analytical tools. Similarly, whilst the observations we made were from *our* engagement, they were carried out after the interviews and hence through their lens. Our observations were made with the experience of listening to doctors and nurses talking, in-depth and for over 80 hours, about their working lives and identities. Our engagement was affected by their accounts. They did not belong to us alone but were influenced by the accounts of the doctors and nurses who we were observing. We cannot be precise about the extent to which our engagements were influenced in this way and, of course, the doctors' and nurses' accounts were multiple and diverse, suggesting different issues and particular interpretations. Observation and engagement offered us a way to 'see' these diverse accounts in practice, to understand how each could be meaningful to the speaker. Clearly, though, our observations and engagement were not made solely though the lens of our interviews. We brought to the process other concerns, perspectives, and experiences: both as researchers and as individuals. And, for us as researchers, watching is not the same as listening. Just as, for the doctors and nurses we interviewed, speaking is not the same as doing. As Knowles (2000) argues there may be a gap between talk and practice: between what people say in an interview setting and what they do in the times and spaces of their everyday working lives. So, *because* observation and engagement are different methods they may offer new insights to 'the silent narratives that are not told by other means' (Knowles 2000: 18)

In carrying out these observations and engagements we followed an unstructured method, building intensive descriptions of space, time and practice across each of our hospitals. In this we pursued an approach more akin to free writing, attempting to capture the physical spaces and activities in minute and sensual detail – smell and noise as well as the visual and to some extent tactile – and also to articulate our own feelings and responses to these times and spaces: thick description (Geertz 1973) but not 'descriptive excess' (Lofland and Lofland 1995 – in Bryman 2001: 278). This method provoked our thinking in a number of new directions, for instance making us aware of the importance of bodily movement: how bodies are held, where people look (and don't look) the choreography of bodies in relation to one another. We would probably have come to this later, through our concern with space, identity and the everyday. But watching doctors and nurses on a busy surgical ward this struck us with a powerful and immediate force. Similarly, using this method forced us to articulate our own sense of unease, as outsiders and perhaps as intruders in certain hospital spaces, for instance the Accident and Emergency room. Unpicking this revealed the cultural discourses through which *we* constructed these spaces, and the activities therein, and to look again at medical and nursing identities in relation to our own.

Analytical approach

With all the essential caveats of the discussion above, we began our analysis of both the interview transcripts and our observations of people's performances and interactions from the position that these were texts of identity, that they were ontological (Somers and Gibson 1994). With the interview material, because of our understanding of what these texts represented, it was essential to immerse ourselves thoroughly in each one to develop knowledge of the content, structure and rhythms of the interview, as well as the narrative in its own terms. Thus, for each interview, our primary practice was to listen to the original tape as we read the transcripts, immersing ourselves in the narrative which unfolded. Listening as well as reading added other dimensions to the analysis, for instance individuals' intonation and voice level and made the process of analysis far more engaged and vivid than our previous experiences of reading text alone. In carrying out this listening and reading, our concern, of course, was to address our research questions and our key concepts, about how working identities are constructed in the times, places and spaces of everyday lives.

We thus employed three main methods of analysis. First, we engaged in very close textual analysis of the interview transcripts, searching for all the places where our key concepts were evident in the talk of our participants. We scoured for references to anything to do with the context of work. We interpreted this broadly as the 'where' and the 'when'. An important aspect also here was the extent to which there were their differences or commonalities *between* the transcripts: between women and men, doctors and nurses, senior and junior professionals. How did they talk about the *where* of their working lives: whether this be in terms of 'space' and/or 'place'? Where and how did they talk about the time aspects, the *when* of their working lives – and how did this intersect with the other aspects of their lives? How did each talk about gender: the differences or similarities between women and men, for example? What was revealed about other aspects of identity such as race, class, age and sexuality, and how did these intersect with gender? Analysing this material enabled us to explore how people situated themselves in relation to their working context, and constructed their identities through it and, also, how they constructed that context through their talk.

A second method of approach to the interview material was narrative analysis. The whole of the transcript we approached as a biographical account, or 'life story'. Whilst we cover this methodological approach more fully in Chapter 6, it is important to note here that this method was helpful in our analysis of all our key areas of enquiry, which we discuss in the chapters of this book. Narrative analysis is a method which emphasizes that the accounts offered in biographical interviews constitute, in themselves, *an opportunity for the generation and presentation of self* (Collins 1998; also Shotter and Gergen 1989). The way in which people talk about their lives, and key episodes within them, reveals ways in which they construct their identities, in the past, present and the future, both to the listener and to themselves. People usually talk about things that matter to them (Cortazzi 2001; Plummer 2001), and whilst this varied considerably between people, there were also similarities. We were interested in exploring these similarities and differences, for they would help to reveal the importance of context in the construction of identities. Were there, for example, commonalities in the life stories of people working in the same professional and organizational contexts?

Leading on from this, a third method of analysis was to explore people's talk for the ways in which they drew on the organizational and professional resources which we discussed at the beginning of the chapter. To what extent did they position themselves using the heritage of subject positions within their professions or organizations? We have seen how people enter professions and organizations to a pre-existing history and culture. To what extent do they draw on this, taking it in to the ways in which they construct their identities, or to what extent do they attempt to modify or resist these and, in the process reconstitute them?

In addition to the interview material, we also had notebooks full of our observational writing. In an attempt to convey a flavour of the liveliness and dynamism of the research contexts, we draw on this directly in our discussion: in the form of vignettes at the beginning of each chapter, and also in the general analysis. Let us now turn to put these, and our other, methodological tools to work and visit the spaces, places and times of Seaside and Lakeside. How *are* identities negotiated in these gendered organizations? How *is* context important? In the next four chapters of the book, we take our three key concepts in turn in order to explore how gendered identities are constructed and negotiated within the organizations of our research. As we have explained previously, this is for organizational convenience rather than for any understanding of these concepts as theoretically separated or distinct. It is of course important to re-emphasize the interwoven and complex relationship of place, space and time. However, by approaching each in turn, we are able to pull out the richness of each concept and consider how it contributes to our understanding of the processes of identity-making in organizations, and the resources and constraints it offers to women and men working within them. We start with an exploration of place and the diverse ways, both discursive and material, in which gendered identities are constructed and negotiated through, within and by each hospital as work*places*. We then, in the following chapters, expand our exploration of the importance of context through the concepts of space and time.

4
Placing Identities

From the crowded motorway to the manicured business parks and out of town shopping centres, the landscape around Lakeside hospital is fast, affluent and modern. Large pale grey buildings set in parklands of lakes and grassy mounds are interspersed with brightly lit supermarkets catering for the upper end of the market. All are surrounded with spacious car parks, in which gleaming new cars reflect the income and the lifestyles of the owners. With its recent architectural renovations and heaving car parks, the hospital blends with its surroundings, presenting a prestigious and dynamic image that supports the management's enthusiasm for being at the cutting-edge of the National Health Service. Reputations are made here: as nurses, doctors and managers acquire national and international renown for particular spe-cialities and innovations. The hospital is big, it's lively and it has a buzz about it. The entrance is glass and pale wood, recessed halogen lighting, carpet and open spaces leading to a café with glass walls, muffins and cap-puccino alongside smart new shops selling helium balloons, cuddly toys and glossy magazines. Local anecdote tells of a place that has re-invented itself over the past five years: from run-of-the-mill to an exemplar of excellence amongst hospitals of its type, placing it in a select band of hospitals one tier below the most prestigious University Hospitals.

The journey to Seaside Hospital meanders through a maze of 1930s semi-detached houses, newsagents, take-aways and funeral directors on the edge of a fading holiday resort. Dilapidated architectural glories on the seafront sit alongside small cafes and boarded up shops. A few fishermen lean over the railings of the short pier, contemplating the sea and their solitude. The hospital sits next to the by-pass on the edge of town. Tacked on to the 1920s red-brick architecture are some later extensions, testament to bigger ambitions in the 1980s and 1990s. Whilst the main business of the hospital is rehabilitation and medium term care of the elderly, there is a minor injuries unit and some innovative outpatient clinics have recently been set up. But a short walk through the hospital produces an overwhelming sense of an earlier 'heyday'. Portraits of benefactors and large bouquets of fresh flowers punctuate the main thoroughfare that leads to the chapel and war memorial in the centre of the building. The support of influential local 'Friends' of the hospital is reflected in the naming of wards and in support campaigns mounted by the local community. Community use of the hospital's canteen – Daphne's – means that it is fully booked at weekends. Outside, the car park is half full and both staff and patients can arrive simply and calmly.

These are two very different places. We chose them for that reason. They are both hospitals, but the gendered organizational and professional resources discussed in Chapter 2 operate distinctively in each, in articulation with the other social, cultural and economic processes that make these places. Over the months that we travelled forwards and backwards to each of them, the days and nights that we spent within them, we were aware of a deepening sense of the particularities of these places. Each demanded distinctive performances from us as researchers, performances that shifted as these places became more familiar, as we accumulated a sense of the layout, the politics and the routines: the complex makings and re-makings of each place. Of course, we were – relatively – infrequent and irregular visitors to Lakeside and Seaside. The everyday working lives of our doctors and nurses are embedded in these places. In this chapter, we begin to explore what difference it makes where working lives are conducted: how the *where* impacts on negotiations of identities in gendered organizations. We begin with a more detailed discussion of our theoretical approach to space and identity, explaining our focus in this chapter on 'place' and, more particularly on workplaces. Chapter 5 picks up these arguments in our exploration of 'space', particularly work-spaces. In the present chapter we use a theoretical approach to place drawn from recent work in cultural geography to explore how identities are negotiated in place and how places are made in this very process. Through our own engagement, and with our interview material, we show how Lakeside and Seaside are constructed as places, as gendered places, and how doctors and nurses negotiate their identities in these workplaces. In our conclusion we reflect on what the concept of place adds to sociological understandings of the relations between gender, identity and organization.

Theorizing space, place and identities

Previous accounts of the relations between gender and organization recognize that whilst gender differentiation and inequality is widespread, the lived experience of particular organizations is diverse. In abstract accounts the conceptual categories are usually sufficiently loose to encompass different expressions of gendered organizational life (Acker 1990, 1992, 2000; Halford, Savage and Witz 1997), whilst empirical studies show distinct configurations of gender and organization. Historical research shows how gendering through formal structural mechanisms (Zimmeck 1992; Crompton 1989) gave way to cultural processes of differentiation, themselves historically dynamic (Kerfoot and Knights 1993; Roper 1994; Halford and Savage 1997). Between sectors, McDowell's study of merchant banking (1997) delineates a specific gender dynamics, which contrasts sharply with Leonard's (1998) exploration of 'women behaving badly' in the BBC whilst both these are quite different to the feminized nursing cultures described by Halford, Savage and Witz (1997). We can be sure, then, that history, social structures, hierarchy and profession/occupation are likely to shape relations between gender and organization. However, for all this attention to differentiation, these accounts offer a shared impression that these historical and social dynamics will work themselves out evenly across space. Indeed, these are *aspatial* accounts: the differences that they describe could apparently be anywhere and are, in the recounting of the research at least, often apparently nowhere. In one exception, McDowell (1997) discusses the significance of the cultural construction of the City of London to bankers' accounts of their working lives and identities. But this attention to the importance of space in organizational life is rare. This is symptomatic of a broader epistemological issue. As Soja (1996) says, we are used to seeing the world as a simultaneously historical and social project. We are far less used to seeing the 'interwoven complexity of the social, the historical and the spatial, and their inseparability and interdependence' (Soja 1996: 3).

Addressing Soja's general point, some recent research has explored relations between space and identity, using a shared conceptualization of the performative and iterative nature of both space and identity (Rose 1999; Thrift 1999; Crouch 2000; Gregson and Rose 2000). That is to say, spaces and identities are understood as done, and done through each other:

We make spaces and places from the geopolitical to the intimate in the living or our lives. And all identities/entities, likewise are co-constituted with the making of these (time-) spaces (Massey, Allen and Sarre 1999: 246)

No longer merely a *backdrop* for the making and conduct of lives, a neutral grid over which meaning is placed (Thrift 1999: 301), space itself is implicated in the construction and performance of identities. As subjects we are not simply *in* space, like apples in a box (Malpas 1999), but are made subject and construct our identities *through* space. This theorization of 'space' shares much with our understanding of the negotiation of identity. (See Chapter 1). Space is understood as the product of dynamic inter-relations and interactions that coalesce 'here'; as potentially multiple, containing 'contemporaneous plurality' (Massey 2005: 9); and as always under construction (Massey 2005).

One rendering of this conceptualization of space is to focus our attention on *place*. Whilst working identities are constructed through discursive resources that stretch across places – including the gendered organizational and professional resources and the symbolic norms and citational practices that animate these discourses described in Chapter 3 – they are always *lived* in place: through the particular histories, meanings and practices that accumulate there. Place shapes our reception, understanding and interpretation of discursive resources available for the construction of working identities *and* place itself offers distinctive resources for the narration of self. Archaeology of the concept of 'place' reveals a deeply contested history, which mirrors theoretical divisions between sub-disciplines in Geography centred on interpretive versus structural accounts and a local versus a global focus. For some place offers the way into human attachment and connection, a focus on meaning and everyday experience (Tuan 1977) and is 'not just a thing in the world but a way of understanding the world' (Cresswell 2004: 11). For others place is static, nostalgic and un-progressive: limited and limiting in both political and theoretical terms (Harvey 1989). For David Harvey a focus on place in the era of capitalist globalization is to miss the analytical point beyond offering an insight to how local states, capital and the rich exploit differences between places for their own benefit. Tackling this impasse Doreen Massey (1994: 2005) offers a re-conceptualization of place that incorporates both the subjective meaning of lived places and the construction of place through global as well as national and local processes (Massey 1994, 2005; Cresswell 2004). In using the term 'place' we follow this account which conceptualizes place as the nexus of historically specific and dynamic economic, social and cultural processes within particular locations. Lives are made and lived in place but this is not to separate this grounding from broader processes and relations. Places are produced through connections and relations in the locale, the region as well as the national and the global (Glucksmann 2000; Massey 1994). According to Massey (1994) '..."a place" is best thought of as a particular part of, a particular moment in, the global network of those social relations and understandings' (ibid: 115). As such, a place may be a city or the corner of a room (Cresswell 2004). The question of scale becomes one of focus rather than of conceptual understanding.

Thinking about our hospitals as workp*laces* is to see them as a dynamic point of intersection: where local, national and global histories are played out, and re-played in the everyday negotiation of identities at work. Thinking about these hospitals as *gendered* workplaces means tracing how the gendered organizational and professional resources, described in Chapter 3, along with other economic, social and cultural relations operating over time, produce distinctive contexts for the making of selves. As Massey (2005) explains

> ... entangled and enfolded within them [particular places] is a multiplicity of trajectories each of which has its own spatiality and temporality; each of which has been and still is contested; each of which might have turned out quite differently (yet in the interaction of these histories has often served to reinforce existing lines of domination) (p. 143)

Like Massey's (1997) account of science park workplaces, the on-going historical construction of medicine, nursing and management can be seen as 'part and parcel of the struggle around the creation of intelligible genders, of certain forms of masculinity and femininity' (Massey 2005: 144) in hospital workplaces. On-going constructions of scientific medicine, rational management and caring nursing are played out and challenged in hospital workplaces across the world, but these are workplaces that are differentiated; made and re-made at the intersection of complex relations, spatialities and temporalities as described above.

The construction of place is also embedded in the material – in planning, in built form, in design and in things and these too may be associated with gender. Think simply of the patients' lounge in a traditional cottage hospital; or an operating theatre full of high technology equipment; or even nurses' uniforms. These material artefacts are not simply the mirrors of discursive, social and economic relations, but themselves are implicated in the construction of place and identities. The material is 'folded into the human world' (Thrift 1999: 312) and exercises agency, exercises power. As Actor Network Theorists insist, our world is constructed out of the activities of both humans and non-humans linked together in temporary and evolving configurations (Law 1986; Law 1992) through the continuous arrangement and re-arrangement of materials – both new and well known – in the routines and habits of daily life (Turkle 1995: Lévi-Strauss 1963). The signi-ficance of the material in the workplaces in this study is immediately obvious in the successive phases of building work at both the hospitals as well as in the furniture, uniforms and generations of medical equip-ment present – in distinctive ways – in both places. Both built-form and artefacts carry the weight of past policies, funding, professional identities and healthcare practices. And both may exercise effects in the negotiations of selves at work.

This then is a non-essentialist, open and dynamic conceptualization of place. Whilst place 'comes with the weight of numerous past associ-ations ... it always depends upon further works of association to activ-ate these associations, let along make new ones' (Thrift 1999: 317). Places are dynamic: the 'simultaneity of stories so far' (Massey 2005: 9). Far from trying to fix the meaning of the workplaces we studied, we recognize multiple and competing accounts of place. Whilst places – workplaces for instance – may be

> ... designed to elicit particular practices (including particular subject positions and emotional responses; [but] all kinds of other practices may in fact be going on within them which they were never designed to admit (but which may become a vital part of those places intelligibility (Thrift 1999: 310–11).

Particular places may carry *many* and *conflicting* meanings. They may be interpreted, lived, and challenged in many ways. However, whilst individuals are active in making use of the discursive resources at their disposal to construct working identities 'they must locate their discur-sive activities within a meaningful context' (Hardy, Palmer and Phillips 2000: 1128). There may be multiple interpretations of place, but there are limits to these. In order to make sense, the construction of place and the agentic use of place in the construction of self, must fall within broadly understood and recognized parameters. In sum, different places offer both *opportunities and constraints* in the expression of self, in making different kinds of lives and subjectivities (Lefebvre 1991). In the remainder of this chapter we focus on workplaces: the places where working identities are constructed and performed. We put our understanding of gendered organizations and negotiations of the gendered self *into place*. Contrary to aspatial accounts, we show that workplaces matter to the ways we have to negotiate our gender identities at work.

Researching workplaces

In this section we examine the resources and constraints that two very different workplaces offer in the narration of identity. What kinds of places are these? How is gender woven into the web of relations that make these places? How are the gendered professional and organizational resources described in Chapter 2 used and re-used, made and re-made by and in these places? Following the analytical approach described in Chapter 3, we begin by exploring the meaning of 'workplace' in both our own engagement with Lakeside and Seaside, and in our doctors and nurses accounts of these workplaces. What are these places like? How did we feel and what did we see? How do doctors and nurses construct these workplaces as they seek to represent themselves? In our discussion of each hospital, we begin with the dominant accounts of place that we were offered. These constructed our workplaces through particular relations with the local and the global, with particular interpretations of the professional and organizational resources described in Chapter 2. Both places are made through relations with 'others', with identification and dismissal: what we are, and what we are not. But whilst particular representations of place are widely evoked, the way that individuals' position themselves in relation to them is diverse. Thus, our effort is not directed towards decoding a meaning for each place. Indeed this would not be possible. Rather we show that that each of the workplaces offers individuals distinctive resources in the construction, performance and presentation of individual identities and that, more than this, individuals use these to produce diverse and complex identities. Emerging through these representations, we show that evoking place draws on a complex interweaving of gender with other resources across a range of scales drawing on both discursive and material resources.

Lakeside Hospital

Constructions of Lakeside as a place rested heavily on connections and comparisons with the outside, in particular through positioning the hospital as national and global player and as a place of excellence in particular specialties. These meanings are constructed as signs that are used to represent the hospital's status, but are used both with approval and disapproval to negotiate distinctive identities. These accounts can be read for the ways that they are interwoven with gender, and indeed we do so below. However, much of this analysis relies on implicit rather than explicit aspects of these narratives. Once prompted on the issue however, the responses by men and women were more notably differentiated. In the final section of our discussion about Lakeside as a workplace we consider these explicit responses to questions about Lakeside as a gendered place, a place that is considered 'masculine' not least by those women who claim to enjoy the resources of global excellence that it offers for the negotiation of working selves.

A global place

There is a large notice board in the foyer of the main entrance at Lakeside. On the notice board is displayed evidence of recent activities in/by the hospital. At the centre of the notice board are press cuttings from local newspapers about recent trips made by a specialist surgical team from Lakeside to Bangladesh. In Bangladesh on a regular basis the team operates fulltime for a month, conducting hundreds of operations and training local surgeons at the same time. Meanwhile, not on the notice board, the local papers report the large-scale recruitment of Philipino nurses for Lakeside hospital, as the overheated economy of the local area makes it harder and harder to recruit in the UK. During our time in the hospital, these nurses begin to arrive and are met with what must have been a bewildering mixture of relief and hostility.

For the senior doctors and nurses at Lakeside, its international connections offer opportunities for the negotiation of identities as career 'high fliers' although they are, after all, working in a provincial District General Hospital. In these accounts, the international connections, relationships and reputations at Lakeside were crucial to the construction of both place and self. Those who talked with most pride about Lakeside's international connections had come from University

Teaching Hospitals and represented Lakeside as a global player to off-set its position some way down the hospital hierarchy. Jessica, for example, had trained as a nurse at Birmingham University Hospital and had spent most of her working life in world class London Hospitals, until leaving work and moving out of London when she had her children. Returning to work after three years, she constructs Lakeside as a place that respects this history. Jessica contrasts herself with the nurses who have trained at Lakeside and stayed there:

> *A lot of people I work with have never worked in another hospital which is actually, I think, a bad thing, but you tend to find that* [those trained in] *teaching hospitals, we are flung all over the world*

Jessica's presentation of self is tied into the places that she has trained and worked, and the kind of place that Lakeside is. She represents her career mobility positively but it is important, for her, that this has led to a place like Lakeside. As a Theatre sister working with an inter-nationally renowned consultant, she has joined the Lakeside taskforce to Bangladesh. This is a source of pride and excitement for her and enables her to maintain her working identity at the cutting edge of medical activity.

This representation of place is also central to Amy's account of her move into hospital management. She represents the hospital as

> *... an exciting dynamic environment where individuals are encouraged to be independent ... The management allow their staff to be empowered ... They take everything very seriously and they're passionate about making sure that this hospital is on the map ... And it's progressive in as much as a lot of the pilot work that is coming down from the Government is conducted here*

Previously working in nurse education at the regional level, Amy had good knowledge of hospitals in the area and could have taken her pick:

> *I mean of the eleven Trusts* [hospital organizations] *that I used to work with, I deliberately wanted to be here, I made a conscious decision about where I would want to go back into practice*

Challenged as to whether, perhaps, her attachment to Lakeside was linked to the *seniority* of her post, rather than this workplace in particular, she was clear:

The status of the organization I think is more the issue, I mean Lakeside is definitely, I think for a general District Hospital, you know, quite high up on the agenda and quite well regarded. And I think the sort of kudos when a major London Teaching Hospital ring up and say 'Oh, can you tell me what you're doing about such and such?' or you're invited to go and speak at Sheffield or whatever. You know I think that gives you a lot of good vibes too.

However, the global positioning of Lakeside was not always viewed positively; indeed it was sometimes perceived as a challenge to notions of identity and nationality. This was demonstrated through the mixed response to the hospital's aggressive recruitment drive for nurses in the Philippines:

I don't know what's going to happen when they bring these new ones in...why didn't they put all the money into trying to get people in this country back into nursing? ... There are loads of nurses around that aren't working because of the conditions and that...I'm sure they could try and entice them back rather than spending money on people that are going to come for two years and then go back home again...and I don't know where they're going to put them to live when they get here...I don't know what they are going to do...and they are going to send all the money back to their families, which is fine, but ...(Sheila)

This solution to the nursing shortage was viewed as yet another devaluation of nursing: undercutting salaries and failing to improve conditions. Furthermore, the grudging acceptance of the Filipino nurses' abilities challenged conceptions of good nurses as 'home grown' or 'London trained'. Through its engagement with the international labour market these nurses *had* to understand Lakeside as a global place, and to revise assumptions central to their own constructions of identity.

Whereas both international and national links were clearly important to many of the more senior doctors and nurses working at Lakeside, links with the local community were hardly mentioned at all, by either doctors or nurses. These were not seen as such an important factor in the construction of either the identity of the organization or personal identities. Reference to the local was only used in the construction of a superior identity. Here it was not only the difference in professional function, but also the spatial separation, however small, which was a clear mark of 'otherness', as Colin (a Senior House Officer) explained

> *General Practitioners get the brunt of all sorts from hospital doctors really. But they're there for it aren't they? They are not on site; they can be slagged off without having to confront them. I think it's pretty poor really, the attitude of hospital doctors, they are very arrogant...*

The representation of Lakeside as a national and international player was tied into the construction of working identities for the more senior managers, nurses and doctors. These tended to be people from well-educated, middle class backgrounds, for whom notions of career and status were clearly very important. Indeed, the use of 'the global' as a positive resource in the construction of identities was differentiated more along the lines of class than gender. For the (predominantly white) nurses at ward level, many of whom came from working class backgrounds, 'the global' was constructed in less positive ways. Race was an issue here, and some resentment was demonstrated at 'foreign' nurses who were seen to be competing for 'local' jobs, even though these jobs could not be filled from the local community at present rates of pay. The global reach of knowledge, telecommunications, technology, and employment markets provided a constantly shifting geometry of social and political relations which provided a range of discourses and subjectivities, some of which were embraced with pleasure, others with more resistance.

An excellent place

> *The office wall of the Director of Nursing Services is lined with certificates, testament to the excellence of the hospital and its nurses in particular. The Charter Mark award for excellence in customer service sits on the window sill behind her desk. As we walk around the hospital we see other certificates displayed; we see the sheer range of speciality and high-tech services that are practiced here. This hospital is a regional centre for most of its activities and, despite its proximity to London, is a national centre for several of these.*

Global constructions of Lakeside as a workplace, and denial of the local, shade into a more specific representation of Lakeside as an 'excellent' place. In part, the connections described above bear testament to this, as the skills and reputations of doctors and nurses are recognized beyond Lakeside. But Lakeside also offers resources *in* place – rather then beyond place – that construct it as an 'excellent' place and which are used by some in the negotiation of working identities.

Andrew qualified as a doctor twenty years ago, graduating from one of the top London teaching hospitals, and since then has built an outstanding reputation as a specialist surgeon. He explains how eight years ago he made the decision to come to Lakeside

> *I didn't want a central London teaching hospital job, although they were all available and still have been available but I wanted – this was a place that wanted a* [particular surgical] *service and didn't have one so I basically came to set it up from scratch*

Lakeside offered Andrew resources which occupy key places within his narrative expression of identity. Specifically, Lakeside offered the opportunity to set up his '*own*' specialist surgical service from scratch as part of a strategic managerial move to overhaul the positioning of the hospital. This offered Andrew the opportunity to 'make a difference' – an aspiration which was central to his account – rather than slot into an already existing service, and to do his 'best' – something he identifies as a key aspect of his identity – reflected in the success of the empire he has built. Being a surgeon is utterly central to Andrew's articulation of identity 'I am a [specialist] surgeon, that is who I am' and Lakeside has enabled him to perform this identity in the way that makes sense to him. For this he is grateful and remains loyal to the organization:

> *Being a* [specialist] *surgeon is a highly tradable commodity, and you know in essence I could go anywhere … but being here is particularly where I want to be. I've had I should think in the last eight years at least half a dozen good offers to go somewhere else but I've always looked at what somewhere else has got to offer and compared it with here and decided here is better. In particular I think in terms of … not having to fight with the administration, having everybody pulling in the same direction. None of these people in ivory towers just trying to conserve their own little piece of the empire …. I can only imagine a situation of moving on … if the whole philosophy of the hospital changed and they said [this] surgery wasn't important, then I would go*

For Andrew, then, the positive place that this organization occupies in his articulation of his identity is linked to his representation of the hospital as proactively and dynamically managed. It is a place that allows him to flourish.

Similarly, several of the nurses made direct contrasts between the resources on offer at Lakeside, with their image of a smaller community hospital like Seaside.

> *I enjoy the pace of it, and the not-knowing, and the speed and things like that [I enjoy being] a skilled nurse as opposed to somebody carrying out your daily activities of living and stuff like that at a cottage hospital ... I suppose it gives that to your identity and with Lakeside ... [using] ... more and more up and coming techniques it is nice to be associated with that* (Rose, junior nurse, Surgery)

Here we see the tensions within the nursing profession played out in an individual account, contrasting the 'hand-holding bed-side nurse' with the skilled professional. Lakeside offers Flack the resources to negotiate a working self that rejects the places associated with the former identity and adopt the latter for herself. As senior nurse on a busy Orthopaedic ward, Diana too embraces the managerialist identity of Lakeside as a workplace

> *I like the buzz of it* [this organization] *and also I am interested in how the hospital is run and the financial side of it and everything else and I think there wouldn't be so much, you know, there's not so much substance to it in another hospital I don't think* (Diana)

Using the resources offered by Lakeside as a place of managerial excellence, Diana positions her self as knowledgeable, capable and highly unflappable. New managerial responsibilities have led her to consider options further up the organizational career ladder. She is currently studying for a diploma in management and already has devolved responsibility for personnel management on her ward and is involved with some ward financial management. In contrast to popular representations of nursing Diana does not see her self as over-worked or stressed-out and is in fact keen to dispel these images, despite being a mother with two children under five years old, and working full-time.

The representation of Lakeside as a 'place of excellence' is used in a specifically gendered way by Martin, a male nurse in his 50s. He has only recently returned to full-time nursing, after a life of being involved in a host of other activities (see Chapter 7 for a fuller account). Money is central to Martin's account: specifically, the low level of nursing pay and the difficulty of being a family breadwinner on a nursing salary. He is highly resentful about this, in general because he sees this as an under-valuation of nursing skills and more particularly because the level of pay has made it impossible for him to work as a nurse for most of his adult life. He has only been able to return recently since his financial circumstances have changed. Nonetheless, public knowledge of nurses' pay causes him some embarrassment with his friends

A lot of my friends are professionals ... I drink with a bunch of guys on a Thursday night, two pilots, Saville Row tailors, there's a whole bunch of us ... earning excellent money and drive Saabs and Mercedes. Although I was probably earning £50 000 a year two years ago, so I was sort of in the same class if you like they find it a little bit difficult to relate to me as a nurse I'm afraid. I don't think they understand it, you know ... cause they know how much money you earn, which is what it boils down to which is how much you earn ... because you're only earning £14 000 a year you're not as clever as they are which is probably right in a way, in their eyes

He clearly feels he has to justify to this middle class peer group why he has chosen to go back to nursing: an occupation which, perhaps especially for men, is regarded by many as potentially rather low level and lacking in status. He does this by constructing Lakeside as 'excellent'

5–10 years ago they used to call it Darkside ... there was no leadership there was no direction there was no, the place was crumbling ... but then something happened ... suddenly the corridors – millions of pounds spent on redecoration and new wards, a new A&E department, a new front entrance ... the charter mark ... so far from being [Darkside] I think it is a very proactive place ... I mean I live in the shadow of [another hospital]... I'd rather travel here ... you can see when you talk to [nurses from other hospitals] that they all want to know what's going on at Lakeside. Because it just seems to be getting a reputation as a place of excellence

This reputation – and its representation in built form – goes some way to ameliorating the assault on both Martin's masculinity and class identity made by the level of nursing pay. This use of Lakeside as a place of excellence is echoed in other male nurses' accounts too. Well used to the ambivalent status accorded to 'the male nurse', they use Lakeside's participation on the national and international stage, the fields of expertise that is has developed and its managerial reputation as a rationale and explanation: yes, OK, I'm a male nurse, but let me explain what that means *here*.

Amongst senior managers there was a prevailing consensus about Lakeside as a workplace, expressed well here by Fiona

> ... *it's pretty informal, relaxed, open, a very open culture. A can do as opposed to a can't do ... its that sort of culture where its 'go get it', cause nothing is outside our scope. I mean we've certainly got that attitude in the management side of things*

Their perception is of an enabling culture, which stretches right down to the wards and to the junior staff

> *I would say that it's an exciting dynamic environment where individuals are encouraged to be independent, working independently but within a team environment. The management allow their staff to be empowered to make key decisions in the way that they want to deliver care ... they take everything very seriously and they're passionate about making sure this hospital is on the map. It's a bit like a family, you know ... so it makes people feel comfortable and secure. It's caring ... it's progressive* (Fiona)

Beyond this however, these qualities are expressed as central to the identities of the managers themselves

> ... *it's enabled me to be what I truly, what I believe is the right way to manage. It's allowed me to be very autonomous, it hasn't curbed my wings in any way and I like that, 'cause I'm that kind of person.* (Fiona)

Here we see how representations of the 'kind of workplace' that Lakeside is, are tied into representations of self. Whilst Fiona subjects herself through a caring and progressive managerialist discourse that certainly stretches beyond Lakeside, the lived performance of this identity is made possible by the resources in place at the hospital. It is a place that has embraced this discourse and has pursued a conscious and pro-active managerial strategy to embed it in organizational practice and corporate identity. The extent to which this is gendered is explored more fully in the next section.

A masculine place?

We have seen above how dominant constructions of Lakeside as a global and excellent place are negotiated by both women and men in the making of working identities, and that class plays a significant part here. The growing ambivalence of the public towards the medical professions means that the traditional assumptions about class and status that were attached to them in aspatial ways are now being refined according to place. Indeed, hospitals themselves are 'classed' organizations – some clearly enjoying more status and support from the middle classes than others. Through its links with the global, excellence in specialist professional care, and training of junior doctors, Lakeside is being constructed as such a place. When we push further and more specifically about the *gendering* of place, we find that gender differentiation also becomes more acute. Whilst the women managers' endorsement of Lakeside as a workplace resonates with suggestions about the feminine sub-text to new managerialism, we found that the relationship between women's managerial roles and their gender identities was rather more ambiguous than this. Alongside claims that a Lakeside management post enabled them to 'be themselves' these managers offered evidence of accommodation and manipulation within the identities that they negotiated at work. This was connected to a sense that 'management' was still properly considered to be a *masculine* role. Amy describes manipulating the managerial process in specifically gendered ways

If Julie is going to be faced with a Board or some quite difficult meeting, she wears a trouser suit. And we all tease her about it. And she says 'oh, I'm power dressing' ... I think that we try to give a masculine image of being very organized and I think that's one of the reasons why we have engaged people like IBM to come in and we tend to, if we're going to make a very big change, get facilitators in and most of them are masculine. That's not because ... Julie and I feel we wouldn't be able to manage the project but it's because we want to give that image of being organized, supported, rational .... Rather than 'lets just sit down together as a load of girls and decide how we're going to do things'

Similarly, when questioned about the impact of others' expectations of her as a woman manager, and if/how this affected her, Alex explained

Not in myself, not in me as a person, but in how I think other people perceive me. Because what I do, I call myself Alex Watson. Now that says it all doesn't it? I'm actually an Alexandra. But I know that if I'm called Alex Watson now that actually, well, I don't know if it confuses, but people don't know what gender I am. So I do use that. Subconsciously more than deliberately.

This continued representation of management as masculine, despite the strong presence of women in managerial roles at Lakeside, is also articulated by nursing staff on the ward-floor, who identify a *'split'* in the gendering of the organization

> *I think it is split. I think the wards are feminine, but the management is masculine. And there are a couple of female managers who fit into the masculine role, definitely* (Drusilla)

> *I think it* [the organization] *is masculine because I think its concerned very much with efficiency, organization. And I'm not saying they don't care about the patients, but their concern for patients is out of giving a service. I don't think they care about the people ... people that actually are the organization. So I think they're more concerned with getting patients and figures off the waiting lists. So I would have to say it's more masculine.* (Wilma)

Here, the nursing self is cast as a feminine self, with management represented in the role of unwanted intruder, sometimes a waste of space and certainly someone who doesn't understand the real practice of nursing. This is despite the belief of nurse managers that they can construct a middle space between the feminine nursing self and the masculine managerial role. Diana for example, a senior nurse from a working class background who, rather to her own surprise, aspires to move into management, plans to take her nursing qualities with her, deploying them to improve (feminize) the managerial role.

> *I'd quite like to go into management so that I could bring a bit of humanity to the wards because it can get very ... very management, you know, or bring it down ... a level ... so that people are aware that management are human or that they are there even.*

The gendering of Lakeside is subtle and shifting, linked to class, hierarchy and profession and particular renderings of these in place. The desire and ability to challenge masculine readings of management is tied to organizational power. As those nurses moving up the hierarchy find ways to re-invent the gendering of management – albeit in unstable ways – the female nurses on the ward-floor feel subjected, but resistant, to a masculine managerialism. For them, the managerial subject threatens the hands-on core of their professional nursing identities, whether this subject is male or female, it is represented as a masculine assault on feminized identities.

Seaside Memorial Hospital

Constructions of Seaside as a place rest heavily on links with the local community, tied to care-led representations of both medicine and nursing. Both these underpin the dominance of a representation of place as feminized, that is used in constraining and enabling ways in the negotiation of gendered selves at work.

A great little facility

> *The day before our first visit to Seaside Hospital the General Manager called us. Would we mind postponing, he asked, there was little local difficulty. Fascinated, of course, we discovered that an internal report considering the closure of the Minor Injuries Unit at the hospital had been leaked to the press. The doctors who worked in the unit, ably assisted by the press, had mounted a demonstration outside the hospital, lambasting the managers and mobilizing the local community. Within days it was confirmed to the press by the hospital trust that it would not close the Minor Injuries Unit at Seaside.*

Seaside hospital provides rehabilitation and medium term care of the elderly for patients referred from the local acute hospital, Churchside. The making of this place was not articulated through global or national connections (although these are still important) but through talk of other local hospitals and reference to the local community. As a large community hospital, with a minor injuries unit and outpatient clinics, Seaside is something special compared with other local community hospitals. But compared with Churchside it is small and old-fashioned offering routine, even mundane, services. These constructions of Seaside as a workplace were used in distinctive and gendered ways by the doctors and nurses that worked there.

The doctors at Seaside split into two groups: those on non-career 'staff grades' employed to cover basic medical responsibilities at the hospital and the consultants, employed by Churchside. Despite our best efforts, none of the staff grade doctors would meet with us. We heard stories about how poorly they were treated; that they were all overseas doctors, mainly Asian; or that they were career failures with no other choices. These doctors' representations of Seaside remain closed to us. But others' representations of these doctors is significant in its' own right. To be a doctor employed on a staff-grade is bad enough within the National Health Service: the status is poor and career options non-existent. But to be a staff-grade doctor at *Seaside* really is the end of the line. By contrast, the consultants spent their working lives travelling between Churchside and Seaside. This movement between places offered them other possibilities for negotiating working identities. According to some observers Seaside enables these consultants to negotiate a *traditional* consultant role in an health service where this is fast disappearing. Jenny, a senior manager explained

> *I think what they see Seaside as is buns actually ... nobody else has got it. I mean* [it's like they think] *'We've got this and nobody else can get it'. They're the* [ones] *that hold the gate ... they've got these 48 beds which are absolutely protected and they can have their names above the beds whereas at Churchside they can't get that ... here they can be the old-fashioned consultant again*

Ward Sister Sarah suggests that Seaside offers the consultants a 'place to breathe' away from the more urgent and arduous demands of the acute sector

> *I think you see part of it is the fact that they're so busy at Churchside and everything is so stressful and completely different that when they come down* [here] *they can sit down and they can have a banter and the decisions are made for them* [already, by the nurses] *and it's a way out really, for a couple of hours*

The consultants themselves endorse this to some extent in that they describe Seaside in traditional terms as friendly, 'a great little facility', somewhere to send their less acute patients for peace, quiet and recuperation. In their presentation of identity, Seaside offers opportunities to present a caring self and to confirm their rejection of stereotypical (surgical) medical identities, as Simon reflects on his medical training

> *What I really enjoyed were the patient communication skills ... I didn't like the then current surgical personality. The rather authoritarian, dogmatic, you know 'This is the way I do it' and making medical students feel small type of person ... I was more interested in the more emotional side of things*

Bernard presented a similar account, describing how he came to resist the authoritarian medical identities that he encountered in training, particularly their lack of attention to the patient at the heart of medical care. He embraces the opportunities that Seaside

I'm very proud to work in Seaside hospital ... the difference between Seaside and other hospitals is its so much consultants [with few other doctors] ... so the consultants are more hands on with the patients and in dealing with the nurses than in a bigger hospital

For the nurses too, the relationship between Seaside and Churchside was central to their representations of self, but in a far more critical sense. For them, Churchside used Seaside as a 'dumping ground' for those patients they had no room for or, in effect, had lost interest in. Whilst the nurses wanted to provide rehabilitation, the consultants sent patients who were difficult to rehabilitate. Any efforts to change this situation were blocked by the consultants, as Sarah reveals:

In the last couple of months, the sister downstairs and I have tried to move things forward; we've faced an awful lot of opposition from the consultants. And I think one of the biggest problems we're finding now is because we're taking a lot of the patients from Churchside, we're not going to be about to change things much because of how the three consultants view the hospital.

The case for a shift in nursing activity is not helped by the fact that none of the nurses at Seaside has a University training, and few have middle class family backgrounds. In these terms they lack cultural capital, this undermines their claims to expertise, and positions them with even less power vis-à-vis the visiting consultants.

However, the local associations between Seaside and the community offered the nurses more pleasurable opportunities for the negotiation of working identities. For Ward Sister Molly, its community engagement is what she valued most about the hospital, and the fact that she and her colleagues were also local people themselves was clearly important to her sense of being professional, and a member of a *special* group of nurses:

I value its ability to supply the community with what they want. In other words, that hopefully if the community needs certain services, we will provide it for them. And I also value that we are all local and that we all want is to give the best possible service to the community. Because it's them who actually kept this open, I think it was about 20 years ago... I think we owe the community a lot...

Here then we see distinct interpretations of the local, made by doctors and nurses and – as it happens at Seaside – by men and women. These gendered differences become more apparent, when we turn to consider the second dominant representation Seaside as a workplace.

A place where nurses can nurse

> *As researchers moving from Lakeside to Seaside, and back again, many contrasts struck us. That after all is an important advantage of comparative methodology. At Lakeside the nurses were rarely close to the patients for any length of time. Some never left their offices. We could see them, busy in front of computer screens or doors were shut as meetings took place. At Seaside, nurses walked slowly with patients along the corridor to the day room or the bathroom. Nurses sat next to patients at the bed-side. The office was busy, a hub of information and exchange, but the nurses came and went during the day never pausing for long unless a shift was over.* (At night it was different, see Chapter 5).

Nurses at Seaside used the local connections and forms of care in their workplace to construct distinctive working identities. As we have seen above they valued their service to the community, and they did not want to be involved in developing 'fancy' services unless it could be legitimated in community terms. They were scathing of the spread of entrepreneurialism and managerialism into nursing practice and throughout, there was an emphasis on the importance of nurses' role at the bedside, providing direct patient care. At the heart of these accounts of nursing identities lies the notion of Seaside as a place where *nurses can still nurse.*

This construction of place was central to Anna's negotiation of self at work. Anna trained at Churchside, and worked there for five years in acute medical and haematology. Gradually she became dissatisfied with what the hospital demanded of her and in particular, the nursing role on offer there. Describing her original motivations to nurse, she says

> *I was a good communicator, I liked working with people. I couldn't have stood a job where I had to sit at a desk. I like working with people, talking to them, finding out and helping them basically*

As a workplace, Churchside exaggerated this conviction, in both positive and negative ways

> *I mean when I first started as a staff nurse I'd trained for three years to actually give physical care to the patients that I was looking after. To then be confronted with being removed from the physical care, more and more*

*into the paperwork and the managerial side of things, which is not what I trained to do. …. and there was a lot of strong feeling for that at the time because we felt so strongly about being taken away from the caring role which we'd trained, which was our role, **that was how we saw ourselves**. That was what we saw ourselves becoming. Then to find out that you were taken more and more away from that … working at Churchside the role that I was being forced into was trying to make me, if you like, into a worse nurse than I knew I could be. (Our emphasis)*

By contrast

Seaside allows you [me] *more scope to* [pause] *maintain the person and to build on the person that you are* [I am].

Also emphasizing Seaside as a place where nurses can still nurse, Douglas – the only male nurse in the hospital at the time – sees quite different potential for Seaside and uses this vision to negotiate his own nursing identity. In coming to Seaside, Douglas has explicitly rejected the acute sector, specifically the masculine identities that it offers:

Its more technical, its more male, if I can think of a word like that. It's more male, yeah? Technical. The interaction that you have with the patient is much less in personal terms. You're dealing with specific problems: dum, dum, dum, dum [said in a mechanistic tone] *… so you never build up a relationship with them. … I have to say I've never met a male nurse that I could model myself on, 'cause I've always thought that they weren't able to make, put the two together and take some of the sort of female-type skills and the more male, and put them together, and actually produce something that was distinctively different in terms of nursing, rather than kidding on you were a woman … and I made a decision I wasn't going to be like that*

Nonetheless, Douglas works hard to reconstruct the nursing roles on offer at Seaside using managerialist resources

I think the sort of person that comes, there is a certain type of nurse who will come to work in a community hospital … maybe I am sort of [person] *… I don't particularly like the high pressure of a very, very acute environment, I don't like it. I don't respond well to it, it freaks me and I don't like it. Um but I still don't see why a community hospital shouldn't be a dynamic and interesting place that moves forward and provides care that actually makes a difference and has a meaning*

Far from being a 'traditional' oasis in a restructuring health service, Douglas attempts to construct community hospitals as a key part of that reform and development. Douglas is critical of the old-fashioned way in which Seaside is managed, describing the place as *'a substantial piece of National Health Service property run like a cottage hospital from the 1950s'* yet he presents himself as someone with the vision to take Seaside into the 21st century: he can see the possibilities. In outlining these he makes use of credentialist discourses of nursing. In sharp contrast to every other nurse we met at Seaside, Douglas endorses Project 2000 and the advanced training of nurses. He is clearly motivated by recent changes and is concerned with effective management in the National Health Service. All of these elements mark Douglas as distinctive at Seaside but rather than rejecting Seaside as an organization which contradicts the way he sees himself, he presents the hospital as one which could, or at least should, confirm these core qualities.

In Anna, Molly and Douglas's accounts we see the complex ways that the resources on offer at Seaside are actively managed in the construction and performance of multiple nursing identities.

A feminized place

The emphasis on a model of nursing where nurses 'can still nurse' is suggestive of traditional feminized discourses of nursing care. Whilst few commented on this directly we would suggest that this is precisely because Seaside is a female dominated place. Gender is camouflaged by the absence of men. As Jenny, a senior manager says: *At Seaside all the nurses are women and all the doctors are men. It fits nicely with what people perceive as right so it doesn't cause* [pause] *it isn't an issue*

Indeed. Seaside is constructed as a feminized place, where conventional gender roles are rarely questioned and where gender divisions within healthcare are maintained. The doctors' and nurses' verbal narratives reveal three aspects to this gendered construction of place, and of their own working identities.

First, several of the nurses explained their presence at Seaside in terms of motherhood. The relatively light demands of ward nursing at Seaside enable these women to combine paid work with their chosen practice of mothering

> *I've always been quite honest, that they* [the children] *come first and this just fits in: no weekends, no evenings .... I think perhaps I could be doing a bit more than what I'm doing at the moment, but then its swings and roundabouts* (Debbie)

This is not the place for a middle class nursing career. This is deeply frustrating to the minority of nurses at Seaside who want this, but not important to the majority of the nurses here. There is a widespread sense that motherhood comes first is linked to the second element in the gendering of Seaside as a workplace: the lack of opportunities for career advancement either within or beyond Seaside

> *My honest view is if you were really career minded you wouldn't be at Seaside hospital anyway ... I know the reason I'm here, I know the reason I'm here part-time [see above] and I'm sure a lot of nurses on the wards, if they're honest, are here for the very same reasons ... I don't honestly think if you're really career minded or a really forward person you wouldn't be at this hospital anyway* (Debbie)

It was widely suggested that community hospitals and the limited opportunities on offer within them acted to deter men from coming to work in them

> *They'd rather be in a district general hospital.* [Community hospitals] *are not sexy. They're not glamorous, they're not thought of highly* (Amanda)

> *It's generally a rehabilitation hospital and its not something that if you're ambitious you're going to get anywhere with really ... that's probably why there aren't many [men] here ... Careerist? No, I don't think that's what's really expected here. I mean there isn't really a career structure as such here ... being that much smaller, the other jobs are not readily available here. You know, you can't apply for a sister's post because there are already sisters here and they're probably going to be here for another ten to twenty years you know?* (Marion)

Third, the construction of Seaside as a feminine place is demonstrated in the reactions to the few men who *do* appear there. We have just seen in the accounts above how the presence of male nurses at Seaside is regarded as an oddity and this is confirmed by Douglas who describes being treated with suspicion because he has not chosen the usual (and more acceptable) channels for male nurses (theatres, intensive care, Accident and Emergency). Towards the end of our research, two new male nurses were appointed into specialist/managerial roles at Seaside. Neither proved a great success. Sarah's account of recent changes suggests that gender plays a significant part in the way that these are working out

I get on with Jim very well ... but it's very difficult, he's generally met with mixed feelings. The way that he projects himself, he opens himself to a lot of ridicule, people don't take him seriously ... because he's quite a feminine man, people just don't see him as management material really ... he's not particularly manly, you can see when people meet him for the first time ... if you watch him when he's with Kim [the new general manager], *people tend to go to Kim because she's got this aura of management, because she's heavy set, she's got this big chest* (laughs) *and she just has that managerial quality ... anyone of that build in nursing seems to command more respect ... Jim is more a very skinny chap ... with Rodney he definitely doesn't like being in a female environment – he doesn't particularly fit in. And he's not one of these men that women can flirt with; he's not a flirty man. Because I always think in a very female environment, you do need a man for women to get on with and exercise that other side of your character. When Douglas was here, he's very flirtatious, it was definitely noticeable. But Rodney hasn't stepped into that role and Jim hasn't either... It happens as soon as the consultants walk in, light hearted flirting definitely.*

This suggests that men are only readily accommodated in this workplace as consultants. All others are problematized. Certainly the consultants themselves represent Seaside as a place where conventional gender roles persist and present this as a natural state for a place like Seaside

I think that the perception of it is that the consultants are men and the nurses are women, and that's a reality here. Whether it's because this is, you know, a community south-coast hospital as opposed to a teaching hospital where you will have dynamic, aggressive, um, career-orientated women who will be up there fighting. I'm sure that's part of it. (Charles)

Here Charles represents a very clear gendering of place. He ties distinctive femininities to particular workplaces. More than this, he absents himself from this, commenting as a liberal bystander, rather than an active agent in the gendered life of the workplace. He can do this at Seaside, where the conventional gendering of professional and organizational life is naturalized.

Summary and discussion

This chapter has begun to explore how the *where* impacts on negotiations of gendered identities at work. Focussing on workplaces, we have seen distinctive medical, nursing and managerial resources used to construct Lakeside and Seaside as particular places. We have seen the complex agentic engagement with these resources in the construction and performance of gendered working identities. Worked through place, these outcomes are nonetheless diverse. Workplaces offer both resources and constraints to individuals in the negotiation of working identities. Through the negotiation of these selves, places are re-produced: though the insistence that Seaside is a place where nurses can nurse, or the active production of Lakeside as 'global' or 'excellent', the distinctiveness of these places is produced. Places are actively produced, not passively received. Places are relative, constructed against other places. We see this in the doctors', nurses' and managers' accounts of what their work place is like and not-like. We see it as doctors, nurses and managers recount their biographies bringing resources from other places with them into accounting for their current work place, and describing their working identities. This attention to spatial mobility underlines an important point. Increasingly, working lives and identities are constructed across multiple workplaces. Of course, these are not erased and over-written as we move on from one to the next. Present workplaces are constructed though past workplaces and, sometimes, projections about future workplaces: place and time are constantly interwoven in this way, through memory, habit and desire. (See Chapter 7). But, at the very least, we cannot assume that working identities are transferable between places. Whilst some elements may remain comparable between orthopaedics in different places, or care of the elderly, the ways in which these are organized and practised, the expectations and routines of social as well as professional life are shaped by the complexities of place. As one senior surgeon at Lakeside, who knowingly embraced the aloof and egocentric identity associated with his profession, confessed with self-deprecation when reflecting on a previous posting in Yorkshire: *'It's difficult to be pompous in Barnsley'*.

Understanding organizations as work*places*, in the way developed in this chapter, is essential to our understanding the relations between gender, identity and organization.

Our use of the concept of 'place' shifts our focus from organizational culture, or 'how things are done around here' (Deal and Kennedy 1982), to take in workplace, or 'what it's like round here' (Glucksman 2000: 146), as well as 'what we would *like* it to be like round here'. Exploring these aspects helps to reveal issues of difference and diversity within organizations. Crucially, we have seen how the making of place – historically, materially and in our narrative accounts – is both gendered and gendering. Each place offers resources that both subject and are used in the negotiation of gendered identities at work. Lakeside offers resources for nurses to resist traditional constructions of nursing, through global connections, reputation and the complexity and size of specialist and management hierarchies. Many doctors too have been shown to enjoy using, and re-emphasizing, the resources of Lakeside in this way. Men in particular enjoy constructing themselves as highly successful, despite working in a District general Hospital rather than a teaching hospital, there is enough for them to construct both the place and self as dynamic, important and cutting edge. We have seen that not only is this interesting in terms of gender, but also class: by emphasizing the professionalism of medicine and nursing through a contemporary, academic approach to care, the middle class status of the professions is also re-constructed. The clear message is: this isn't a job that can be done by any old person: you have to be special (clever) to do it, a particular kind of doctor or nurse, man or woman. However, we have also seen that there are limits to this sort of social mobility – many of the nurse managers have confessed to feeling out of place in managerialist spaces, and feel the need to deploy a range of performative tactics to support their right to be there.

Similarly, Seaside offers resources and constraints that are both gendered and gendering, but which are also negotiated in creative ways. We have seen how many of the female nurses enjoy serving the elderly people of their local community in the way they feel they deserve – slowly, patiently, sympathetically – in short, drawing on 'feminine' skills. This construction of both the workplace and workplace identities impacts in interesting ways on Douglas, who, although he feels he has found a place where he can negotiate the sort of masculinity he desires, attempts to resist the conception of Seaside as 'purely' feminine. In his attempts to credentialize Seaside and, in the process, his own nursing identity, connections can be made with Martin's negotiations at Lakeside. Both men struggle with what they see as outsiders' views of male nurses: non-masculine men engaged in women's (and, therefore, low level work). In their negotiations of their identities they attempt to draw on alternative discourses of both gender and class to re-emphasize the skill and ambition necessary to be a good nurse.

This chapter has argued that the notion of workplace is a rich and deep concept, which can incorporate organizational culture, but also places this in a wider empirical and theoretical framework. We argue that this approach has a number of distinct strengths. First, at the heart of the concept of 'workplace' lies both the large and the small, the specific and the general, the local and the global. Workplaces are highly specific yet this specificity is wrought from social, cultural and economic processes operating at global and national as well as in the locale. To see organizations as 'workplaces' refutes an 'inward looking enclosure' recognizing instead 'local articulation within the wider whole' (Massey 1994: 115). Second, the notion of workplace spans boundaries between academic disciplines and theoretical approaches, recognizing the complex articulation of the social/economic the historical and the spatial and of the discursive and the material. This offers a richer and deeper engagement with 'organization' and understanding of the articulation of gender and identity at work. Third, our use of the concept of 'workplace' recognizes both structure and agency, and the iterative relation between them. Workplaces are done, they are performed, but certainly they are performed through the constraints and resources of history, economy and discourse. Places carry already constituted meanings, but not in any essential form. These have to be constantly activated and reactivated if they are to persist. Fourth, and finally, the progressive notion of place developed by Doreen Massey (1994, 2005), and used in this chapter allows for difference and diversity, in a way that is partially captured by the concept of 'sub-cultures' but which reaches beyond this. The meaning of 'workplace' is contested and dynamic: produced in the everyday in ways which may differentiate not only between clearly defined groups but which may shift and slip between groups and even within individuals. This is to remind us of our central point: workplaces are both used and made in the negotiation of gender identities at work.

5
Spaces of Identity

It is 4.30pm in the Accident and Emergency department at Lakeside. The waiting room is half-full and has an un-nerving sense of tension and boredom. Each time the doors open, heads turn with curiosity and apprehension. A&E is a liminal zone: anyone could appear at any moment, in any kind of condition – in pain, in distress, drunk. The nurses and doctors are sealed-off in an inner sanctum – a large square room with curtained bays and a central doctors' station. As an outsider, this space is intimidating. There are sick, injured and frightened patients in every bay; unfamiliar sights, sounds and smells. I try to make myself as inconspicuous as possible: there seems no legitimate way for me to occupy this space. Based in the centre of the room, the all male group of doctors inhabits the space with ease. In between periods of urgency, communicated largely through speed of movement rather than speech, the doctors' gather at their station, backs outwards, quiet, intently focussed on each other. The nurses do not enter this huddle but continue with their routine business. As the doctors' conversation turns to plans for the evening's entertainment, one stretches his arms above his head and pushes his chair out to stretch his legs and, doing so, blocks a main thoroughfare. A nurse side-steps smartly to avoid him. He doesn't notice her.

It is 2.45pm on a rehabilitation ward at Seaside. The post-lunch lull has given way to a palpable sense of expectancy: the consultant is due for his weekly ward round at 3pm. The ward is extra-tidy, the paperwork up to date and all the last minute jobs are done. The patients are in bed, or sitting quietly in the day room, watching TV and reading magazines. There is enough space on this ward to make a corner for myself and a benign disinterest from the staff that makes it easy for me to be here. The ward sister stands at the top of the ward, where the consultant will be arriving shortly.

She takes a deep breath, pulls her shoulders back and runs the palms of her hands along her hips and thighs, smoothing her already pristine uniform. Walking smartly along the main thoroughfare of the ward, she does one last check then turns to smile and greet the consultant as he enters.

Introduction

In this chapter we shift our attention from representations of place, as they are used to negotiate gender identities at work: to look at the lived spaces of everyday life. Whilst the previous chapter showed that gendered identities are negotiated through representations of workplace, this chapter concerns space as it is inscribed on, and performed in, the gender identities of doctors and nurses as they inhabit the spaces of their everyday lives. Whilst doctors and nurses may construct coherent (albeit competing) representations about the 'kind of place' a certain hospital is, working lives are lived within wards, cafeterias, operating theatres, waiting rooms, staff-rooms, management offices and corridors: sharply differentiated spaces that both demand, and are produced by, distinctive working identities. Here we endeavour to unpick the iterative and dynamic gendering of these spaces as they are used and produced in negotiations of identity. This means that we pay attention to the ways that organizational spaces are used and produced in the negotiation of working identities. Like the previous chapter, here we analyse our interview texts to explore the ways that people talk about the spaces of their working lives. We also make greater use of our observations in different hospital spaces, particularly focussing on the ways that spaces are animated by the embodied performances of the women and men who move through them. This means a direct focus on the materiality of lived experience: the practices through which individuals become subjects (Nash 2000). These embodied activities are ways of negotiating identities in gendered organizations.

The chapter begins with *our* description of the differentiated spaces in each of our two hospitals, drawing attention to both the material and the symbolic, as well as our own reactions to these spaces of hospital life. This starting point does not imply that we see space as pre-constructed – outside of human activity – but to understand space as always already under construction. The aim of our text is to convey the complexity and differentiation of hospital spaces as they are encountered, made and re-made in everyday working lives. Our question is this: how are these multiple and fragmented organizational spaces used and made in relation to working identities? More specifically, how/do these spaces inscribe identities? And how/are these resisted? How important is gender here, and to what extent is the relationship between space and gender differentiated? Before exploring our own empirical material further, the chapter discusses our theoretical approach to the spatialities of embodied identity, drawing on broadly Foucauldian approaches as well as on non-representational accounts of everyday practice developed in contemporary Geographical theory. Attempting to bring these perspectives into a productive dialogue, the chapter continues with our empirical analysis, exploring what our doctors and nurses, women and men do and how they feel in their relations *to* the spaces of organization, as they move *in* these spaces and as they move *between* the micro-spaces of their everyday lives.

Spaces of organization

Lakeside Hospital

Sunlight streams in through the large glass atrium at the front of the hospital. Plants are tastefully placed against curved backdrops. Colourful ceramics are displayed in glass cases. There is no smell. Walk a bit further and these impressions start to slip. The café has glass walls, muffins and cappuccino, but chipped institutional-green crockery and old-fashioned formica-top tables. Further on, the blue carpet stops, replaced by shiny, but worn out linoleum and peeling polystyrene ceiling tiles, hard grey surfaces and metal windows as you enter the unrefurbished 1960s build. Long corridors stretch ahead with wipe-clean surfaces, strip lighting on ceilings, closed doors off with bluntly descriptive, but sometimes incomprehensible, nameplates (SCBU, MRI scanning, Theatres). Some efforts are made to relieve the functionality of the corridors: local students' artwork is displayed and the series of small gardens beyond the windows are being redeveloped in a range of styles, like so many examples from garden makeover T.V. shows (Japanese Zen here, sculpture garden there). Accident and Emergency at Lakeside has its own entrance, separate from the glass atrium. There are no boundaries – physical or social – between A&E reception and the outside world. You step immediately from outside into the waiting room, and unlike any other area of the hospital, everyone has a right to be there, 24 hours a day, 7 days a week, and the staff have a duty to take them seriously. There is a strictly policed boundary between the waiting room and the treatment area. Nurses and doctors do not appear in the waiting room: the receptionist operating border control between the two spaces controls access to these professionals – she is socially and spatially in control. If the going gets tough she can pull down the shutters, sealing herself on the 'private' side of the border, but this rarely happens. The nurses and doctors work in the treatment room. Here there is a sense of timelessness and the room feels a long way from anywhere (although, of course, it is in fact very close to the entrance).

The Management Suite also feels a long way from the rest of the hospital. Added as another new extension, it is accessed by mean of a glass and metal bridge leading off from one of the old-style corridors. The bridge is decorated with large black and white photographs of (gendered) hospital activity: a mother with a premature baby, two male surgeons with facial masks operating under bright lights, a male nurse doing 'resusc(itation)', an old woman chatting to a woman social worker. The management Suite itself is impressive: a large light and airy space, with contemporary chairs and movable screens. The silence is noticeable: people 'pad' about, their movement noiseless and cushioned. Back on the wards the contrast is stark. Each ward is named simply by a number, with a layout and style that shows little variation. Bays of 6–8 beds are sectioned off from a long central axis with single rooms for the most seriously ill. These spaces are marked by their drab uniformity and conformity – curtains, bedding, furniture and decoration reflect a 1970s attempt at 'brightening things up' with floral borders and pink paint. The dark ward corridors do not even have this distinction; they are in dilapidated order, and littered with objects on trolleys: laundry trolleys, the drug trolley, oxygen cylinders, patient record trolleys, even crash trolleys. There is obviously no point in putting these things away, or attempting to 'make things look nice'. It is always busy. There might always be an emergency at any moment. There is little personalization anywhere on these wards, the walls, the nursing station, the reception desk – no photographs or postcards, bits or bobs. The wards are cramped, hot and stuffy: they feel confined (and confining). Members of staff have little control over the temperature or lighting. There is some natural light by the beds, but none along the main ward axis. As you leave the wards, the main corridors seem cool, breezy and empty with the promise of another destination. Just off one of these corridors are the Postgraduate Centre and Doctors' Mess: both live up to the sense of promise. We are once again back in the new build, with its plush carpeting and shiny fixtures. Here the emphasis is on style and comfortable expense – more corporate conference centre than institutional National Health Service.

Seaside Hospital

At Seaside, a new entrance hall has been smartly 'tacked on' to the older building behind with modern automatic doors that open and shut continuously, letting in the biting sea air. A nod has been given to contemporary design: glass and beech veneer are in evidence, but the colours are 1970s institutional: dark green paintwork, pale green walls. To one side is the restaurant, 'Daphne's' which, despite the dated pink walls, pink furniture and funereal flowers, is clean, tidy and comfortable, busy and indeed often full with customers from the local community as well as patients' relatives and members of staff. Nearby an un-named door leads up a stairwell to the management offices, newly built and smartly furnished. The doors are open and managers and administrators work with quiet camaraderie. Downstairs again, a central corridor leads through the hospital, past large bouquets of fresh flowers situated at incidental points and major meeting places. This is a hyper-clean, well-resourced and very much cared for hospital. The 'Friends of the Hospital' (local dignitaries and business people who act as advocates and fundraisers) are frequently in evidence: portraits of benefactors and other corporate memorabilia hang alongside the displays of leaflets and reproduction works of art. The chapel forms a central focus, outside of which a large wooden board remembers citizens of the town who died in the two world wars. There are three highly distinctive wards in this hospital, each with a proper name commemorating an influential 'Friend' in the hospital's history. Entering each ward is by means of long highly polished squeakily clean corridors, and each one gives off the feeling of orderly calm: no major events will take place, many beds are unoccupied as the 'patients' sit in the day room or shuffle up and down the corridors.

The wards are self-contained and, spatially, at the end of the line, situated as they are on top and the edges of the building, they are not thoroughfares, they lead nowhere. The overall colour is pink: pink walls, pink furniture, and–again–pink flowery borders. One ward is markedly different however: situated in an older part of the building, it is larger and old-fashioned in style, with a 'Victorian' air. The main activity centre of the hospital is the Minor Injuries Unit, which is newly designed and furnished space. Yet even here the atmosphere is one of civilized calm. The furniture is comfortable: almost domestic rather than rundown institutional. Coffee is made to order using a household kettle: 'would you like a biscuit with that?'

The spatialities of embodied identities

Different spaces, then, both within and between the two hospitals. Each organization is a dynamic composition of 'all manner of spaces, conforming to all sorts of metrics and metaphors' (Thrift 2003: 2022). The practices through which our doctors and nurses, women and men negotiate gendered working identities are constituted in and between these sharply differentiated spaces. These identities are on-going, done in the practices of everyday life and embedded in and through particular spaces and spatial relations. This directs our attention to the *embodied* subject. Identities are done by and through bodies: embodied practice is both expressive and constitutive of identities (Crouch 2000). This is profoundly spatial. Our ways of living as bodies derive from the relations the subject has to objects and events in space:

> ... these are not reflective or scientific properties of space but are effects of the necessity that we live and move in space as bodies in relation to other bodies (Grosz 1995: 93).

Identities are performed by bodies in constant interchange with their surroundings. As Gatens (1996) argues:

> Identity can never be viewed as a final or finished product ...The human body is radically open to its surroundings and can be composed, recomposed and decomposed by other bodies (Gatens 1996: 110).

From this perspective our surroundings, our environments, the spaces of our everyday lives are far from passive. They are, rather, 'a manifold of possibilities' (Thrift and Dewsbury 2000: 415) and limitations.

Exploring the spaces of identity requires attention to embodied performance, examination of how people act and re-act in the spaces of their working lives. In more practical terms this means that we need to explore how identities are performed through the positioning of objects and people in space; through access to (and exclusion from) these spaces; and movement within and between spaces. These complex 'spacings' (Crouch 2000) are simultaneously conceived, perceived and lived (Lefebvre 1991): they are abstracted and designed, by planners and policy makers; they bear meaning constructed from a myriad of competing and shifting sources; and they are experienced and animated bodily, as we move within and between them.

One way to develop this is to trace the exercise of power over the embodied subject. The working body, for instance, is subject to overt surveillance and discipline about where and when it should be located, how it should move and position itself in relation to others and to objects. But we must also recognize the exercise of disciplinary power in mundane and routine embodied behaviours (Foucault 1977) or 'styles of the flesh' (Butler 1990). For both Butler and Foucault, the body is a surface that is inscribed by the power vested in social practices. Bodies are acted upon discursively in particular institutional settings – workplaces, for instance – bearing 'taken for granted practices in which bodies are disciplined and normalized' (McDowell 1999: 50). Working bodies are inscribed through aesthetics of bodily style and presentation (Witz, Warhurst and Nickson 2003): so far as we are concerned here, how we move and space ourselves in relation to the people and objects in the spaces that we work. As Bourdieu (1984) states

> one's relationship to the social world is never more clearly expressed than ... in the space one claims with one's body in physical space, through a bearing and gestures that are self-assured or reserved, expansive or constructed 'presence' or 'insignificance' (1984: 474)

From within feminist geography, and beyond, this engagement with space has been read in gendered terms. Using time-space geographies, it has been shown that generally women's and men's patterns and range of movement differs, as men's lives produce larger scale and more linear geographies whilst women's lives produce localized and more complex but repetitive movements (Rose 1993). Beyond this literal mapping of gendered spatialities, imageries of home and the domestic are woven into understandings of femininity whilst exploration and adventure, the claiming of new territories have been central to white western masculinities connected to the activities of colonialism (Segal 1990) but resonate still today. Of course, it is not only the 'where' of spatial movement that is important but also the 'how'. In relation to sex and gender, both 'man' and 'woman' are produced through 'regimes of corporeal production' (McDowell 1999: 51), including gait, posture, movement and relations to other objects and subjects in space. It is (in part) the repeated citation of gendered bodily norms, by sexed bodies that produces gender, both subjectively and discursively. Whilst masculinity works through expansive bodily posture and authoritative movement, embodied femininity encompasses the constrained/restrained and tentative occupation of space. These gendered spatialities are intertwined with professional discourses associated with medicine and nursing, particularly in relation to movement (quick/slow) and relations with bodies (distanced/engaged). Whilst a 'doctor' is expected to be 'quick' and to engage in specifically distanced (emotional) or proximate (examination) relations with patients, the 'nurse' is represented as both slower and closer to patients (emotionally as well as in physical cart).

However, whilst we are certain that disciplinary power is inscribed on the embodied subject, in gender specific ways, we need to extend our theoretical and analytical framework beyond this in two key ways. First, these embodied and spatialized representations of sex/gender and profession are just that: representations. They suggest the ways that gendered and professional identities *might* be inscribed on working bodies but this is not the same as knowledge of how working identities *are* performed bodily in the spaces of everyday life. Discursive representations of embodied professional and/or gendered identities certainly warrant investigation at the level of everyday life, but – of course – we would not expect to find a seamless correspondence between discursive representation and embodied practice. The relation of embodied individuals to these discourses can only be *explored* and should never be assumed. In both theoretical and empirical terms, this leads to a focus on everyday practice: what people do and how they feel as they create and navigate the spacings of their everyday lives in the construction and performance of identities. Whilst recent debates in organizational studies have also paid increasing attention to the agential subject (Benhabib 1992), showing how people resist, manoeuvre and play with discursive practices in their working lives (Iedema and Wodak 1999; Newton 1999) these are based almost exclusively on *talk* about representations of ideal-type subjects. For instance, interviewees are asked to comment on particular discursive subject positions, or authors' present their own deconstruction of interview texts to make claims about the nature of the working subject. In distinction, here we are concerned as well with '… the arts of what people do … in real time, through the expressive qualities of the body' (Thrift and Dewsbury 2000: 420)

Second, we must recognize that the body is not only discursively inscribed: it is also fleshy, material and sensate (Shilling 1992). The body is not only 'done to' but is also generative; it has 'configuring abilities' (Harrison 2000: 504). Thus, for Harrison (2000) the key question is not 'what does a body stand for?' but 'what does a body do?' For the proponents of non-representational theory (inspired by Thrift 1996, 1997), this means a focus on action before thought, the pre-discursive: on bodies that re-act and in that re-action make themselves subject. Individuals are '... understood as effects of the events to which their body parts (broadly understood) respond and in which they participate' (Thrift 2004: 60). However, in both theoretical and methodological terms we find it difficult to be clear about boundaries between the 'pre-discursive' and the discursive. Embodied response and practice is rarely an independent or singular act but is rather related to, and done in (if not determined by) representational contexts (Crouch 2000; Nash 2000). As Seamon writes in his *Geography of the Lifeworld* (1979) the un-reflexive body-subject learns behaviours through repetition over time, behaviours that come to be perceived as 'automatic', 'habitual', 'involuntary' and 'mechanical' (p. 41). Movements, for example, 'become familiar when the body performs them several times and incorporates them into its world of pre-reflective understanding' (p. 48). This is not to re-prioritize mind over body. Rather it is to recognize these as relational. Non-representational theory draws our attention to the fleeting, subjective and affective moments of organizational life (Conradson 2003) but, as Dewsbury (2003) argues, following Deleuze (1991); it is the relation between sensing and making sense that matters, that it comes at all, rather than which comes first, that is important.

This understanding frames the remainder of this chapter, which is concerned to explore how gender identities are negotiated in and through the multiple and fragmented spatialities of organizational life. In researching these questions we have used both interview text and our own observations. Interviews offer doctors' and nurses' reflections on what they do, and how they feel, in the spaces of their working lives. Whilst often our observations confirmed these verbal negotiations, gaps also opened between talk and practice. We saw activities and responses that were never mentioned in talk, embodied engagements with working spaces that either people did not want to talk about or, perhaps, that 'cannot adequately be spoken of' (Nash 2000: 655). Whilst non-representational theorists draw attention to the potential of 'wilder empiricism' (Dewsbury 2003: 1927), including theatre, music and dance (Thrift 1997), to make this 'world come alive', we agree with Conradson (2003) that 'a more general attentiveness to everyday doings, habit and improvisation' (Conradson 2003: 1989) can also enable a 'more lively and creative account of organizational space' (Conradson 2003: 1989). Close *engagement* with the micro-geographies of habitual practice (Nash 2000), the body- and place-ballets (Seamon 1979) of everyday life, offers a way into that which is un-spoken, perhaps un-sayable. (See discussion of our distinction between engagement and observation in Chapter 2). However, we are wary of the assumption that researchers can access that which their subjects cannot. As Nash (2000) has argued, this implies

> ... a new (or maybe old) division of labour separating those who think (especially about not thinking or the non-cognitive) and those ordinary people out there who just act (Nash 2000: 662)

Thus, we repeat: these are *our* observations, borne of *our* engagement with the spaces within Lakeside and Seaside hospitals. Certainly we suggest that these offer insight to the unspoken but these claims are provisional. Similarly, we persist in presenting our doctors' and nurses' spoken accounts of their engagement with organizational spaces and what this represents to them. Whilst these are undoubtedly partial, limited by the interview context and more fundamentally by language as a representational system, these texts express something of *their* embodied engagement with organizational space and this remains important to us.

In the rest of the chapter we examine the minutiae of embodied activity in the multiple and differentiated organizational spaces that comprise our two hospitals. We explore how identities are performed through access *to* (and exclusion from) these spaces; and through movement *within* organizational spaces. In particular, we focus on the ways these are gendered – what differences exist here between men and women? What do these tell us?

The spatial practices of bodies

Relations to space

The multiple and diverse spaces of hospital life bear an invisible map of inclusions and exclusions that mark the territories of the working subject. Mapping these territories allows us to open up some very particular spacings of identity, related to both profession and gender. Specifically, this section explores the embodied accounts of spatial restriction and spatial freedom, a binary at the heart of gendered spatialities. It shows that the conventional privilege of (masculine) travel over (feminine) confinement is contingent and open to subversion.

In both hospitals, nurses as a professional group are most confined to specific organizational spaces. Whilst doctors' responsibilities usually require them to move from consulting rooms to wards or theatres as well as between wards, nurses are commonly rooted in place, attached to a localized territory, usually a ward. There are some exceptions, most notably for nurses working in Accident and Emergency for whom the diverse nature of emergency admissions means regular trips with new patients to all parts of the hospital. Notably, significant numbers of male nurses are found in Accident and Emergency nursing, whilst nursing on mainstream wards (excluding Intensive Care) is almost exclusively carried out by women. Across our two hospitals there was only one male nurse working on a mainstream ward, and indeed he had chosen this explicitly to mark himself as different from the usual performative expectations placed on male nurses. (See discussion of Douglas in Chapter 4). The wards are staffed almost exclusively and certainly most consistently by female nurses. Among these nurses, a sense of their hospitals as a set of multiple and diverse spaces barely registers. Their working day began with a set route through the hospital into 'their' ward, where they would stay for 8–12 hours often without leaving. Their role of hands-on care for named patients, combined with staff shortages has cut breaks to a minimum, and nurses have least access to any recreational or study space (McMahon 1994; CSAG 1998). This effectively denies nurses access to the other spaces of the hospital, both physically and emotionally. The ward-space is, for many nurses, all they have and even these workspaces are not 'theirs' since the shift work pattern of nursing means that someone else is always in 'their' space, even when they are not there. This may explain the lack of personal imposition in the construction of space by the nurses, which we noted above. Of course, the nurses make some informal private space for themselves, whether this is the transitory 'borrowing' of sluice rooms, corridors, washrooms or offices. At Lakeside, successful lobbying by nursing staff on the surgical wards brought them a (small) staff room of their own, which allows for some relaxation, discussion of non-work issues, and thus other identities to surface. Conversely, however, it also functions to confine nurses to the ward area even more denying any reason at all to leave the ward during a shift.

Conventionally, the spatial restrictions placed on nurses – especially in relation to the freedoms experienced by doctors – might be read in negative terms. Restriction represents constraint, powerlessness, a 'lack': an impoverished relation with the organizational spaces of identity. However, in clear distinction to this, nurses' confinement was not widely resented. Rather it was experienced and used in more positive ways, linked by a common sense of 'home', associated with belonging, warmth and at-easeness (Seamon 1979). Other spaces were not longed for, but derided

I never go on the other wards! (laughs) Very rarely, no, no. If I go down to [another ward], to be perfectly honest, I view them with somewhat amusement (Sarah, nurse, Seaside)

Whilst to the outsider, the differences between working as a nurse on one ward rather than another lie only in the nature of the patients, for these nurses the home ward – whatever its speciality – became a basis for the construction of difference and loyalty

I think you just feel comfortable in your own area, don't you? Because everywhere else is going to be different from here (Carole, nurse, Lakeside)

This is a very happy ward definitely ... I mean even going to the ward next door I notice a big difference ... there seems to be more people that aren't quite happy in their jobs (Gaby, nurse, Lakeside)

Spatial confinement led to a strong territoriality and an almost domestic relationship with the ward, that echoes the traditional ties of femininity and 'home'. This was especially marked at Seaside, as Sarah reveals in describing her feelings when a part of 'her' ward was taken over for another purpose

... effectively the ward lost a tremendous amount of space, it lost that identity, and I couldn't walk through the door and feel the whole area was mine anymore ... I was very lost for a long time

I'm very home orientated and the ward's my home whilst I'm here. I take everything very personally and the care has to be just so and I'm very neat and tidy and very organized....this is an extension of how I run my home in many ways

This domestic sentiment was echoed in the spatial practices of the nurses on the wards at Seaside. All bar one of these nurses was female. The office was a safe haven, in constant use where the nurses sat round talking, their feet tucked under them, enjoying coffee, biscuits and a chat. Douglas, the one male nurse, used the office in this way too, apparently comfortably engaging with and re-making the space along with the other nurses there. There was little sense of embodied urgency expressed in their relationship to space; but many were emotionally attached, demonstrating a fierce loyalty to their ward expressed through a sense of intimacy and territoriality.

In contrast to the ward nurses, most doctors at work traveled extensively within and beyond the spaces of hospital life. This offered them a range of differentiated spaces within which to narrate working identities. Their privileged access to certain 'doctor only' spaces present an opportunity to live out their status and superior position in the professional hierarchy of healthcare. As we saw in Chapter 4, the consultants at Seaside have particular spatial freedom, moving regularly between two rather different hospitals in their working week. Their representation of Seaside and the local acute hospital as different places offered these doctors alternative resources to negotiate rather different working identities. However, once at Seaside, their movements were limited. With the exception of ward rounds – once at Seaside, doctors stayed in their offices. These rooms, with their closed doors and restricted nurse access acted to confirm their status as well as helping shape what it means to be a doctor at a hospital such as Seaside: a rarely seen, solitary 'expert'. As a far larger hospital, with a far wider range of responsibilities and resources, Lakeside offers its doctors many potential resources for negotiating identity. The to-ing and fro-ing between the multiple spaces of theatres, personal offices, consulting spaces and wards or the Accident and Emergency Department meant these doctors' relationships with the various spaces of the hospital were altogether more fluid and mobile, as well as being a lot more visible. There was a greater choice of spaces in which to perform their working identities. For surgeons, operating theatres offered a 'pure space' for the surgical identity, a space where, they say, they could relax free from the demands of managerial culture and concentrate on their 'real' business.

> *Operating theatre is a very special place ..., it's usually quite relaxed.. there may be music in the background, anaesthetists and people you see quite regularly, and there's usually just quite a lot of chat ...it's nice being in theatre because you can leave your bleep with the receptionist and you're in a sanctum and no body can get at you* (Nina, Registrar)

> *the doctors used to treat that as a time when they could be themselves, and say completely irreverent things about everything, whereas when they were in front of patients they've got to be in their position of authority.* (Deidre, nurse, Seaside)

But they have too the choice of other spaces. Both the Postgraduate Medical Centre and the Doctors' Mess, offered greater and more varied opportunities for the construction and performance of identities than either the personal offices or ward space allowed at Seaside. Lakeside doctors use these spaces regularly and value them highly both in terms of the variety they offer as well as the prestige they confer on those privileged enough to use them. It is these facilities in particular which help to differentiate the hospital as a large centre of teaching and learning, helping to reinforce the identity of consultants and junior doctors that they are not 'run-of-the-mill', they are part of a dynamic, cutting edge organization. In addition, these doctors' facilities are not open to nurses or patients, and this separation of social space serves to create a sense of being special among the doctors:

If you have your own space and it's away from the patients, I mean all the other hospitals I've worked at, the restroom, the cafeteria you share with the patients...I don't think that's right really. It's nice, it's very friendly, it's quite small, it's probably very clean, it's very well equipped, we have good access to the labs...it's almost like a little centre point, because all the General Practitioners come here, they just come down here to have lunch (Rachel, junior doctor)

However, this sense of community was disrupted both by hierarchical divisions within the medical profession, and between medicine and other healthcare professions. In the Doctors' Mess spatial practices reinforced seniority and authority as Greg, a Senior doctor at Lakeside explained:

There's a consultants dining table ... it's not designated as such, but they all sit in a little group and no-one else sits on that ... You wouldn't dream, you wouldn't dream of sitting there ... occasionally they will lower themselves and sit with their juniors ... but you would never go and sit with them ... There always used to be a consultants dining room ... you know, napkins and table cloth and silver knives and forks and all the rest of it ... they perpetuate it by having their own table. Unspoken, but it's there.

Here, spatial practice perpetuates traditional hierarchical divisions. The consultants have the privilege of choice; the junior doctors accommodate themselves to the invisible boundaries imposed on them but maintain a sense of expectancy that they might, one day, be chosen. Organizational travel and access to multiple spaces for doctors at Lakeside also substantiates the distinction between medicine and nursing, as well as their hierarchical relation. As Alistair, a Surgical Consultant and Diana, a Ward Sister, explain:

The postgraduate centre at lunch time, that is quite an interesting place and I think that is unusual because all of the doctors go there for lunch...a great opportunity to meet people, but it also means that you never have lunch with any of the nurses and radiographers, or any of the junior medical staff (Alistair)

I mean on the wards you're integrated with the doctors, but then they go off for meals they go to the mess, or they go to the post-grad centre and they've got their own restaurant. We don't often see the doctors in here [the public restaurant] (Diana)

However, the apparent spatial freedoms offered to the medical staff at both hospitals have their downside. As doctors are intermittent visitors to the wards, they are constructed as outsiders to ward life which – to some extent – undermines their power and destabilizes performances of the confident, autonomous and superior professional. Doctors need the nurses to update them, or to find supplies, and they are well aware that this is the nurses' space. (See below for further discussion of this point in relation to movement and walking). Furthermore, travel between multiple spaces means moving through public as well as professional spaces and opens doctors up to unpredictable demands, as Andrew (Surgical Consultant at Lakeside) and Bernard (Care of the Elderly Consultant at Seaside) explain

I can't appear on the corridor, I can't appear on the ward, I can't be on the end of a phone without people wanting me to do something all the time... I couldn't be a General Practitioner, because it would not only involve me it would subsume me, I can see that, by having the total personal contact with patients like that. At least I don't meet them in Sainsburys (Andrew)

You can walk down the corridor having a joke or immersed with a colleague about something and you suddenly bump into the relatives of the patient and often its very awkward. You completely feel as though you shouldn't be doing that sort of thing because you know that, rightly or wrongly one doesn't want the patient or the family to feel that the person looking after them is anything other than a strict professional who knows everything (laughs) and it can be awkward (Bernard)

The Accident and Emergency Department at Lakeside operated as an exception to the accounts above, for both doctors and nurses. Here, the prevalent spatial rules were reversed, with doctors more confined spatially and nurses more mobile than their peers elsewhere in the hospital. Indeed, the distinctiveness of these spatial practices were explicitly used to mark out the special nature of A&E work.

> *A&E has got its own staffroom its got its own community, and you don't actually go anywhere else...that's why I don't come up here [to the management suite] ever, even the canteen and stuff: you just grab some food and go back to A&E* (Rav, Junior Doctor)

For nurses here, the transient nature of their patients and the need to move those admitted to the hospital out of A& E quickly meant that they often had the opportunity to visit other parts of the hospital as they moved patients about. Indeed, this aspect to their particular work was relished and used as a key marker of their 'special' status in relation to ward nurses, as Kay (an A&E nurse) demonstrates:

> *Most people recognize me because I'm forever taking patients to all the wards...they [ward nurses] don't really get around; they probably go to x-ray or theatres and nowhere else really...*

Discussion

Inclusions and exclusions across the multiple spaces of hospital life play a central role in doctors' and nurses' negotiations of the working self. This map is a gendered map. Who is allowed access to what works, in part, through gender distinctions and is used in gendered ways in the negotiation of identity. As we described in Chapter 2, the historical emergence of medicine and nursing as professions was intertwined with gendered representations and expectations of spatial practice. To this day, nursing remains – in one account – strongly tied to femininity and domesticity, to closeness and being rather than distance and doing. Whilst nurses' spatial restriction to the wards might be interpreted within masculinist hierarchies as stasis and confinement, this is reinterpreted and animated productively within nurses' accounts as safety, arrival and belonging: a 'homespace' (hooks 1990). Whilst this is, clearly, situated within a thoroughly gendered context that continues to insist on confinement as limitation, these nurses show how their 'homespace' offers possibilities for resistance (Duncan 1996), and we will pursue this further in the next section. In contrast, the travel opportunities for doctors represent activity, privilege over restriction and doing rather than being. Some of these hospital doctors are women (although rather few remain in hospital medicine beyond training) but, arguably, they are accommodating to a spatialized discourse that resonates with representations of masculinity rather than femininity. Whilst women doctors had the same access to multiple spaces within the hospitals as did the male doctors *at their level in the hierarchy*, hospital consultants are overwhelmingly male (EOR 1998; EOR 2001) and the resources of organizational space are still used to underscore power and privilege. As a consequence, key sites of medical privilege took on a predominantly masculine identity, which the junior doctors – both women and men – had to accommodate themselves to. But, whereas all the male doctors expected to stay in hospital medicine and hoped to gain access to these spaces of privilege as their careers developed, none of the women doctors was certain she would stay long enough for this. (See Chapter 6 for detailed discussion of this point). For the women doctors these spaces seemed unattainable, not only now but ever. Finally, it is important to recognize that doctors' organizational travel does not always represent control, and can itself be experienced as constraining. Doctors movements are heavily determined by 'the bleep' – dictating where they should be and when, often in impossible ways (Walby et al 1994; see Chapter 6 below). In addition, travel across organizational spaces can open doctors to multiple expectations that are difficult and uncomfortable to manage. In sum, we have seen so far that gendered spaces are important in the negotiation of self, but that this is an active production. The power relations invested in particular interpretations of space are contingent and open to destabilization. Most of this account has relied on talk, but our last point about power rests more heavily on our observations of doctors and nurses as they go about their daily practice. In the next section, we begin with a stronger reliance still on these observations of spatial practice although, as you will see, occasionally verbal representations are stunningly incisive.

Relations with space

As well as differences in access to space, differential professional and gendered relations *with* space were present in *movement* through and within the spaces of the hospitals. *Walking,* for example, is a particularly important spatial practice: the walker brings to life the resources and limitations offered by particular spatial configurations, and makes these exist as well as emerge (De Certeau 1984: 98). In relation to our concerns here, we might say that the walker both uses the resources of organizational space in the everyday expression (Augoyard 1979) of professional and gendered identities, but is also constrained by them. But it is not only the *where* of walking it is also the *how*: comportment, posture, orientation, eye contact, and pauses: all tell rich stories of relationships and power networks.

On the surgical wards at Lakeside, for example, the ward nurses move quickly in the constant performance of their tasks: responding to the constant ringing of buzzers, visiting and checking each patient, making them comfortable, administering drugs, taking blood pressure, whilst all the while returning to the nurses station to complete their paperwork, log things onto the computer and answer the phone. They move with purpose but in repetitive, chore driven ways – always busy, always doing something, buzzing around repetitive spatial patterns, communicating with each other in passing, snatched conversations. Built into this ceaseless pattern of activity, in which nurses seem to have little control, these nurses use their bodies to marginalize the doctors, turning their bodies and avoiding eye contact. The message is clear: 'we're busy, and we haven't got time for you', 'we're not your handmaidens', 'you'll have to come to us if you want something'. In this the nurses' contest professional hierarchies. They render the junior doctors, in particular, uncertain, and they display their unease in hesitant and slightly bowed and almost childlike bodily postures. In contrast to the nurses' constant activity, doctors are either still – the thinker – or moving purposefully towards a goal – the doer – the nature of their work means they are usually going somewhere specific for a one-off visit, and they move differently. As we sat on the surgical ward at Lakeside a male doctor came striding along the central thoroughfare towards us. He didn't see us but, as he swept past, his unbuttoned white coat flapped outwards creating a breeze on our faces. This speed and style of comportment asserted direction, authority, an unquestioned purpose. Our observations of women doctors show them to be less ostentatious, both in their speed of movement and posture. Their occupation of space was less comfortable. We repeatedly saw young women doctors walking with their arms crossed over patient notes, held against the chest, heads down in thought, purposeful but closed and – perhaps – defensive. Relations between the women doctors and the women nurses were also uneasy. There was no ready accommodation of women doctors, by virtue of their sex or different embodied approach on the wards. The intertwined class and professional differences were too long standing and significant for this.

On ward rounds at Lakeside the gendered and hierarchical differences within the group of approaching doctors can be read, simply from the bodily styles of movement. But the doctors act as a group in relation to the nurses on the ward, communicating with each other in closed groups: backs outwards, quiet, almost whispering. For 'important discussion' it appears, nurses are not needed. Nurses do not even try to enter these huddles, displaying disinterest, perhaps even disdain, whilst they continue with the 'real', practical activities that actually need doing whilst the talk goes on.

At Seaside, the different type of tasks and responsibilities that the nurses undertake mean that things are less frantic and there is far more sitting down, and chatting and sometimes time to talk. One nurse at Seaside articulated this difference absolutely in terms of embodiment and movement:

You get two types: you get pretty girls with ponytails who are fairly slim and who walk around very quickly, and they tend to work on surgical wards. And then you get people who are a bit more like me, who are sort of a bit rounder, a bit slower and tend to sort of be edging towards medical nursing. And it's really true (Linda)

Walking here was calmer, as patients were less critically ill, many sitting in the day room enjoying a read, a quiet snooze, a cup of tea, or a chat. Activity for nurses thus peaked at certain times of day: getting the patients up in the morning, ward rounds with a consultant, putting the patients to bed again at night. Perhaps for this reason walking the ward became more of an event, and as such some were able to reflect on it as an expression of personal work identity. For example, the combination of 'walking' with the 'wearing' of the uniform was particularly important to some to confirm their sense of their working identity.

I put this uniform on, I'm a completely different person ... It is bizarre, it comes out in even the way I walk. [pause]It's [pause] I never walk the way I walk in this ridiculous dress. I don't do that at home. If I'm walking down the road ... I'm dragging my feet. I'm constantly in trainers, I just wander. Here, head up, and I walk straight, like a determined walk. You walk as if you're going somewhere, even if you're not, even if you're popping to the kitchen to make a drink, you'll walk in that manner (Amanda)

Douglas, a male nurse at Seaside also saw walking as a central bodily practice in the performance of his working identity as a male nurse. The wards themselves were sometimes felt to be like a theatre, where one was constantly on display and subject to performative demands:

It actually is quite difficult; it's something you have to learn to be because it's like a theatre. 'Cause you walk on and you're on show, to a certain extent, 'cause somebody's looking at you, yeah? And you've got to learn how to do that, to feel comfortable doing it

Douglas' sense of 'being looked at' and display reveal the disciplining power that is embedded in 'the gaze': both from patients and from other colleagues (Foucault 1977). Indeed, as Foucault argued, the architectural design of 'the ward' exploits visibility and reinforces the sense of surveillance. In hospitals, like schools and other public institutions, the surveying and controlling gaze is one of the techniques for producing abstracted and appropriate performance in terms of both profession *and* gender. For example, Douglas recounts the pressure on male nurses to adopt a particular practice in relation to practice

... you know, be like a floor-walker in a shop ... You walk up and down the ward but you never touch anybody. You know, you direct people. And I've met lots of male nurses like that, yeah? ...they've never seen them; they've never touched the patient

However, Douglas 'made a decision I wasn't going to be like that'. In this rejection of these masculine spatial practices, he constructs an alternative masculinity which is central to his nursing career, and directly linked to his identity as an out gay man.

The way one walks is thus not only read by the walker themselves, but by also by others. Bodily comportment conveys both power and authority, as Douglas reveals in his description of his ward manager,

She is quite traditional, and you can tell by the ... way that she walks about the ward and the way she carries herself and the way that she acts and behaves. It's actually very much the quite traditional sister. .... [later] I mean you can see in the way she walks up and down the ward, it's sexual. Hyper-sexual. It is sexual. I mean she doesn't wear that uniform like a piece of work-kit, yeah? It's like power-dressing, yeah? [chuckles] That's sexual. ... And she's seductive. It's the way she stands, the way she moves, the way she smiles at them [the consultants]. Um the way she uses her eyes. It's sexual. And it's about them being controlled.

This sense of ownership and the construction of outsiders extended to the hospital manager, who broadcast his discomfort on the ward to Douglas through is bodily style

> *He is not comfortable on the ward ... he doesn't know how to do it ... he comes on the ward, and he is uncomfortable, he feels out of place, even with me ...and he sort of shuffles uncomfortably.*

Whilst this manager would prefer nurses to visit him, and has set up open meeting times to encourage this, they won't go; to enter managerial space is not something the nurses will willingly do:

> *This is an open thing and nobody goes. Well of course nobody goes, because it's up those stairs up into his lair where it's nice and comfortable for him to be.* (Douglas, nurse, Seaside)

This suspicion was echoed at Lakeside, where the marked difference between managerial spaces and healthcare spaces was used to underscore a sense that managers were over-privileged and even parasites on the under-resourced healthcare professionals who were, after all, the 'real' business of the hospital. Annabel, a nurse at Lakeside sums this up:

> *Lovely nice carpets, nice office, lovely up there for them...I don't know what they do, but they can get on with it!*

Discussion

Bodies in movement are central to the grammar of narrating identity. To walk away, to walk past or turn one's back: these are all ways of expressing identity in relation to others, with the contingent aspects of gender, class, race and age all being intimately involved in the performance. Movement between and within organizational spaces relies on the continual and complex articulation of spatial rules and resources: access and exclusion; speed and direction; posture and comportment; the positioning of bodies in relation to other people and things – clipboards, drug trolleys, even cups of tea. Movement offers different possibilities for the negotiation of identity yet these articulations are situated within habitual choreographies of space, which our doctors and nurses, women and men, perform in their everyday working lives and as they negotiate their working identities. These movements may be planned and strategic, or un-thought, unreflexive embodied reactions but they are clearly – in part – constitutive of professional and gendered identities at work. In this brief account alone, we have seen that movement bears the imprint of power: professional power, gendered power and resistance to both. Movement animates, but may also rework the hierarchies of professional and gendered power. Male doctors continually reconfirm their status and rights through the ways they walk, the spaces they occupy and the contact they have with others. It appears that their negotiation of a particular hegemonic identity is done with unquestioning confidence. However, these performances are sometimes deliberately ignored by the female nurses, thus presenting a challenge to their meaning and power. Women's ways of bodily performance may reveal a more tentative and uneven relationship with power and a less sure negotiation of their working identities as people of some status. However, women's consciousness of being 'watched', of being subject to the male gaze, means that they are used to a sense of performance. Some are able to exploit this with enjoyment, using movement and posture to control and excite. This sense of performance was be shared by Douglas, who explicitly positioned himself as an outsider (as a male nurse, as a gay male nurse, and as a gay male nurse in a community hospital). Douglas was acutely aware of spatial performances at work, and uses the ways he walks and moves between patients to convey an identity of engagement and contact with the more caring side of nursing. These shifts in the performance of movement reveal the contingent, provisional and ongoing nature of negotiations of identities.

Summary and conclusions

In this chapter we have argued theoretically, and seen empirically, that organizational spaces are complex and dynamic constructions, provisionally composed from a variety of resources continually woven together to produce opportunities and constraints that are used – both deliberately and, perhaps, without thought – to negotiate identities in gendered organizations. Hospital spaces bear gendered histories and meanings, embedded in their architecture and design; the kinds of objects which are selected and their positioning within particular spaces; the activities that are carried on within them and the practitioners responsible for these. Different gendered threads are woven throughout these abstract, symbolic and lived spaces of everyday life, providing differentiated environments for the women and men who conduct their working lives within and through them. Difference and inequalities are woven into the very architectural fabric, and familiar hierarchical relations are routinely reinforced and maintained in distinctive ways, between the sexes in medicine, in nursing and between the professions. However at the same time, since meanings can never be fixed in or to spaces, possibilities for redefinition and challenge are ever present. People draw on the open, unbounded quality of space to reinvent relationships and identities, to reinscribe the ways in which space is used and understood. Women, or junior nurses and doctors, can gain the upper ground of spaces and challenge the structures of power and relationships, negotiate an alternative identity. This may be only ever unstable – achieved in one moment and lost in the next, but it is in this minutiae, in the fleeting bucking of routines and the momentary bursts of revolutionary energy, that little victories may be won and enjoyed.

All this we were able to observe in our periods of active engagement with hospital life, and we have used these observations to convey a flavour of the value of watching the ways people move about, noting what they do with their bodies, where they go, who they stand near or move away from, who they seek out and who they ignore. As watchers of these performances we were able to make our own analyses of the identities that people were negotiating: these were how they appeared to us, these are the assumptions we made. Of course these may be read differently by others involved in the relationships – the way we read the exercise of power for example, may be simultaneously understood in a different way by others. However, we would argue that this multiplicity of interpretation and meaning only serves to underscore the richness of looking at the relationship of the body in space. Indeed, it was through our continual watching of our doctors and nurses that the importance of gender was reinforced for us. We have to admit that at times we would come away from interviews feeling that we were barking up the wrong tree – as gender was denied with an indifferent shrug, or a bored sigh. We would meet for coffee in the canteen and ask each other – *have you met anyone who thinks gender is significant?* But as we looked around the canteen – at the separated tables of female nurses in their starched hats gossiping whilst eating their slimline yoghurts, to those of young, white-coated male doctors, sprawling across tables, laughing about football as they tucked into their chips – we could see gender all around us. Clearly, interviews and talk were not sufficient to tell us what happens in gendered organizational life. Attention to the embodied subject – to the ways people move about and use organizational space – offers the opportunity to go beyond the spoken and in the process extend our understanding of the complexity and subtlety of the relations between gender, identity and organization.

We would argue that this approach is important in two key ways. First, it shows that far greater care is needed in thinking about 'organizations'. Certainly, there are aspects of organization that transcend the particular spaces we have discussed in this chapter. Personnel policies, for example, dictate the terms and conditions of employment whilst, so far, national agreements determine doctors' and nurses' pay. But however important such factors are in shaping working lives, these lives are not defined or conducted solely through such policy documents but in the embodied and differentiated spaces of hospital life. As we have seen, gender is made distinctively within these spaces and this must be taken into account if we are concerned with the negotiation of working selves in gendered organizations.

Second, our approach insists that we develop a fuller account of gendered organizational spaces, an account in which history and materiality are central. Access to space and movement in space are not only made in the present, but bear the weight of historical associations and precedents, past negotiations *embedded* in the present (Halford, Savage and Witz 1997). The on-going construction of nursing spaces and medical spaces is always in response to the already constructed spaces of hospital life, whether in re-iteration of earlier constructions or as a challenge to them. In this we include both discursive constructions of space – the meanings and understandings that underlie practice – and material constructions of space – the built form, interior design and objects that construct space. Through developing a fuller understanding of organizational spaces in these theoretical terms, the possibilities for and constraints on embodied *practices* by women and men working within organizations can be better understood. And it is through such opportunities and constraints that on one level, the power relations between gender, identity and organization are determined and formed.

6
Everyday Times

Introduction

Early in the morning at Lakeside the nurses start preparing for the daily scramble for beds. Patients are roused with cheerful clatter and brightly told that they are 'going home today', bags are to be got ready, and relatives notified. New nurses appear, and the night nurses tell them of the night's proceedings. The nurses here are always – or so it seems from the outside – trying to catch up and never getting there. Later, surgeons and junior doctors appear in fast moving convoys, their dialogue rapid and unintelligible to us before moving on, leaving a residual rocking of the swing doors behind them. In the corridors beyond, the Surgical Business Manager joins the throng: the Consultant is also the Clinical Director and we see the Business Manager asking him to sign off on a major equipment purchase. He does this without stopping, steering himself seamlessly into his office. Through the open door, we see piles of papers in his in-tray. Outside in an ante-room, a long queue of out-patients are waiting to see him. We wonder what time he will get home tonight...

We arrive as the night shift settles in on Nightingale ward at Seaside. The last patient is put to bed, and the pace slows. The nurses gather in the staff room, sharing snacks, magazines and stories. We are welcomed as a new form of entertainment – the nights are long and not always busy. Occasional waking patients are helped with kindness and patience, and we can hear gentle murmurs of encouragement and support: a trip from bed to the bathroom and back might take half an hour. The sister sits in her office, a still and silent, watchful presence. By 6am, just as we are drooping, the patients are being woken, and breakfast is underway before the day shift arrives. The handover is calm and ordered, but the

100

pace is picking up. Relatives, social workers and physiotherapists begin to move through the ward spaces, carefully monitored by Sister White. The morning drifts by rather peacefully, the nurses working quietly with the patients. At 2pm sharp, the Consultant arrives from the acute hospital, eight miles away, and the weekly ward round begins. There is a slow and sociable progression around the beds: patients have their weekly chance to see a doctor and learn whether they will be discharged. When the ward round finishes, the mildly flirtatious banter we enjoyed listening to between the Consultant and the Sister continues as they move into her office.

The next two chapters explore how gendered working identities are negotiated with and through time. We show that time is a central discursive and material resource in the making of gender identities at work: both constraining and enabling as gender identities are contingently negotiated with time and across the places, spaces and times of individuals' lives (Taylor and Weatherell 1999; Holmes 2002; de Certeau 1984). Developing this account, we recognize the multiplicity of times (Adam 1995) implicated in negotiations of the gendered working self. Whilst calendar and clock time are dominant in work organizations, healthcare work and hospital life are simultaneously shot through with other renderings of time, from within and beyond working lives. So, argues Lefebvre '[j]ust as Cartesian geometry is a reductive way of understanding space, so too is the measure of time, the clock, a reductive comprehension' (Lefebvre 2004: xi). Rather, as Adam claims, 'there is no single time, only a multitude of times which interpenetrate and permeate our daily lives' (Adam 1995: 12). Following this lead, our temporal approach to the study of gender identities at work, emphasizes the simultaneity and mutual implication of different times in the negotiation of gendered working selves. In the next two chapters, we explore the gendering of working times and trace how these times are used in the negotiation of gendered working selves. Furthermore, we show that the availability, meanings and uses of these times are *themselves* subject to change over time and space. This allows us to further explore the contingent and contextual nature of gendered selves as they are negotiated at work.

Both of the following chapters explore the temporal negotiation of gendered working selves in a different way. Whilst this chapter concentrates on time in *everyday* working lives, Chapter 6 concentrates on *lifetimes*. However, the difference should not be overstated. Lifetimes are not fixed but continually (re)constructed in the present; whilst everyday times are embedded within wider social, cultural and economic contexts (Silva 2002). In theoretical terms, the difference between the chapters is – again – one of focus, not categorical distinction. In the remainder of this chapter, we explore the implication of *everyday time* in the negotiation of gender identities at work: time as it is constructed, experienced and used in everyday working lives. This is complex and differentiated. The complexity of everyday time lies in the multiplicity of times it encompasses. Of course, everyday working time is about the measurement and meaning of clock/calendar time: How much time is spent at work? How much time is allowed for particular tasks? And how is this experienced? But other times are interwoven too. Bodily times, memories and other commitments in time (and space) may be embedded in daily time at work in routine and mundane ways and/or appearing in unpredictable flashes and moments (Sheller and Urry 2003). To add to this complexity, these everyday working times may be differentiated over both time and space. The construction, meaning and use of time may be distinct between day and night – for example –in different parts of an organization, or between home and work. Finally, it is important to repeat: these everyday working times are not, necessarily, derived from present everyday relations. They may have long histories, connected to the emergence of professional discourse, the organization of the National Health Service, or inter-professional relations. But they are lived in the everyday lives of the doctors and nurses that we met, and in their living they are made, re-made and – sometimes – transformed.

Our aim in this chapter is *not* to present an exhaustive account of everyday hospital time (cf. Zerubavel 1979) but, rather, to examine the constraints and opportunities of everyday time as doctors and nurses negotiate gendered selves at work. We do this by once again looking closely at the talk of our interviewees to explore how daily working time is framed and represented in relation to the self. Specifically: to what extent is the relationship with time gendered, and how are gendered working selves negotiated *using* daily time? And *over* daily time? Our observational methods are also important here. Time is both visible and embodied: we could *see* men in white coats rushing about at Lakeside, talking to each other in snatched, clipped sentences, constantly looking at their watches as they scooted down the corridors. They performed 'being busy'. In contrast, we could *see* the pleasure taken by the women nurses in their relaxed discussions at Seaside, where, as they walked slowly down the corridor with a patient, leaned against the doorway or hugged cups of coffee, *time was taken* to care, to ask about the night before, or to gossip about the latest machinations from management. Indeed the attitude towards us within each hospital was different also: at Lakeside we were often ignored as people almost stepped over us to get on with their work. At Seaside, time was taken to ask whom we were, whether we had kids, where we lived.

We begin our discussion with an overview of previous research on time, gender and healthcare work, exploring medical work, nursing work and management in turn. Building on this, we show that distinctive patterns and representations of time have been central to both the *definition* and *gendering* of these different forms of healthcare work. Nonetheless, and in distinction from previous sociological accounts, we argue that time takes multiple and contested forms within medicine, nursing and management. In the remainder of the chapter we explore how these multiple and gendered times are implicated in the negotiation of gendered selves in specific working contexts at Lakeside and Seaside hospitals.

Time, gender and healthcare identities

Hospitals are 24/7 organizations. They require continual cover from healthcare professionals and managerial synchronization of a complex mix of activities, resources and patients, subject to a highly unpredictable workload, in terms of admissions, the progress of disease and illness and the time necessary for care. Medicine, nursing and management are positioned distinctively within this temporal order. Indeed, we see at once multiple, and clashing, temporalities driven by differences between hours of work, daily routines and, more fundamentally, different conceptualizations of time (cf. Glucksman 1998). These distinctive temporalities are central to both the definition and the gendering of medicine, nursing and management and to discursive representations of working identities in healthcare.

Sociological research identifies time as a key marker of the medical profession, both in the *amount* of time that medical training and practice require and in the class status that this heavy time commitment carries (Zerubavel 1979; Frankenberg 1992). Doctors work longer hours than are expected from most other occupational groups: it has not been unusual for UK hospital doctors to work over 100 hours/week (Pringle 1998). These hours have been unpredictable: doctors are expected to see patients through particular crises, however long that takes (Zerubavel 1979); to respond to their 'bleep' immediately wherever they are and whatever they are doing (Walby, Greenwell et al

1994); and to regularly forego sleep. This time commitment has been central to the 'traditional conception of the professional as inseparable from his (sic) occupational role' (Zerubavel 1979: 53). Through its time demands, the profession consumes identity, becomes synonymous with it: the person is the doctor. At first glance, doctors' submission to the temporal demands of their profession bears some striking similarities with domestic time (Pringle 1998), tied to dominant cultural representations of femininity, where work is all consuming and never finished. However, whilst domestic time is commonly represented as lacking status and power, the time required of doctors is a cornerstone of professional status. Indeed, medical time may be 'the most valued cultural capital that doctors have' (Pringle 1998: 11). Furthermore, in the medical conceptualization, time is intellectual and expert whilst domestic time is embodied, emotional and – usually – represented as unskilled. Lastly, the power of all embracing medical time lies, for Frankenberg (1992), Zerubavel (1979) and Pringle (1998), in the representation of a medical career as a privileged *choice*, rather than a constraint or burden.

Despite this, the British Medical Association (the professional body representing doctors in the UK) has been active in pursuing limits to doctors' working hours. In 1991 the British Medical Association successfully negotiated a 'New Deal' which limited junior doctors' hours and introduced regulated shift working for the first time (British Medical Association 2004). This obliged National Health Service employers to limit junior doctors to an average maximum of 56 hours/ week. This *professionally-led* restructuring of doctors' working time was backed by legislation in 2001 and 2003 making it illegal for junior doctors to work longer hours, or without sufficient rest. Hospitals were also encouraged to introduce 'bleep policies', employing more senior night nurses to reduce calls to doctors. Alongside these changes, demands for more flexible and 'family friendly' working hours have gathered strength. In 2005, the British Medical Association and the National Health Service Employers negotiated a new contract enabling job sharing across the range of hospital training posts. This is represented as a direct response to the rapid increase in the numbers of women entering medicine in the UK. Women now take up 61% of all places in medical schools, and will outnumber male medics by 2012 (*The Scotsman* 11/04/05). With relatively few women doctors staying in hospital work, particularly because of the incompatibility of working hours with family life, these changes are represented as an essential policy intervention to halt the haemorrhage of qualified doctors from UK hospitals.

Meanwhile, previous sociological studies of nursing suggest that a key distinction between nursing and medicine lies in the 'boundaried' nature of nursing time, compared with medical time (Zerubavel 1979; Frankenberg 1992; Walby, Greenwell et al 1994). Zerubavel (1979) argues that whilst individual doctors have a continual obligation to their patients – even if they are not actually with them at all times – individual nurses are easily replaceable by other nurses who can provide continuity of professional care. This, he claims, means that 'whereas physicians stop when work is done; nurses stop when the shift is over' (Zerubavel 1979: 54) being associated with their professional role only 'within the temporal boundaries of their duty periods' (ibid: 56). This suggests that nursing is a 'job', rather than a 'career', an important class distinction as well as a gendered distinction. Because of the boundaried nature of nursing time, both Zerubavel (1979) and Frankenberg (1992) agree, nurses are cut-off from their professional identities and activities, operating clear distinctions between work-time and break-times, and between public and private. These distinctions between nursing and medical temporalities are read as expressions and mechanisms of power. In the healthcare context, the lack of boundaries is a 'symbol of almost sacred power' (Frankenberg 1992: 5). The demand for continuous presence signifies a mystique and status that is denied to nurses, who are, supposedly, interchangeable and diminished for this (Frankenberg 1992).

However, this representation of nursing time can be seen as an effect of the *already* gendered nature of nursing; and of the hegemony of clock time in previous sociological accounts. Since nursing care is coded as feminine, linked to the 'natural' capacities of all women, rather than to the acquired professional expertise of individuals, it follows that nurses would be interchangeable (so long, perhaps, as they are women). Claims about the boundaried nature of nursing time also rest on an impoverished concept of time, specifically on clock time which 'does an injustice to the resonance of nursing experience' (Jones 2001: 154). Rather, Jones (2001) argues, it is unlikely that a nurse would leave in the middle of a crisis because a shift was over, whilst s/he might replay events and attempt to resolve on-going issues even when off shift. This sense that nursing time cannot be bounded by clock time is located within a concept of 'process time' (Davies 1995) that underpins professional nursing discourse. Here, the amount of time that nursing takes cannot be specified: it takes as long as the patient needs; and the boundaries are fluid. Whilst this bears some similarities to doctors' commitment to 'see a crisis through', process time requires a sustained and open ended relationship (Davies 1995) rather than the management of a particular problem. Nursing knowledge is generated through regular and intimate contact. Bathing a patient is not only about cleanliness, but allows monitoring of pressure sores; talking with a patient is not idle chit-chat but gives insights to both physiological and psychological conditions (Davies 1995). The time spent on these routine tasks is also time spent developing professional nursing knowledge and care. Process time is determined by the carer's evaluation of the patients' needs, led by an 'other' orientation which puts the care receiver's interests first, showing understanding, empathy, flexibility, affection and respect (Davies 1995: 279). This conception of nursing time is tied to dominant cultural representations of femininity, as Odih (1999) explains, where the 'feminine ideal is expressive of a '"relational" mode of engaging with the world' and 'acquiescing to the demands of others' (Odih 1999: 17). In these terms, feminine process time is embedded in present social relations, linked 'indissolubly' to context (Davies 1995; Odih 1999). It is difficult to predict in advance how long an activity will take. It is hard to measure or even account for, since fluid boundaries mean that process time may be spent thinking about or acting on a patient's needs even when the nurse is doing something else, even when s/he is at home, at the supermarket or asleep. In this sense, the link to context is not tied just to the organizational setting but to the context of a patients' condition and needs which, in a nurse's thoughts, may extend beyond the boundaries of the hospital.

However, Davies (1995) argues that whilst a patient centred, holistic approach demands process time, nurses in today's National Health Service are increasingly managers, devising, assessing and monitoring care plans that others, especially nursing aides carry out. For more senior nurses, taking on managerial tasks – including budgeting, ordering and personnel management – undermines process time and increases the practice of taking paperwork home, as nursing temporalities are refashioned by managerial time.

Sociological deconstructions of time in management discourse highlight the dominant representation of time as linear, homogenous and controllable (Keenoy et al 2002; Noss 2002). Within this formulation, time is a mechanism of measurement and control: of productivity and planning, looking backwards to audit and forwards to implement change (Noss 2002). Indeed, it is 'hard to see or name what the present exactly is' (Noss 2002: 50). This contrasts sharply with the essential contextualization of process time, described above, and chimes a chord with discursive representations of masculinity. Connected to representations of masculinity as rational and purposive, defined through control, reason and logic (Kerfoot and Knights 1996; Seidler 1989; Odih 1999) linear time allows a 'perpetual transcendence from the contextuality and particularity of human and "trivialises the specificity of the finite moment" experience' (Odih 1999: 16). Rationality, reason and control are underpinned by linear time.

This account of time has been central to the managerialist restructuring of the National Health Service over the past two decades. At its core, much of this has been about acceleration, speed and challenging the temporal limitations of public healthcare. The drive to reduce waiting lists, to increase throughput, to audit productivity and to reward these 'efficiency gains' with stars and greater independence for the most successful hospitals, all represent the imposition of this linear-rational model of managerialist time across the National Health Service. Paradigmatic of this has been the rapid expansion of day surgery and the introduction of the booked admissions programme for inpatient surgery. Day admissions for both elective and emergency surgery have dramatically increased (Bolton 2004) whilst the booked admissions programme attempts to take managerial control of waiting lists by booking fixed operation dates. Previously, elective surgery was fitted around the demands of emergency patients, according to surgeons' evaluation of shifting medical priorities. Now, administrators determine the operating list denying surgeons' expertise and autonomy in prioritizing cases, requiring them to free their diaries months in advance and preventing (some of) them opportunities to take up lucrative private work as it arises (Ham, Kipping and McLeod 2003). It has even been suggested that in the past some doctors deliberately maintained long waiting lists and waiting times as an indicator of their popularity and status (Ham, Kipping and McLeod 2003). The drive to cut waiting lists not only removed this tactic but subjected doctors to conceptions of time driven by managerialism, rather than professionalism.

However, whilst it is undeniably the case that the new managerialism in the National Health Service has been driven by a rhetoric that conceptualizes time as linear, rational and controllable, recent organizational research offers an alternative perspective on the structuring of management time. However managerial time is represented, Keenoy et al (2002) show that the 'timescape' of the managerial decision making process is not linear but, rather, draws on 'a sometimes confusing complex of temporal reference points' (Keenoy et al 2002: 195). It appears, they continue that decision processes implicate not only ongoing judgements about the perceived past, present, and future of the organization but, simultaneously, the perceived and projected pasts, presents and futures of the individuals involved in that decision process (p. 195)

The representation of decision making as rational, in a linear temporal framework, is Keenoy et al (2002) argue, a post-hoc rationalization 'that homogenises a complex of sometimes incommensurate individual rationales' (ibid). In this sense, time passing permits the rationalization of chaotic, diverse and emotional processes into a more familiar managerialist script. Thus, conclude Keenoy et al (2002) management is better represented as 'the enfolded events of ... numerous temporalities' (2002: 187)

In sum, we can see that different temporal practices and different conceptions of time are linked to different forms of work within the National Health Service and that these have been central to the gendering of this work. However, in these representations we see a complexity that belies essentialism. There are multiple and contested constructions of time *within* medical discourse, nursing discourse and managerial discourse. Furthermore, whilst we can see that these complex professional and managerial temporalities resonate with particular discursive renditions of gender, exactly how these discourses are implicated in the negotiation of gendered selves remains an empirical question. Whilst theoretically, we can see that these temporalities are powerful in representing normative possibilities for gendered selves, as we have argued throughout this book, how women and men, doctors, nurses and managers negotiate their working selves is contingent and, potentially at least, dynamic. The gendered temporalities described above are situated within a myriad of other discursive resources, thorough which identities are negotiated and re-negotiated within working life. These temporalities, like other discursive resources are contextually specific. Thus, rather than attempt to produce a general account of organizational time, in which the specificities of the research context are represented as a weakness to be 'deliberately ignored', as Zerubavel (1979: xvii) does, we suggest that the particularities of context – space, place and time – are central to understanding the ontology and epistemology of time, what time is and how we come to know it. Rather than abstract time from context, in what follows we explore the talk of our doctors and nurses to see how everyday time is experienced, constructed and used to narrate their gendered selves at work.

Our exploration draws on our theoretical discussion above to frame key themes that emerged in the interviews with the doctors and nurses. Time was a continual reference – it spilled over into almost everything that was said as people talked about their selves at work. In particular, pressures were revealed around the amount of time that work demanded from lives and identities and the speed with which work had to be performed. Identities had to be negotiated against and through these pressures.

All the time?

The amount of time that *both* doctors and nurses devote to their working lives is central to the representation and negotiation of working selves. For doctors, this finds a shared reference point in their common training. As Simon explained:

> *I think there is a rite of passage about medical training ... it is a real test of stamina and a battle against adversity in a way. If you come through that then, yes, you are a better person, you're someone who is resilient, able to withstand pressure and able to withstand bad, long hours, lack of sleep and those sort of practical things ...It becomes a way of life and it is a full-time way of life, you know?*

In their discussion of this stage of their medical training, little reference was made to gender differentiation. Overwhelmingly it appeared that young and single women and men submitted to its temporal rigours. Once they started to talk beyond their basic training, we found significant differentiation in the meaning and place of time in negotiations of working selves: differentiation in which gender, age and speciality as well as place play a central part. Medical time has a gendered sub-text, most visible in the surgical specialties at Lakeside. There are two aspects to this. First, the construction of time is singular, total and determined by goal driven rationalities, linked to a masculine representation of the surgical self. Second, surgical time denies a place for alternative masculinities or for women surgeons who, it is assumed, have a feminized relationship to time linked to the body clock.

The total time demand that surgery makes is linked to familiar representations of the surgical identity. As one locum at Seaside, himself a drop-out from surgical training, put it

> *Are all surgeons big-headed, loud-mouthed, knife-wielding maniacs because that's the personality that becomes surgeons? Or do you end up like that because you've done two years one-in-two?* (Steve)

For Steve, these time demands are given as the reason for abandoning his surgical career (although he had failed the exams several times!). Having just met the woman who he later married he *'wanted a bit of a life'* so opted for General Practice. He expresses no regrets, claiming *'I probably, certainly, am a much more pleasant person to know as a General Practitioner'*. Conversely, Andrew– a Consultant surgeon at Lakeside – describes how surgery replaced an earlier religious vocation: *'I lost my vocation and put it all into medicine'*. To clarify, he continues

> It wasn't ... the sort of caring sharing side of it. It was the dynamism, particularly surgery ... the dynamism and the instant difference of surgery. You do something and it's better (our emphasis)

Surgery held the promise of being someone who could put things right, quickly and permanently: defining a problem, dealing with it and moving on. But just as Steve feared, Andrew explains

> I have no doubt that the thing that has first place in my life is being the surgeon and family and other relationships take second place ... I am the surgeon, that is who I am, that is what everybody perceives me to be. And I have very little existence outside of that. I don't get time.

This is not just a job that *takes* a lot of time. Rather, the need for a perpetual presence *defines* surgery

> In all surgical specialities you will find consultants in at night doing things, and structuring their on-call to be available for emergencies and not doing anything else. And that is the culture: that is the surgical culture. If you're on call for trauma, you don't do any private practice, you don't do any elective orthopaedics, we are there waiting for the emergencies to happen...But in medicine, they're on call and they're at home, or they're at a clinic somewhere else ... and you know there is friction between major departments in the hospital because of those kinds of attitudinal things

Yet, this is a pleasure – something Andrew is 'hooked on'.

> I couldn't not be a surgeon ... it's very deeply ingrained within me doing this. I can't imagine another lifestyle

despite attributing his failed marriage directly to the temporal demands of his job. He claims no other interests or 'hobbies' at all, although he has five children. As he says: *'I spend my time here'*. He is dismissive, of the New Deal, angry even, as it undermines surgical constructions of time that are, for him, the hallmark of his profession

> *I think opportunities for juniors ... in surgical specialities, have been stolen from them by other specialities, who form the negotiation committees that actually restructure these hours ... the surgical trainees who really want to get on, deplore the fact they're not allowed to do more time and get more experience. So their training has been devalued*

Ambitious junior doctors in surgery, he confirms, continue to work punishing hours, but now they do it 'free and for gratis'. Nonetheless, the regulation of junior doctors' hours steals time that Andrew expected to have as a consultant. He can no longer rely on an army of willing and ever present assistants. This also denies him a professional class status

> *They don't have to do the long hours and, you know, the philosophy is "Oh its 9–5, I'm going ... it's a job now, not a vocation ... Nowadays, surgeons are just, they're almost tradesmen ... with the same attitudes to availability and responsibility and its much more shallow on the whole*

Here time, specifically the bureaucratization of time, is tied to a repositioning of medicine in class terms. Despite this, Andrew is positive about managerialist interventions at Lakeside, willing to spend time on managerial tasks and to speak the managerial language of time. Whilst he dislikes being pulled away from

> *... the surgeon model as a person who intervenes, to so many other things in terms of organization and accountability and governance and all the rest of it*

He manages this by adding managerial tasks on top of his surgical workload. Furthermore, he says

> *People who have done what the administrations have wanted have seen their department expand and the people who've resisted have not. Every time I see an initiative I tend to look at it and respond to it positively ... So I recognize that, you know, which side my bread is buttered.*

And adds: '*to the victor the spoils*'. In this Andrew has successfully nego-tiated managerial demands and representations of time into his project of the surgical self. In gender terms, we see the strategic accommoda-tion different masculine temporalities drawn from medicine and man-agement. But this demands almost superhuman effort. For Greg, a Senior doctor in Surgery at Lakeside, this is sometimes too much. Re-iterating Andrew's construction of the time-consumed surgical iden-tity he emphasizes '*there's nothing a surgeon hates more than not operat-ing, particularly if it's not for a valid reason*' for instance attending management meetings about '*paperclips*'! For Greg there is a constant subjective battle between his preferred surgical identity – linked to the knife, '*re-arranging people's plumbing*', and being '*an arrogant bastard*' – and demands from management, and indeed from his profession, that he displays a more 'user-friendly' and conciliatory identity to both colleagues and patients. This takes time, and he says

> *I resent it when I can't be bothered to put the performance on and I know I'm not … performing how I should be performing because I can't be arsed, cause I'm tired, over-worked, stressed or whatever … And the choice is you either do it and make yourself unhappy or you go around being this obstreperous git and make them unhappy and I usually choose the latter*

Here we see clearly that temporal shifts take place in Greg's negoti-ations with medical and managerial time: sometimes he will be this person, and sometimes he will not.

There is no question for Greg that surgery demands a total time com-mitment and, for him too this is tied to a particular surgical identity:

> *I don't think the faint hearted can survive a surgical training, which is essentially, what? Ten, eleven, twelve years of pushing yourself*

This he links explicitly to gender

> *Surgery discriminates against women because it is a long hard training. And it is just not amenable, particularly, to doing, you know, part-time, flexible training. I mean the Royal Colleges are working hard to make it attractive, and saying you can do this part-time, but you can't. Its long hours, you know, lots of work at night, hanging around your boss for experience. It's a very practical subject that you can't actually just go home and read the book … its very demanding physically in that respect.*

And it's still a very male dominated bastion, and there's still an awful lot of sexist surgeons around ... So it's a bit of a self-perpetuating cycle really [laughs]

Here, gendered time is critical to Greg's construction of the surgical identity. At Lakeside, there was only one woman surgeon, represented by her colleagues as an outsider and as difficult, although as highly skilled in her specialist area *'away from the crash and thump'* (Andrew) of heavy orthopaedics. Below consultant level there were a number of young women working their way up the surgical ladder. Nina is in her late 30s, a surgical registrar, with a highly successful career. She is clear that the temporal regime in surgery is linked to a masculine status claim

You know, you're meant to be perceived as being tough and, well [affects a macho voice] *'I was up operating all last night, didn't get any sleep' you know 'got up again at 6.30'*

Whilst she pokes fun at this, she does not challenge it and – contrary to Greg's claims – has proven herself quite able to achieve in this context. However, an intermittent but persistent gender narrative appears within her account of everyday time as she struggles to accommodate a nagging desire to have children with the all encompassing temporal demands of a life in surgery and, indeed, her ambition to become a Consultant. In thinking about the organization of her everyday time in the future, Nina tries to negotiate a way to be a mother and a surgeon but the temporal regime of surgery offers no way to conceptualize this:

[other women in surgery] *none of them are married or have got children. Quite where that comes in I don't know, but I have sort of got to face that*

Others saw the choice more starkly:

Well for females it is completely different...with constraints as to having a family, of getting married and having children it is completely different because I think a lot of women who would have stayed and gone into surgery tend not to because of family commitments and they may get side-tracked into general practice, because the hours are a little better (Asha, Junior Doctor, Lakeside)

As Sinead explains, ultimately

> *Being a consultant is a very demanding job and you have to have a keeper at home to look after everything. Do you know what I mean? You can't go home and then have lots of work on top of that ... I couldn't do it myself I don't think*

Within surgery, it seems, that the best women can do is to accommodate themselves to masculine constructions of the surgical identity and accept the temporalities that underpin this. They must ignore the gender identities that are thrust upon them as women, discount their outsider status within surgical sociability and emulate masculinized practices of surgery, in particular showing total devotion by committing all their time to their profession. Surgical time is simply not compatible with caring time.

Outside surgery, and away from Lakeside, the temporal pressures on doctors working in Care of the Elderly at Seaside are less acute, as Steve observed earlier in his choice of General Practice over surgery. Nonetheless, here too, the temporal demands of medicine are central to their negotiations of self. For Simon, there is ambivalence about this. He describes a journey, when he was a young doctor, and a conversation with the stranger who sat next to him. After a while, and without any discussion of his work or medicine, she said 'You're a doctor aren't you?' Now Simon is aware that he has 'become the doctor', but this is something that he is not entirely comfortable with

> *For me, medicine is a life. I mean I don't think medicine is a job that ever goes away ... I think it is a life, and in that sense, you know, I wish I could think of myself as a father and husband first but I can't really, I think of myself as a doctor first.*

Amongst all the doctors at Lakeside and Seaside (with the exception of Charles, who we discuss below) we see an ambivalent response to the restructuring of medical time, though managerialist interventions and professional demands for change. Whilst there is anger from the surgeons, there is resignation amongst the Care of the Elderly doctors, who know that they will have to carry some of the juniors' workload. In both cases there is a fear of de-professionalization, a loss of middle class status, linked explicitly to the restructuring of time and – by extension – to the entry of women into the profession, since it is women's demands that are sent to underpin recent changes. The reduction and regulation of hours undermines professional status in both the development and practice of expertise. There is doubt, and even derision to the notion of part-time working and so, in effect, to transformation in the gendering of the profession, either in terms of admitting alternative masculinities or permitting maternal femininities.

As quick as you can?

In this section we turn our attention from the *amount* of time spent at work to the nature of time as it is experienced *within* these working hours, in particular the *intensification* of hospital medicine and nursing over recent years. With the rise of general management in the National Health Service, heralded by the Griffiths report in 1983, increasing productivity has been a major item on the managerialist agenda. Two of the principal strategies used to achieve this have been the devolution of managerial responsibility and the increased throughput of patients. This has resulted in more work for healthcare professionals, met partly through increasing hours, but also through a faster *pace* of work during working hours. For nurses, intensification, combined with persistent under staffing, undermines both boundaried and process time. Listening to the nurses talk, using temporal discourses more akin to the masculine construction of medical practice, it was clear that nurses were regularly transgressing the boundaries of their shifts. There was a sense of regret over the loss of feminine process time in particular. This was explicitly contrasted with the discourse of 'task oriented' time, for example by a ward nurse at Lakeside, who described Lakeside as a 'masculine' organization

> *Because they're very task orientated: you've got to get this done, and you haven't done this and you haven't done this. They don't really give you time.*

These complexities in nurses' subjective experience of everyday working time were highly contextual, working themselves out in distinctive ways between particular specialties, between Lakeside and Seaside, and also in connection to position in the nursing hierarchy.

On the surgical wards at Lakeside, nurses were struggling to accommodate the temporal demands of managerial tasks, and managerial constructions of time, with their roots in nursing process time. These tensions generated ontological insecurities that operated at the level the self. Alice is a nurse in her late 30s who has worked at Lakeside for ten years 'on and off'. She is critical of the demands placed on her, even as a staff nurse, to work long hours and skip breaks:

You know half the time, we don't get breaks, and yet you have rushed around up the corridors and you see they [the managers] are getting their trolleys of coffee and freshly cut sandwiches and yet they are not worried that we have been on a shift all day without a break

She describes how her working hours have expanded, to levels that resonate with the construction of medical time:

They expect so much of you, and at times I feel...they don't want you to have an outside life. You are supposed to give 100% to the hospital and forget your family, which you just can't do. ...there was one occasion ...when I started at lunch time and I stayed until half past one in the morning because the ward was shut at the weekend and they had so many emergencies and the idea was that we opened it for one or two, about then they filled the ward up and I was the only one there. I kept saying 'I can't cope! I can't cope! You are bringing in one emergency after another' but they didn't seem to recognize that.

This is connected to both the increased demands of the National Health Service and the professionalizing strategies of the profession. Of course, professional leaders are absolutely opposed to extended hours, and the exacerbated pressures described above. But in Alice's comments we see the reality of new managerial and clinical responsibilities for nurses in a resource limited health service. Tensions over the length of the working day are exacerbated by the increased pace of work, which undermines nurses' ability to operate with 'process time'.

We have a very high turnover, I mean 24 hours is really the maximum patients are staying, a lot of short cases. So there's a constant momentum to get people out. I mean 7 o'clock in the morning I'll come on duty and I know that I have got to provide 10 beds, even though those 10 beds are full. So I know that by 8 o'clock I have got to have at least half of those beds empty and the next lot in. And there's no nursing in that, there's no way you can nurse. And this goes on all the time ... And sometimes it really gets to you because I think, well, I came into work today and I threw people out, but in my mind as a nurse, I know I shouldn't have ... Its not nursing ... To me nursing, I would put it as, I look after some-body's needs... [but] we are taught that you are discharging somebody to get the bed

For Alice, the situation has become so acute that for the first time since she was three or four years old, she is considering abandoning a life in nursing. The task orientation of her working life prevents her from caring and undermines her sense of self

> *If I have a good day, if we have not been rushed off our feet and you have time to spend with the patients, if you feel you have given them adequate or enough time, chance to chat, then yes I feel I have enjoyed the day. But most days aren't like that. I usually go home thinking: Have I done this? Have I done that? I wish I had spent a bit more time.*

In contrast to Lakeside, the attraction of Seaside for many of the nurses working there was precisely that it was a place where these temporal demands could be avoided. (See also Chapter 4). At Seaside the ward nurses stick, largely, to their break times and shift times without difficulty. The exception to this is those nurses in managerial roles. Linda described how she felt perpetually on shift,

> *I need to be available to my staff because I've got the twenty-four hour responsibility, so that unless I'm actually away, if I'm at home I'm kind of on-duty, yeah. ...I'm available if people ring and there's a problem with covering, I tend to come in and cover it and then think about what I was going to do that afternoon [laughs] some other time. ... the time I object to it is if I get a phone call and I've actually got something planned and I end up, and sometimes I cancel it in order to make sure that everyone here's covered because I feel the responsibility to the other staff and the patients. ... But I mean people always were, I mean if you think, I mean local General Practitioners always were available. I mean that's just, I mean some jobs are like that.*

Here we see the explicit connection of the new nursing roles with medical time embodied in the professional committed to 24/7 responsibility. Similarly, the even more senior nursing managers at Lakeside recounted tremendous long hours, and a sense of unbounded responsibility

> *I leave at 7.30 in the morning and I'm home by 7 in the evening. If things are still going on at 7, I'll stop ... what I'll do often though is go home and then come back and we meet half past 8 to half past 10 (Alex)*

In this time commitment, Alex echoes the surgeons' accounts in the previous section explaining – reluctantly – that her work takes primary place in accounting for her self

> *Sometimes I do think my husband is a sterling number 2, and perhaps he should be number one*

However, Amy explains, for her this commitment is not simply tied to the managerial job that she does but to her personal history, specifically her nursing past:

> *I think it's also to do with the fact that nurses always feel they can't, that everything has to be finished …I think in my job I haven't got anybody else to hand it over to, so I tend to take work home with me. But I think that there is an understanding that we don't work for 37½ hours a week in managerial capacity. So therefore there is an organizational expectation that the job must be finished and that a job must be done.* (Amy)

Here then we see the representation of *both* nursing and management as totally time committed. Amy is using both managerial and professional nursing discourses to explain her time commitment, mixing the discursively masculine and the discursively feminine in the way that she describes her everyday working time, and drawing on the past as well as the present to negotiate her identity.

Doctors at both hospitals also recounted the impact of intensification on their experience of everyday working time. Whilst some doctors just seem to be able to soak this up, others find it more challenging to their sense of work identity. At Seaside, Simon explains:

> *The average medical take at Churchside was about 12–14 patients a day, now it is 19–20, OK? It's gone up at least 50% … You're meant to do what you did before, and more, and carry on … the junior doctors' hours business has meant that more and more of everything has to be done in the 9–5 period, because you can't do a teaching ward round at 8 o'clock in the morning any more, because that's against junior doctors' hours. You can't say 'we'll go round those patients at 6.30 this evening' because the doctors have all pissed off home*

In this context, he wonders, how should he be a doctor? Throughout his interview, Simon placed a high priority on communication with patients, rejecting the surgical identity in favour of a more communicative and caring identity that he associated with Rheumatology. But with the increased workload, he questions this

Helping the patient to make the decision with you requires so much more time and explanation that it's almost not worth it sometimes I feel. You know, sometimes it would be so much easier to say 'well we know this is the best way to treat it' You know, do you really need to know why or can I spend the next 20 minutes seeing someone else?

Even in surgery, Alistair at Lakeside agrees

It is just more and more is expected of you and some of these things you want to do. You want to do your job better. You want to give your patients a better deal and explain things to them better

But

I am fed up going home at night, every single week day, exhausted. My wife patches me up, I go to sleep, and then start it all over again

Here we see the very real pressures of intensification in today's National Health Service: the continual pressure to fit more and more into the working day. Dealing with this is not simply a practical question, although there are profound practical difficulties and costs, but also a question about the performance of professional and work identities – as intensification reconfigures who it is possible 'to be'. In this section we have seen doctors, nurses and managers using multiple constructions of time as they talk about these identities. These often transgress traditional and gendered temporal constructions within occupational boundaries, and reveal a sense of unease with the identity performances which have been negotiated.

Finding time

So far in this chapter we have explored the effects of everyday working time on the negotiation of gendered identities. In particular, we have focussed on the temporal demands that are made of our doctors and nurses, both in terms of the amount of time they spend working and in terms of the quality of that time, specifically the increased pace of everyday working time in National Health Service hospitals today. However, we have seen that these demands are complex and that the personal negotiations talked about by different people reveal the existence of multiple outcomes, both between and even within particular individuals.

In this section we build on this diversity of outcome by turning to explore more overtly tactical actions. The interviews revealed the pressures of time on people, but they also showed us how some of the doctors and nurses were agentic in their relationship to time. These people seek to *find the time* which offers them the material and discursive resources for constructing the working identities that they desire. In what follows, we discuss three such tactics which we found came through in our interviews: first, mothers' use of the different working hours available in nursing to negotiate a compromise between family and work; second, nurses' use of night shifts to find time to care; and lastly, doctors' and nurses' choice of specialty and workplace.

Whilst part-time work, and even reliable shifts, had not yet been introduced for the women working in medicine at Lakeside whilst we were there, we found extensive evidence that women in nursing used the range of working hours available to find the time they needed to negotiate a compromise between being a mother and being a nurse. Annabel presents a life story typical of these accounts. Having left work to have her eldest child, she was soon 'desperate to come back' and describes the development of her nursing career from that point on as follows:

> *I came back on the twilight job in A&E, which was 9pm – 1am for a couple of months, then it became 9pm till 1am Monday to Thursday and as things have got busier, the hospital's changed, so those hours went up … I had a second child which I just had ordinary maternity leave for and then I came back because I was working part time and my husband was looking after the children whilst I was at work, because of the hours I worked*

> **Right, so you don't do any nights now?**

> *Occasionally, if I, mostly if I request them. Sometimes it suits me, like for the 6 weeks of the summer holidays if I do 4 nights that will be 40 hours one week and then the next weeks nights off then I've got a week of annual leave that gives me two weeks off in the holidays and just one week of annual leave*

We should be clear here. Part-time work and night shifts are low status (Brooks and MacDonald 2000) in comparison with full-time and day shifts. But, at Lakeside at least, it is clearly not a 'dead zone' (cf. Halford, Savage and Witz 1997) in which these nurses are permanently stranded. The negotiations that these nurses at Lakeside are making are a temporary compromise, rather than the permanent relegation of career to second place behind family (cf. Hakim). Theirs is a temporally specific tactic, using variations in working hours, to maintain both career and family through the early years of their children's lives. And even once back to full-time days, the shift system in nursing permits pleasures less known to parents working the standard office day, as Drusilla explains

> *So far as I'm concerned it's better than working 9–5. 'Cos I'm at home in the mornings or the afternoons. I mean I'll be at home at half-past-three this afternoon … sit in front of the TV and watch Telly with Victoria, and watch Playdays, you know?*

Drusilla clearly finds pleasure in the way in which she can negotiate a satisfying work identity with her identity of the 'good mother' (see also Chapter 7). However, night shifts as a temporary necessity to tide mothers over. Rather, for some, the quality of time at night means that nurses can find time to devote to care, to process time, rather than being driven by the managerialist, task-orientated conceptualization of time. It was widely agreed at both hospitals that nights were insulated (to varying degrees) from recent changes to nursing temporalities. Ruth, on Accident and Emergency explained

> *We had a chap in on nights and he had had a stroke and he was so grateful for what we had done and that was so nice and we knew that we were able to do things which on a day like today there is no hope of being able to do*

This tactic of using time to find time was used to greatest effect by Brenda, who had worked as a night sister at Seaside for over 15 years. Alienated by the restructuring of both nursing and the National Health Service, the introduction of academic nurse training and the imposition of managerialist agendas Brenda finds that neither her profession, nor her organization, offers her the resources to uphold her self-identity as a traditional nurse. In the combination of Seaside and nights, Brenda has found one of the few spatial and temporal locations where she can continue to negotiate her working identity.

One exception to this endorsement of nights comes from the only male nurse at Seaside, Douglas, whom we have met before. For this man, isolated both by sex and sexuality, nights are experienced as an unpleasant concentration of all the things he hates about nursing. Dominated by older women, he describes the sociability at nights in terms of exaggerated femininity and heterosexuality emblematic of the way that 'bossy big arsed women' have dominated nursing, in his experience. Whilst Douglas is at Seaside because it enables him to negotiate a place where he, as a male nurse, can care in a way that is underpinned by a concept of process time, the exaggerated femininity of this time at nights is simply too much for him.

Douglas's presence at Seaside leads us to the second tactic, used by both doctors and nurses, to find time within the temporal demands of their professions and organizations. For the nurses at Seaside, this is a place where they can spend caring time with patients, something that they see as difficult in the acute sector. As a male nurse, in particular, Douglas had felt pushed into management and/or technical specialities in acute nursing, something that he consciously resisted. Amongst the doctors at Seaside too, we found the tactical use of specialism to enable relations with working time, connected to the negotiation of particular working selves. The wards at Seaside still conducted weekly ward rounds, in a traditional manner. We were told that on ward round day, the wards would be especially spic and span, and so we made arrangements to be present on the day that the consultant was due. Indeed, there was a palpable sense of expectancy. Once the consultant entered the ward, he set the pace. The nurses were fully focussed on him, and his expertise and judgement was final.

I think the old ward round though, really hasn't come on that far ... No, I think the consultant [acts/thinks as though] 'I'm the man who makes all the decisions. Everybody's' you know 'listening to me' and what I say is ... The pace is very slow and its also really quite a social affair. (Sarah, Sister, Seaside)

The timing, routine and pace of the ward round facilitated an old-fashioned medical masculinity. The nurses represent this as a game

I think the consultants know in their heart of hearts that its really a game, all their decisions are already made because it's a multi-disciplinary – we work very much as a multi-disciplinary team. And when they come we just tell them what the decision is ... I think they probably realize that we will do whatever we feel is best for the individual regardless of what they think

Nonetheless, the consultants' power was backed-up by Trust policy that only they could discharge patients at Seaside, so this could only happen weekly, whatever the patient's progress. We were told how the attempts to allow nurses to discharge patients had met with strong resistance. Here the authority of the doctors continued to over-ride pressure on beds, despite management acknowledgement that nurses had the competence to determine when patients were fit to leave the hospital,

However, in contrast to old-fashioned gentleman consultant, at Seaside we also found the most striking example of a newly emergent medical subjectivity. Charles was 38 and a consultant Rheumatologist. His extraordinarily linear career narrative was centrally shaped by temporal considerations

> *After you qualify you've got to decide very clearly where you want to go, medicine, surgery or General Practice. And within those, you can decide where to go. So you make a very clear distinction, do I want to work in a hospital, yes or no? If it's, 'I want to work in a hospital', then it's do I want to be a medic, or do I want to be a surgeon? .... Um, and then after you've got your exams, then you decide which of those directions you want to do ... do you want to be training until you're thirty-eight or thirty-nine, or do you want to be independent and a consultant by the time you're thirty-four, which is what happened to me ... So basically, can you see yourself in theatre, can you see yourself up at three in the morning operating, can you see yourself being on call every third night? Or do you see yourself doing a nine-to-five job with no on-call experiences? ... For me it was very easy to say I wanted to do Rheumatology. The quality of life. I wanted to know that I wasn't on call*

Here we see a rational problem solving approach more akin to managerial discourses of time, than traditional professional representations. In contrast to Andrew at Lakeside, where managerial time is tolerated and used as a resource in the consolidation of a surgical identity, Charles draws on a managerialist construction of time as part of a broader discussion on the shift in medical identities

> *I think that there has been a general change in terms of the attitudes of medical students. They're not as scared as they used to be, they are confident young people now, and they think about their rights, they think about working contracts, they question things much more. Um, they're*

> *much more prepared to say, 'Look, I'm being asked to do unreasonable things,' or, 'The physical and mental demands are too much ...' it's becoming a modern society, as opposed to a throwback to the old system where the doctor was a privileged individual, at the top, but felt that they probably had to work for it to get there. But once they were there, they'd made it. Now it's all changing.*

Here we see an increased use of managerial middle class assets, enabling Charles to maintain status despite his challenges to the professional middle class assets historically associated with medicine.

Summary and conclusion

From the rich descriptions presented in the accounts of our doctors and nurses, we can see the multiplicity and complexity of everyday times that are circulating within healthcare work: coalescing and reforming around medicine, nursing and management distinctively in different contexts, noticeably between specialties, places and times. Whilst we argued in our introduction that these everyday times resonate with broader constructions of masculinity and femininity, the main focus of the chapter has been to explore how these are felt, used and practiced in the working lives of our doctors, nurses and managers: how gendered working identities are negotiated against and through these times.

Clearly, the temporal demands of working in today's National Health Service are immense, both in terms of the amount of time demanded and the intensification of work within that time. Every one of the doctors, nurses and managers that we spoke to echoed in one way or another. These demands exercise enormous power in the negotiation of gender identities at work, subjecting individuals through their rigours. Indeed, for the most of the consultants at both hospitals, the combined demands of professional time and managerial time (since the devolution of general management in the National Health Service) left little sense of *negotiation* at all, little time, or space or place, to be anything other than the total doctor. This was expressed in explicitly gendered and classed terms. First, as something that demanded a masculine relation with time. Whilst this was open to women doctors climbing the career ladder, great doubt was expressed about this, both by the senior male doctors already up the ladder and the young women themselves. A mothering self simply could not be negotiated within the everyday times of a successful surgical career. But these women had other options, and the negotiation of a future time, where a medical career and motherhood could be possible was an underlying refrain in their accounts. Looking back to the past, some of the male doctors, for whom their gender had made family and career possible expressed regret that they too had not made such negotiations and that, now, it was too late. Second, the time demands of medicine were expressed as a cornerstone of middle class status. Professional assets depend on a total time commitment (or at least the appearance of this) and a consumed identity. Whilst one individual in particular, Charles, is drawing on other middle class assets, specifically managerialist constructions of time to negotiate an alternative masculine medical identity, this was derided by most.

As the National Health Service demands more 'efficiency' and 'productivity' from nurses, and the nursing profession repositions nursing as a middle class career (rather than a vocation) the escalating temporal demands on nurses, especially at Lakeside, produced similar accounts of the loss of self, the loss of a sense of negotiation. Nonetheless, we found nurses at both Lakeside and Seaside making active use of the multiplicity of times and spaces in the National Health Service to negotiate identities that were more desirable to them. In particular, the use of shifts work, night work and particular specialties opened temporal regimes with which these selves could be negotiated. We should be clear, again. Night work, shift-work and care of the elderly are all low status forms of work within nursing in terms of professional prestige, career opportunities and the financial rewards associated with these. Often, these forms of work have been presented as only a 'second best' alternative for women nurses with young children who, given half a chance would prefer to be in full time work, on a day shift, and perhaps moving into a more exciting speciality. Whilst this may well be the case for some, we did not hear these stories. The nurses who chose these forms of work were negotiating working selves that they were comfortable with. Selves who had time to care for patients, time to practise nursing in the way they were trained, time away from doctors (often, actually, away from men, since male nurses do not tend to work nights and, as Douglas explained, the feminization of nights can be exclusionary) and time to be with their children and families. No doubt they should be paid fairly and – from our perspective – their contribution should be more fully recognized. But what these nurses are doing is clearly engaging in the creative negotiation of gendered selves with the everyday times that are available to them.

This is echoed in the Seaside nurses' accounts of their reasons for being in a Community Hospital, during the day as well as night time, and the scope this gives for the negotiation of a caring self. Doctors at Seaside too make this point, both in their narratives of early career choices and their descriptions of the current temporalities that these specialties continue to offer particular resources for the negotiation of self. The timing and pace of the ward round at Seaside, in particular, was something that enabled the continued negotiation of a traditional consultant identity, something that the doctors clung on to and that even the nurses, although they found it frustrating to wait for the doctor once a week, treat with bemused tolerance.

Our attention to importance of everyday times in the negotiation of gender identities at work, and the theoretical approach that we have taken to this suggests a number of key points of importance in the broader study of gender, identity and organization. First and quite simply, it insists that we transcend conventional divisions between public and private, work-time and family time, clock-time and social time and explore further the simultaneity of these in the negotiation of gender identities at work. Second, our empirical study highlights the importance of context in the study of everyday times. The availability, meanings and uses of time vary themselves across time and space. Time is contextual (Mandanipour 1996; Rosengren and de Vault 1963). We cannot make a general understanding of time, that is abstracted from the contexts that produce and reproduce those times (cf. Zerubavel 1979). Third, attention to the repetition of familiar times, and the active seeking out of these times, indicates how a consistent sense of self might be negotiated, however contingently. Nonetheless, it is clear that we are all subject to a slowly shifting kaleidoscope of times, some of which offer the opportunities to both confirm and deny this consistency.

7
Lifetimes

Our research at Lakeside takes us round and round the spatial grids of the hospital rather like hamsters on a wheel. Yet as we walk to and fro, from the surgical wards to A and E, or from the canteen to the Postgraduate Medical Centre, we encounter the full diversity of staff employed here. Shy faced junior nurses giggle together as they walk past in huddles, whilst older Sisters march past confidently in their blue dresses, with an altogether more efficient sense of purpose. Junior doctors sweep by, their white coats flapping and their stethoscopes swaying, whilst besuited, bespectacled Consultants pass with seemingly less urgency. Sitting in the Doctors' Mess, we watch the doctors circling with their trays, deciding which of the diverse groups to join. Here we can see the broadness of cultural and ethnic backgrounds and experiences in the hospital.

The spaces of Seaside are altogether quieter and peopled by a less diverse group of workers. The young are rather a rarity here: the staff are predominantly white women nurses at various stages of the middle aged spectrum. Whether on the wards or in the canteen, they chat to each other in a way that – on the surface at least – suggests mutual understanding and shared experiences. Exceptions to this rule are soon spotted – particularly the doctors: all male, occasionally Asian, often removed from the banter of the nursing staff.

But what are the stories behind the rich diversity of doctors and nurses whom we met – the people of different ages, different classes and different ethnicities who all come together in the organizational times and spaces of Lakeside and Seaside?

In this chapter we turn to look at these life stories more closely. As in the last chapter, we show that time is a crucial resource in processes of identity-making. In the ways in which the doctors and nurses at Seaside and Lakeside talk about their life histories, past experiences and predictions for the future, the broader dimension of lifetimes is added to our discussion on the activity of producing and creating gendered working selves. This underscores further the simultaneity and mutual implication of different times in the negotiation of gendered identities. We have seen how these are continuously negotiated in everyday times, but they are also situated in the wider span of people's lives. Events and happenings, stories, memories and reflections, hopes and ambitions, yesterday, today and tomorrow: all these provide central material and discursive resources in the making and remaking of gender identities at work.

This chapter draws back therefore to look at the narratives women and men use to talk about the whole of their lives and experiences to date. These 'stories of lives' are doubly fascinating: it is not only the incidents of lives which are of interest, but also so are the rhetorical techniques that are used to describe them. Together these reveal the individuality of personal histories, the range of different experiences that the women and men, doctors and nurses, have had in their lives and careers, and the variety of ways in which time is used in talk as a key resource to construct gendered identities. Whilst the choices and decisions which have been made in life, as well as the 'epiphanies' – the important and interactional moments which have left marks on people's lives and identities (Denzin 1989) – are often used as key markers in the construction of identities through the recount of lives, the ways in which this is done can be quite diverse, and gender is revealed to be a key differentiator in the ways identities are negotiated.

Life stories are also interesting in that they can also show the important ways in which larger social, political and cultural contexts shape lives: not only gender, but also profession and the changes in the National Health Service can all be seen to impact on and interplay with people's lives and identities over their life course. These broader contexts are often integral to the ways in which life episodes are recounted and understood. A look at life stories thus makes a crucial contribution to the aims of this book. It extends the methodological approach to the analysis of talk which we have undertaken in previous chapters to take a broader look at the scope of the doctors' and nurses' lives, and to explore the unfurling interrelationship between gender, personal identities and wider social and political events. This exploration reveals the rich variety of ways in which personal identities are framed, gendered and negotiated through the constraints and opportunities offered by particular social, professional and organizational contexts that women and men meet in their lives.

However, we are not claiming that each of our respondents gave us 'neat and tidy' whole life stories to play with. The enormous differences in the ways in which people talk about their lives mean that whilst some give some rich indications about the ways in which their identities have been negotiated over time, others may give very little to go on. This was true of both men and women. The accounts, and the ways in which stories and events are plotted (or not), thus also reveal the different ways in which 'time' is understood and drawn upon in the making of gender/identities, theoretically and conceptually. Some people make full use of it, whilst others prefer to use it in a more limited way. This attention to the temporal aspects of people's narratives: not only in terms of the ways they talk about pasts, presents and futures, but also in the different perceptions of time which are drawn upon, can open our eyes once more to difference, and importantly, the diverse ways in which gender identities are negotiated at work. However, the fact that life stories are not always offered to us neatly 'on a plate' means that we need analytical methods to deconstruct the temporal aspects of people's narratives. In the next section therefore, we start with a discussion of the theoretical and methodological frameworks we employ in our analysis.

Theorizing time, lifetimes, and identities

When people talk about their lives, epistemological notions of past, present and future are constantly intertwined. Stories are told which may shift over time and space, as past events and episodes of life are recalled. The future is often pondered upon, and the past and the present may be drawn upon to inform it. It is within these temporal and multi-layered narratives that identities are formed and presented,

> a temporalizing process in which multiple selves speak: the self of the story teller and the selves of all the different experiences of one's life. These multiple selves merge, double back, laminate and build on one another, and provide the context and occasion for the production of the larger story that is told. (Denzin 1989: 73).

The telling of a life event or story is thus simultaneously a process of identity-negotiation. The self is presented in this way or that way, and time may be drawn upon to substantiate embellish, or even fantasize. Thus this telling of a 'larger story' is influenced by social and cultural as well as personal factors. For example, Denzin (1989) has noted the importance of the *storytelling role of western culture* in the telling of lives.

This means that people tend to characterize or locate themselves within a processual or sequential movement of 'life stages' such as childhood, adolescence, adulthood, and old age or life episodes or rituals (Somers and Gibson 1994) such as going to school, beginning work, marriage, children and retirement. Through such frameworks, people embed themselves within relationships and stories that shift over time and space, revealing the relational nature of identities, as well as an approach to time which is largely linear. Such life stories thus reveal the importance of the overlap in the chronology between individuals' lives, their relationships and the social structures within which they are, and have been, embedded (Steedman 1992). Their experiences reflect the structural, cultural, professional and organizational aspects that impinged upon them and moulded or constrained their actions (Dex 1991) at the various times in their lives. It is through these that identities are constituted and reconstituted in time and over time, precluding any notion of categorical stability. The past, or lapse of time, is thus a crucial factor in understanding present identities and relations.

Within such chronological descriptions of lives, differences are revealed however. People draw on a variety of understandings of time in their life stories, particularly in the relationships they see between past, present and future. Roberts (2002) has also discussed this, commenting on the fact that some people see the past as gone for ever, 'done and dusted' so to speak, whilst some see the past as ever present: still having an influence over the present and even the future. These perspectives may be enriched further through *'time orientations'* – general moods or outlook, such as nostalgia, prediction and reminiscence, which may be given in people's talk about their lives: perhaps through metaphors and other figures of speech. Thus how time is perceived affects how life and identities are constructed, how people talk about their past and present lives, and how they see the future and how they might act in it (Bellaby 1991). The exploration of how people talk about their lives and use time thus shows us their attitudes to work, organization and profession now, then and in the future.

Further differences are revealed in the way that not everyone operates from a chronological approach to time. Just as we saw in the last chapter, the rich and different ways in which people talk about their lives underscore the fact that there are alternatives to those understandings of time that draw on the 'start to finish' mentality of linear processes. They show us the mutuality and simultaneity of time: how we can hold different understandings of and approaches to time together, at the same time. Mead's (1932) thoughts on time are useful here: he argues that it is only through the present that the past and future are constructed, and thus our experiences and predictions are ever subject to change:

> the past and the future [are] expansions of the present, rather than the common conception of a sequence proceeding from the past, to the present to the future. The reconstruction of the past and the anticipation of the future arise from the same foundation, the reality of the present. The past therefore is not a fixed condition of a structured time period but will vary in accordance with any particular present. (Petras 1968 in Roberts 2002).

According to Mead, the past cannot be seen in any way as fixed, neutral or factual therefore. It is created and recreated through talk in the present. Schutz (1971) is in agreement here, claiming that all we can do is reflect on past 'performances', and that any meaning related to these is inevitably an outcome of our present consciouness and relationships. The ways in which people talk about their lives can thus be only ever understood as in the moment: this may change tomorrow, and may be very different to yesterday.

This is an argument that is also central to Ricoeur's (1984, 1985, 1988), work on temporality. Temporality is intimately connected with narrativity: the ways in which our lives are actively emplotted in our talk about them. Chronological time may be used to give the 'illusion of sequence', but as individuals reflect on the past, contemplate the present and rehearse the future, they may move between different 'time perspectives' in their narratives.

> Lives have to be understood, as Erben (1998) argues, as lived within time and time is experienced according to narrative. Narratives – of past, present and future – are the means by which biographical experience is given understandable shape (Roberts 1999: 21)

In talking about their lives, people thus actively construct their lives and life events into an intelligible whole through these narratives or temporal 'plots'. People rarely simply replay the chronology of the past as it occurred (Cortazzi 1993). It is through plot that experiences are timed, made meaningful and assembled into a story (Miller 2000). However, Miller (2000) notes that the 'plot' of a story can never be complete: ambiguities exist and of course our lives continue while the ending is unknown. There will also rarely be a single 'plot line' as narrators draw on the variety of cultural resources to tell their tales. Important here – and again, these provide an alternative to simple chronologies – are Levi-Strauss's (1963) notion of 'myth', and McAdams' (1993) notion of *character* or *'imago'*. A myth is 'a special kind of story', that we construct 'to bring together the different parts of ourselves and our lives into a purposeful and convincing whole' (McAdams 1993: 14), whilst an imago is a 'personalized and idealized concept of the self'. McAdams argues that we all consciously and unconsciously fashion such main characters or imagos for our life stories, and we use these to construct our identities. These are thus both cultural resources that may influence how people understand their selves and lives, and which may be drawn upon in their narratives, providing additional frameworks through which people negotiate their identities. They can have great power in structuring an account, such as the archetypal (masculine) story of 'the hero': the call...the journey...the battle...the return (Denzin 1989), or the myth of 'the unhappy childhood' or the characters of the 'selfless mother' or 'self-made man'. Public myths and characters may thus intertwine with private ones, as people integrate their remembered past, perceived present and anticipated future (McAdams 1993).

The ways in which temporal narratives are constructed is thus intricately implicated in the negotiation of our gendered identities. In the ways in which life stories are told and 'self-narratives' are constructed, attempts are often made to provide connections, coherence, movement and purpose (Gergen and Gergen 1984: 174–5). These explanations are however usually complex and multi-directional, as individuals continuously select, summarize or resequence events and their meaning (Roberts 2002). In the process, time is constantly manipulated. There may, for example, be compression of sometimes long and actually eventful periods of time in order to dwell on other periods deemed more significant. Further, life stories are not, and can never be, fully coherent or unchanging, but always in a state of 'becoming' (Roberts 2004). It is, therefore, not one self which is constructed, but multiple selves , as 'past selves are re-visualized and revised, whilst future selves are rehearsed in thought and pictured in action' (Roberts 2004: 176).

From all this, it can be easily seen that the putting together of a 'life story' is by no means an easily accessible or simple process therefore, either by the narrator or by the researcher. As Stanley (1993) argues, the past often has to be recovered in traces and hints by the researcher rather than appearing before us whole and entire. People may refer to the past in fragments of speech rather than tell coherent 'stories'. Like snapshots, they are not panorama but partial views (Bellaby 1991). From the point of view of the person doing the telling, in the interests of being interesting or relevant, events may be selected, compressed, shaped, recreated and reconstructed for the occasion. Recollections of lives are also affected by memory. Memories are shaped by the perceptions then, and later retrospective interpretations and current concerns of the teller. These produce selections, compressions and expansions. Further, as Passerini (1990) and Portelli (1998) have recognized, memory is not simply an individual activity, but may rely on group, generational and more formal public accounts, which all interrelate with individual accounts in complex ways. Professional and organizational 'memories' thus interweave in personal accounts of careers and lives. Cortazzi (1993) argues that this effectively doubles the interpretive aspect of a narrative from the teller's point of view: it concerns both interpretations made at the time of the events and those made later in or through the telling. In this way, narratives are a dynamic dialogue between past and present.

All this means that what results is a particular and very individual construction in a particular and very individual context. In the context of the interview there is an interplay between what people are able to tell about their lives and what they perceive to be of interest to their audience (Coleman 1991). The 'stories' which result may be partial and incomplete, revealing the importance of individual differences in the selection of events and experiences which make up the content of the story, and in the extent to which this material has been integrated and restructured (Coleman 1991). This was very evident in our research: whilst some would launch into long speeches about their lives with little prompting, others would constantly check with us that this was what we wanted: '*you can't be interested in all of this, surely?*' Some thought we were there as consultants to the National Health Service and as such either could not possibly be interested in the detail of their lives, or should be treated with caution in what we were told! We thus ended up with a wide variety of biographical narratives, in terms of the amount of the life story that was told.

Lifetimes and gender

In the last chapter, we argued that although Time, like Space, is a gendered concept, there are no simple binary divisions to be found between men and women's relationships to and conceptions of time. The above discussion of the complexities and diversities of life stories and time perspectives helps to reinforce this argument. Men's experience of time cannot be reduced to the linear and progressive, nor can women's time be linked solely to their biological rhythms, or reckoned through the prism of the family. We also saw in the last chapter that men and women share experiences of emotional and social time; both struggle over time for work and leisure. Categories of time need to be destabilized therefore to provide a richer analysis to cope for the ambiguities and diversities that are to be found.

However, in daily life, and over the course of a lifetime, time does place competing and simultaneous demands on women and men in gendered ways, and as such is clearly a gendered resource. Whilst for both women and men, time is continuously relational, gender difference reveals itself in the ever-shifting hierarchy of importance and the demands of lives as time slips by. Holmes (1995) has demonstrated how women's time is experienced in multiple ways, integrally linked to the spaces they occupy and the locations they live in as well as to their biological possibilities. She suggests four different conceptions of time: industrial, domestic, biological and individual as a way of distinguishing between differing demands upon women's use of their days and lives. These reveal common experiences as well as retaining individual life rhythms. 'Industrial time' is the term used to describe time as linear and progressive, the most dominant public time which governs the experience of time outside the home. It is the time governed by the clock, characteristic of capitalist notions of time management and efficiency. The ways in which this kind of time needs to interplay with other conceptions of time means that it is often a locus of struggle. 'Domestic time' for example is not so easily regulated. By definition, it is determined by the spaces of home that women occupy, and these are strongly influenced by discursive constructions, both historical and contemporary, as well as class and geographical location. They are subject to immediate conflicting demands and integrally linked to family time. 'Biological time' is also difficult to regulate: menstruation, pregnancy, childbirth and lactation as well as the life rhythms of menstruation, menopause, ageing and death. Cross-cutting all of these is 'Individual time' – the time of events and daily life. This is a complex category, in some ways specific to gender and class and yet at the same time even more personal, subject to the individual's idiosyncrasies.

This recognition of a multiple, complex, gendered sense of time elucidates the ways different understandings of time impinge upon women's lives in particular in immediate and often contradictory ways, but also helps us include the impact of work, organizational and professional change on women's lives. For example, the changing experience and understanding of time that has permeated the National Health Service over people's lifetimes is particularly striking in the female nurses' accounts of their lives and careers. The ideas of rational scientific management, progress and efficiency that we talked about in the last chapter, which now shape their working lives, compete sharply with previous conceptions of giving the patient enough time for care, as well as the other domestic demands they may have on their time. Many of the women's narratives about the specific developments and events in their lives also challenge any conventional notions of chronological time. As Holmes notes, women experience such events in different ways from each other and at varying times in their lives – 'history does not move in straight lines – it is fractured and runs off at tangents' (Modjeska 1990). By and large, women's lives are rarely single-minded progressions towards predetermined goals (as are some of the men) but a pattern of repeated events and rhythms with unpredicted and unpredictable disruptions. However, as we shall see in our discussion below, exceptions to this do exist.

In the remainder of this chapter we turn to focus on the temporal narratives that the men and women at Lakeside and Seaside used to tell us about their lives. In many ways these mirror, reinforce and extend the arguments made in the earlier chapters on space and place, adding yet more pieces to the jigsaw puzzle of identity construction in gendered organizations. Close analysis of the transcripts thus revealed that, whilst there was some overlap, some clear differences in narratives were to be found between the women and men located at the each of the two hospitals. This suggests at one level that people who narrated similar 'types' of life stories and experiences were attracted to – or ended up – in similar 'types' of organizations.

Our methodology here draws on the theoretical approaches and methodologies to analysing and understanding lifetimes that we have discussed above. That is, we engage in what Denzin (1989) has termed 'interpretive biography' – in which *we* create accounts and representations of lived experiences. In order to do this, we looked at the ways in which lifetimes were narrated according to plot, or to character, as well as the way in which different time perspectives were drawn upon to discuss past, present and future. We also looked closely here at the differences between the ways in which women and men talked about their lives. Clearly, not all the narratives made use of all of these techniques, but in many of them one approach seemed to stand out to us, and we have used these to explore the differences in the ways in which people present their identities through narrative. Whilst people may have repeatedly evoked a certain theme or approach however, we are not claiming that these construct identities which are coherent or singular. Multiple resources are drawn upon, and the combinations of plot, character or time perspectives that were pulled together into one person's narratives are complex and may constantly change.

As Derrida (1972) has pointed out, there is no clear window into the inner life of a person, for any window is always filtered through the 'glaze of language signs and the process of signification'. We are of course therefore totally 'up front' about the fact that these are our interpretations. In short, these life histories are not treated as sources of fact but as social constructions made by both our interviewees and ourselves. We look for framing devices for the stories we were told, in many ways therefore providing more coherence than was ever there in the original telling. However, if 'the intent of the biographical project is to uncover the social, economic, cultural, structural and historical forces that shape, distort and otherwise alter problematic lived experiences' (Denzin 1989) then analytical methods are necessary. Yet, taking on the cautions of Denzin (1989), we try to never lose sight of the individuals who live these structurally shaped lives.

So how did women and men talk about their lifetimes, and how did they construct themselves through these biographical narratives? One of the most common approaches was to emplot lives according to a broadly chronological model, within which variations could be seen. Some narratives could be described as 'future oriented', whereby the past is framed in relation to the future, which is looked towards with hope and ambition. The underlying myth here is that life is planned for future gain: the 'best is yet to come'. Other narratives are more grounded in the past whereby the past is looked back upon with some nostalgia, framed as being more important than the present, as a better time, which has now gone. The future in this form of narrative offers either the chance of release from the present, or is regarded as an even bleaker state of affairs. Clearly, within these broader perspectives to time, different narratives, myths or storylines abound. However, some gendered patterns could be discerned, and these offer us a window on the importance of lifetimes as a key resource in the negotiation of gendered identities at work.

Chronological approaches to lifetimes: future-oriented narratives

The ladder

A popular narrative was to describe life stories in terms of a structured career model, in which a future-oriented, 'onward and upward' identity was very strategically planned and controlled. These narratives demonstrate the impact of profession on people's life stories, and senses of self, as well as wider social pressures on the middle classes to develop purposeful 'careers'. Lives and identities are negotiated in relation to the gaining of credentials and career structures laid down within professions and organizations. This *'Ladder'* narrative was particularly evident for many of the male nurses and doctors, for whom there was always another qualification to be applied for, and another promotion to go for. Medicine has a particularly clear relationship to the onward march of time, and this for many men, this is part of its key attraction:

> *when one looked at the structure of medicine, it was a very clearly defined structure. I mean you just go up to it and have your rewards at every stage* (Charles, Consultant Seaside).

Careers could thus be clearly planned and followed through:

> *I always wanted to be a doctor ...Somebody reminded me at a reunion that I said in the first week we were in medical school 'I'm going to be an orthopedic surgeon'...* (Andrew, Orthopedic Surgeon, Lakeside)

The majority of the doctors we talked to, at both consultant and junior doctor level, were clearly from middle class backgrounds, and the 'ladder' approach to life was an extension of their private school backgrounds and parental expectations. However many of the male nurses we met were from working class backgrounds, and for them one of the attractions of nursing as a career were the clear opportunities for social mobility. Credentialism was therefore something that was totally bought in to, and indeed relished.

> *It was a very difficult course – you have to be very committed to what you feel you are going to gain at the end of it. [However] I know where I want to be and I know what I have to do to get there. You are learning new ways of developing yourself which nurses need to be able to do because it is a very adaptive environment that you are in. If you feel you are static, you will end up being static, and you will not progress* (Cameron, Project 2000 theatre nurse)

As these men narrated the quantifiable building blocks of their work histories, differences in their emotional approach to time, and the future, could be discerned however. In particular those doctors who had now 'made it' to consultant level were reflective on the impact of the profession on their personal identities, and the ways in which these have shifted and changed over time:

> *You change as you go along from being really quite sort of fun and matey with the nurses, and having a laugh, and going out with them, to slightly start to distance yourself, partly because of the expectation of the role that you're carrying, which is that you'll have to be, to a degree authoritative, you have to make decisions, you have to guide people, you have to make decisions about patients and that you are the ultimate decision maker in terms of the management of a patient's condition. And I think that goes hand in had with just getting older, having other responsibilities. Getting a mortgage, getting a family. All of those things all happen at the same time.....So the person I am in my thirties is totally different to what I was, six or seven years ago. And sometimes I sort of miss that...* (Charles)

The more senior people had become, the more the ladder narrative was seen as carrying some heavy costs once 'the top' was reached. The future was now not so clear-cut. The substantial amounts of time that they had donated to their work over their lifetimes meant that now in the present, reflecting both 'backwards' and 'forwards', they were conscious of how much their senses of identity were constructed through work, and home lives had been marginalized:

> *If I'm not here doing it, I'm at home preparing to do it and preparing an article about it, or reading about it, or talking about it...I don't get time, as I said my marriage has failed...I don't have time to pursue any hobbies and I spend my time here...*(Andrew, Consultant).

Although the strategic approach that Charles has taken to his life has worked for him, he admits that it has taken him over:

> *So I am a doctor throughout my whole psyche. But that's what I've been training for all my life, I mean the amount of bloody exams that I've done and things like that...You've been basing your whole life on this particular career. And the satisfaction that you've had is through achieving goals over the last ten years or whatever. Every time that you get more money, that you get a pay increase, you get a step up the ladder, that is your gratification.*

Although predominantly a masculinist narrative, the ladder metaphor was by no means only appropriated by men. Once again, class is found to cross-cut gender, and career mobility was clearly important to many of the middle class women. Most strikingly, the female nurse-managers also narrated their professional lifetimes and identities in strategic terms. However, they did differ from the men in that none of them initially entered nursing with the *intention* of moving swiftly onwards and upwards, coming into the profession with quite traditional feminine motivations:

> *I remember just knowing that I wanted to help, I wanted to care for people...I know it sounds a bit corny, but it was the reason, I would not have wanted anything else* (Fiona)

Many of them became goal oriented very quickly however, and this has sustained both the approach to professional life and the negotiation of professional identities:

> *I always knew, I always wanted to...when I was doing midwifery I loved it so much, I wanted to be head of midwifery, when I was training, that was my goal. I knew then I was aiming for that. And I suppose I've always had a goal, I've always known where I wanted to be, and I suppose the more I've moved into positions, the more I've known what I want to be, my next position's going to be a Director of Nursing or Operations of whatever. So I do know that, I know that's what I'm looking for now. I've always liked a challenge as well and I like making change...if I was to describe myself, I would say I was a mover and a shaper as opposed to maybe a stayer...*(Fiona, Senior Manager)

Amy remembers quite deliberately deciding she wanted to promote herself out of the constraints of her initial nurse identity:

> *I felt very uncomfortable in the way we had to dress, and we had quite starched aprons...I felt like I was a glorified air hostess and that just wasn't for me. Also within that ethos you were very much a handmaiden to the doctors...I just felt very uncomfortable.*

She decided very strategically to develop her career, and negotiate a different sort of working identity. Her memories reveal the important intersections of space as well as time in this process:

I needed to, for my own career, to be part and parcel of something that was more dynamic, to be able to demonstrate in my C.V. and in my career that I was engaged in exciting and new and innovative changes... I felt in order to progress my career, I needed to be in London, seen to be in a London hospital...somewhere big, with a big name, if I was going to make the move...I felt there was a perception by managers that if you came from a big teaching hospital you'd be quite a different type of animal.

For those doctors and nurses who narrated their lives according to 'the ladder' metaphor, time is perceived as a relatively simple chronological sequence. There is always a 'next step' to be aimed for, which is, of necessity, perceived as a higher goal. Among the nurse managers only one had a (single) child to care for, and all of them acknowledged that their lives were dominated by work. The men were all fathers, but their children were only mentioned in passing – they too narrated their life-times according to the steps that their careers had taken. It was only the consultants, who had technically 'made it to the top', who had started to consider that their life's narrative may be due for a change. As Alistair ponders

I used to think what a great way to run your life-work hard, professional work then just come home and put your feet up. Now when I go home I usually am working til the early hours of the morning...I wonder if now my work has just completely taken over...

The vocation

Some stories were narrated in no less a future-oriented perspective, but identities were constructed through a discourse of vocation rather than career. Nursing careers in particular had been chosen and pursued as a way in which something tangible could be given to society and others. Further, Seaside was constructed as being the sort of place which enabled the fulfillment of vocation and the performance of vocational identities, and was explained in some people's life stories in these terms. For example, Sarah is a ward sister for whom nursing, rather than management, has always been '*a big part of who I am*'. She remembers her first, uneven attempts to find a job which was meaningful:

I'd done a degree, I'd done secretarial work, I'd worked in marketing...and I just couldn't see the value of it, I think more in a sort of spiritual way if you like. I wasn't getting, I didn't feel I was giving anything to society and

I felt that I ought to be doing something where, that someone would take notice of at the end of the day that's something different had happened because I'd been there.

She enjoyed the caring aspect of nursing, and remembers that in the early days of being a nurse, the fact that she was doing a 'nice job' was important to her: *'people approve of nurses'.* She always knew that she was not 'the type' to go into the acute sector. She remembers feeling that she was different to the other nurses during her training. Seaside immediately struck her as a place that she would enjoy being in: looking after the elderly in a small community hospital fulfils her sense of vocation and enables her to negotiate an identity she feels comfortable with. She has no plans therefore to change things in the future: *I'll still be doing this kind of thing in five or ten years time.*

It was not only female nurses who constructed their life stories through a vocational identity. In contrast to the consultants at Lakeside, Bernard, a Care of the Elderly Consultant at Seaside, also negotiates his identity through a discourse of care and empathy. From the early days he remembers that

I wanted a career where I spent a lot of time dealing with people because I was a people chap, and solving problems was the way to help. Medicine has the most mix of science and intuition and empathy with people...

Although his training emphasized scientific over other skills: *'one wasn't encouraged to demonstrate the normal human characteristics of feeling sorry for people',* as the years have gone by, it is the caring for people side that he has enjoyed most:

As I was going on it became clear that dealing with people was even more important

In contrast to the cynical weariness of the consultants at Lakeside, Bernard clearly loves his work, describing it as 'absolutely fantastic!' He looks forward to his future with energy, which includes more of the same, is looked forward to with energy and enthusiasm.

The journey

A less structured, but still future-oriented perception of time was revealed in the narratives which saw lifetimes as more of 'a journey'. However this view of life, as a series of 'adventures', or meandering stays in various 'ports', *was* a gendered narrative – of masculinity, as well as of time. These were men whose lives were not so much driven by a sense of career progression as by the search for an interesting life in which a rewarding job (in terms of satisfaction if not finance) was part. They were not from the privileged backgrounds of some of their peers, and perhaps therefore were not so tied by strict class-based expectations. For some, their narratives amounted almost to a sort of 'pilgrim's progress' as they recounted their experiences, often literally full of travel and journeys, as they have shifted back and forth between nursing and other working identities. For example, Colin, a Senior House Officer who had come into medicine as a mature student, had tried out several other careers first. Going to university was clearly an achievement in itself, but he had no clear sense of direction beyond this. Each time he started a new career, he remembers being worried about what the future might be like, and what he would be like as a person in that job:

> *I was sort of lured away by the thought, well I don't want to be a teacher for 45, 50 years, having looked around me at some of my teaching colleagues who were older...I felt I've got nothing to lose by trying something else...*

Martin, the A and E returnee nurse whom we have met earlier, had been equally restless. His narrative of his life was a literal journey around the world, as he moved on from one job or country to another. Within this journey, he variously constructs himself as a nurse, traveller, sailor, or wealthy/failing businessman. Rather than being the primary driving force of his past life, therefore nursing has always been there as a security net. However, both men now talk in terms of having 'arrived' at the final stage of their journey. Loving their present careers, they see that their continual searching for 'something better' has finally enabled them to negotiate an identity which they by and large enjoy performing.

In sum, the, future-oriented narratives were found to be more likely to be held by men than by women. Although it would be to overstate the case to claim that all men's orientations towards time were futuristic, it was interesting to note how this orientation to time dominated 'masculine' narratives, including those of *women* who had successfully followed a more traditionally masculine approach to their careers and negotiated their ways into senior positions. Class was an important factor here – many middle class women share the ambitions and expectations of their male peers. Looking to the future implies a willingness to change, and this is seen to be an essential part of contemporary professional identities within both medicine and increasingly nursing. It is also an organizational expectation at Lakeside. This contrasted with an equally strongly set of gendered narratives in which identities were negotiated and constructed through *past* events.

Past-oriented narratives

The golden years

Many of the older female nurses looked back at the past as a 'golden era': a time when the profession was better organized and truer to itself, and a time when they were happy with their working identity. They tended to be older nurses, who felt the skills and values, which they had acquired long ago at the beginning of their training, were now no longer held as important. Past time was therefore particularly dominant in the narratives of these nurses, with an oppositional 'then and now' discourse framing the way in which they constructed their professional lives. The past was looked back to as a time when things were much more predictable – when 'who was who' and 'what was what' were clearly known. The present, in contrast, is viewed as rather unpleasantly unpredictable and unstable: the rapidity and breadth of the changes leaving them regretful as to what has been lost.

At Seaside, it was within the nurses of Nightingale Ward that an almost tangible sense of regret could be felt about the changes that the passage of time had brought. This brigade of predominantly older nurses were described as 'backward-looking' by some of the other nurses in the hospital, and clearly shared an affinity with how they felt about the past, present and the future. Pam is a good example: she is a night nurse who has been at Seaside for over 35 years. She remembers her childhood as being shaped by 'wanting to be a nurse' from an early visit to Great Ormond Street at two and a half:

From that day, I wanted to be a nurse. Nothing would sway me at all. In all the years of growing up, I wanted to be a nurse and that was it.

Pam's memories reveal a fond affection for the past and a sense that the changes within nursing have very much been for the worst:

Everything was…it was their ward and nothing was going to be wrong with their ward. Whereas today well you know, if it gets done, it gets done, if it doesn't, well tough, somebody else can do it tomorrow.

I think some of the older members, especially those that have been in the hospital for twenty or thirty years...mourn the passing of proper uniforms. We still wear caps down here...I still mourn the passing of the apron. That gives my age away!

Pam's narrative of her early career reflects the pleasure she found in it. This rather sadly contrasts sharply with how she describes the present:

Up until now, I would have said that I was extremely happy in my work. But nowadays, not so happy. Not so satisfied. You don't know from one day to the next what's going to be happening in your particular job...the respect that you have as a nurse, in the old days, has disappeared dramatically. I don't think that nurses are held in the same regard as they were, even ten years ago.

Pam reflects on the changes within nursing which have happened over the course of her career with a sense of loss: *I can't believe how things have changed.* Treating each other with respect, and having a real sense of pride in the job are the key things to have disappeared. Now, the future is a sea of uncertainty which they all find very unsettling:

Nobody knows from one day's end to the next whether you're still going to have a job! And if you are still going to have a job, where it's going to be or what it's going to be...

This has meant that Pam now feels very differently about her jobs as she nears the end of her career:

I'm getting to the stage where if money was no object, I would go tomorrow...

The epiphany

Not all those who looked back to the past did so with regret. Some used the past to explain their present identities as the result of a key moment of identity renegotiation. These were women who had almost in spite of themselves experienced a kind of 'conversion' to or within the profession. The stories were of epiphanies, in which the nursing profession was acknowledged as having changed identities and the course of lives. For many of them, there was thus a real 'moment' of surprise as they discovered new aspects of themselves, and realized that this was more than a job, but a life and a set of identity performances that they could – and wanted to – become totally committed to. Class was also important here, as the change of heart about nursing was often a result of class-based assumptions and expectations.

Jessica, a theatre sister, recalls how at 18 she entered nursing 'out of desperation'. Her middle class background meant that she was expected to go on to university, but she was tired of full-time academic study, and couldn't bear the thought. The compromise was to train at several of the top London teaching hospitals – not because she wanted to become a nurse, but because it enabled her to kick her heels and leave home with her parents' (reluctant) agreement. Nursing was thus a means to an end:

> *I thought I can do that for three years; I can always go and do something else at the end of it. I never thought of it as a lifetime career.*

At first she remembers being put off by the heavily gendered image of nursing:

> *That contributed to my poor image of nursing before I went into it. That is one of the reasons why I thought it was like a big shop girl, and I thought it was a very lowly job. It was only when I actually did it that I realized what an important and very involved job it was.*

She acknowledges how nursing changed her younger self:

> *I went in with a very lofty opinion of myself, thinking it was going to be so easy, and that it was way beneath me to do this nursing, and I had the shock of my life because it was a really tough course...I felt so small and insignificant, that I'm a nothing really, and yet all these people were turning to me for help, and I found that quite...a buzz. I loved it.*

Drusilla, also a Sister at Lakeside, had experienced a similar career epiphany. However hers was very much a working class background, and she came into the job expecting to spend a lifetime caring for others. Beginning her narrative with the declaration that she had always wanted to be a nurse, she describes herself as 'the typical vocation type' who had 'always been interested in helping people':

> *I just wanted to look after people. Even probably during my training I didn't want to go any further than being a hands on nurse.*

However, much to her surprise, she has become fascinated by the intellectual demands of nursing and the changing demands on the profession. Her present identity makes a stark contrast with her early plans:

> *But that's changed and my ideas have changed…Because of the way that the attitudes of the public to nurses and the expectations that people have on us, you know within the National Health Service and outside of it, you have to want more for yourself because you'd just go insane otherwise. You can't stay – if you're trained as a qualified nurse; you can't stay as hands on any more. Definitely, nursing has changed. I mean I'd be quite happy to go into management now.*

Both personally and professionally, she is pleased with the way the present contrasts with the past, and the new identities she has been able to negotiate. This is particularly the case when she considers the power relations between nurses and doctors which she puts down to increasing credentialism and responsibilities for nursing:

> *I think that's why doctors' attitudes to us are different. I mean, they used to say jump, and we'd jump. And that's certainly changed. I mean, the ward round I was doing earlier, I gave the doctor such a dirty look at one of the comments that he made that he actually apologized. Well, I mean that wouldn't have happened in the past…*

Serendipity

The sense of falling into the profession by accident that came across in some of the nurses' narratives of the past was shared by many of the female doctors. However if an epiphany was to occur, they were still waiting for it! Class was again important here – these were middle class, intelligent women who were clearly expected to 'get a good career'. Becoming a doctor was something which led out of being 'good at science', rather than due to any sense of vocation. As Rachel, a Senior House Office in Accident and Emergency at Lakeside explains:

> *I don't think it's because I wanted to be a doctor at all. I don't think when I went into it I thought 'I am going to be a doctor'. It's so far in the future you don't think about it. I really liked the sort of biology, chemistry type subjects, and couldn't think of any other, anything else that I could do both of those at the same time really…*

This rather ambivalent entry into the profession was shared by Nina, who at Registrar level has been the most successful in career terms of the women doctors we talked to:

> *It was a bit of a mess really: I mean, it wasn't driven by a vocation as such. I just went to university and first started studying natural sciences, which I did for a couple of years and realized that I didn't want to be a scientist. But not too sure what to do next, and medicine seemed to be the logical thing to go into I'm afraid...*

This seemingly casual control over their futures still dominates both women's narratives. Both in their thirties, they also both mentioned motherhood as a future possibility, without really having much of a plan as to how to 'fit it in'. The hectic pace of their everyday working lives may partly explain the rather passive, fatalistic approach to both the past and the future – it *is* hard for them to find the time to do anything else. Further, the expectations of their class make it difficult to step off this predetermined plan of how their lives should go.

So far we have discussed the different temporal narratives through which men and women draw on either the future or the past to construct their work identities in particular ways. Time is used as a key resource here to in the construction and narration of identities. Through focussing on the future, present identities are deferred to other, 'ideal type' identities, which are ever being negotiated. By looking back, present identities are contrasted with other identities that may be more preferred. Although different in the direction of the focus, these gendered, class-based narratives share a common, underlying understanding of time as *chronological*. Other people's narratives however were dominated less by discussions on the linearity of time, as through the narration of key episodes through which a certain character or 'imago' (McAdams 1993) was constructed. Once again, this was a gendered activity: as we will show, these were in the main male characters, and the process of constructing identities through them was a predominantly masculine activity.

Character narratives: the hero

A traditionally hegemonic version of masculinity was revealed in those narratives of male doctors and nurses in which they positioned themselves as a 'hero'. Here, time was experienced through a series of key incidents which were constructed as contributing positively to their sense of themselves as heroic – a maverick but especially competent professional, easily able to challenge death, and 'cure' those near to it. These men were less interested in aspects of 'care' – they enjoyed the sharp-edged drama of 'saving lives'. This would preferably involve utilizing their superior surgical skills or knowledge of cutting edge, complex technology. Time was often used as a resource through which to intertwine medicine with other traditionally masculine activities such as military involvement or masculine sports. For example, Greg is a surgical senior house officer who is also heavily involved in the Territorial Army. He had originally intended to be a forensic pathologist and '*cut up dead bodies*':

> *Dead bodies, murder, fascinating. I just thought that was the ultimate career.*

His memories of himself as a boy reveal a sort of Boy's Own narrative of being fascinated by murder and death:

> *I had my little library of famous murder...the history of the Yorkshire Ripper and Jack the Ripper and the Boston Strangler biographies, and all that sort of stuff. Um, slightly macabre for a 14 year old...*

His epiphany happened at medical college, when he realized that the actual work didn't allow him to perform the sense of identity he was looking for:

> *By Christ, it was boring, and two, I was crap at it...What I wanted was a big ideal of being a forensic pathologist, and doing post-mortems and cutting up dead bodies – the day to day tedium of actually looking down microscopes at slides of pink and blue stained bodies that all looked the same to me, just bored me rigid....so it all just spiralled down a big dark hole really.*

In contrast, surgery attracted him, primarily because he admired the 'arrogant' personalities of surgeons. He has very strategically negotiated his own identity in relation to this, which he thinks is a necessary quality because of the nature of their work, and the amount of time they dedicate to it – both in lifetime terms and in terms of the day to day commitment.

At the end of the day, for you to decide that by cutting up somebody open and grabbing hold of their bits, rearranging their plumbing, you can improve their life, then I think you have to be fairly confident in your knowledge, in your own abilities, your technical skills. It's not a place for the faint-hearted...It's bloody hard work knowing that if you slip, if your handiwork gets a bit shabby, then they all die in front of you.

For Greg, the physical nature of the work and the long hours it demands over the years make it necessarily a male domain, adding to its 'heroic' quality

Surgery discriminates against women because it is a very long, hard training...It is long hours, you know, lots of work at night, and hanging around to assist your boss for the experience... It's very demanding physically...

Indeed, for Greg, 'time' is integral to the appeal of the job. Its rigorous training demands and long hours culture all contribute to the 'heroic' qualities which he enjoys incorporating into his identity.

The dutiful son

Another gendered character narrative was that of 'the dutiful son': not only a masculine discourse but also a racialized one which all the Asian doctors referred to. Freccero (1986 in Denzin) in his discussion of auto-biographical narratives has suggested that male narratives tend to be stories of separation from their parents, and indeed many of the white male nurses at Lakeside talked about their father's disappointment with their son's decision to become a nurse. Both Cameron and Martin for example mentioned that now, as adults, they are not really very close to their fathers – becoming a nurse represented part of the passage from child to adult, and proved to be something of a breaking point in the relationship. This could also be in part a result of working class expectations of suitable masculine careers – the feminized associations of nursing might make it difficult for men of an earlier generation to accept as suitable occupations for their sons. In contrast, the Asian doctors talked a lot about their parents, and how, in their early childhoods, the identity of 'being a doctor' was constructed as the most desirable of vocational achievements.

Rav, a Senior House Office who intends to become a General Practitioner, explains that his decision to become a doctor was influenced by his working class parents' dreams of social mobility:

> *It was a bit of family pressure as well, only-child pressure – that they want their son to be the best, a doctor. And that's what it is in Asian eyes, so it was a bit of pressure in a way.*

> *(My) Parents, I would say started mentioning it from the age of 10... I would say seriously myself, fourteen. My dad's unemployed and my mother's a factory worker – basically for their son to be a doctor is sort of an Asian Dream.*

For Nem, now an A and E Consultant, becoming a high flying doctor was very much a result of his middle class background – part of the family tradition, and as such is '*in my blood*':

> *My family were medically minded – three of my brothers are doctors. [I made the decision] when I was about six or seven...very young.*

Nem's life had been clearly mapped out ahead of him, and his family's broad and international involvement in the medical profession has meant that he has always had a clear idea of his future – what was ahead of him, and what to expect at each stage. Time has had a predictable quality – his elder brothers have told him what to apply for, and where, at each stage. He has had to work hard, and accept step backs in time – having to do several years of repeat training when he came to the United Kingdom. His present future however now feels quite secure – time, place and space have come together, just as was planned in his childhood. In contrast, Rav, a British-born working class Sikh, lacks these sorts of family connections, or what he sees was the 'right background' to get in to medical school. He has had a more lonely task to negotiate his Asian identity and the working identity his parents want for him against the norm of doctor identities, based as they are in the middle class:

> *I was lucky to get in because of the amount of people from influential backgrounds...there is a rigid old boys network running – male, white and sporting...rugger-buggers...*

The maverick

Douglas, a senior rehabilitation nurse at Seaside, uses time, professional and organizational change, as well as his sexuality, as resources to construct himself as 'different' to his female colleagues, and also to other male nurses in the acute sector. He positions himself as a maverick, a commentator on the hospital who is able to see things more clearly than others. He draws on his own past experiences and those of the hospital to narrate this identity more fully:

> *I came into nursing through having done lots and lots of different things, I mean very different things. When I came into it, I hated it, I abhorred it. I nearly gave it up. I couldn't stand it. I couldn't stand the traditional dictatorial – how can I put this without sounding nasty?...bossy women's syndrome, yeah? That you get on the wards, you know, bossy, big-arsed nurses, bustling down the ward and telling everybody what to do? And it's still like that, it hasn't changed that much!*

One of the reasons Douglas had come into nursing was his sexuality as a gay man.

> *I had trained as a telephone engineer, I'd worked in engineering and all that kind of stuff. And I found it really, really hard to be myself because I worked in an all male environment, rather than an all female one, and that was really hard.*

Douglas had expected to find things easier in nursing. However he still felt 'different' from both the female nurses and the male nurses he met during training. He had to make an early decision not to conform to the common male nurse model of being distant from the patient: not touching, communicating more with the doctors than the patient. As Douglas explains:

> *I made a decision that I wasn't going to be like that...as a nurse, I wasn't going to be like that.*

Although Douglas despises 'the hard, cynical nurse' model which he feels dominates much nursing yet feels that over time he has had quite deliberately to change his identity to fit in with the expected performances of being a nurse:

> *I think I have had to change to survive...and to start to play the game to a degree...*

At Seaside, he feels he is 'different' from the other nurses at the hospital is because he has invested less, emotionally, in any single ward. His identity has thus been formed in a more fluid way, having spent time in many different areas of the hospital. This marks him out as different from many of the others who have remained in the same ward for years, such as the staff in Nightingale: '*those people have never changed and it's very territorial...*'. As part of his bid 'to play the game', as well as to appear different from the '*traditional bits of wood*' at Seaside, Douglas has embraced the developments within the nursing profession enthusiastically:

> *what I'm trying to do is actually make something happen here that makes a difference, that actually changes the culture of the building.*

Douglas uses the future to indicate his lack of full identification with the hospital and his colleagues. His narrative is peppered with throw away comments such as '*I'm getting out soon anyway*', '*I hate it. I'm moving*'...concluding

> *It'll be a while, it'll be about a year and a half. I mean, I'm desperate to work somewhere where innovation actually means something, that things are introduced and questioned...*

The mother and the gendered jigsaw puzzle of time

In contrast to the range of male characters, there was only one strong character-driven narrative that was routinely drawn upon in the women's talk. The character of 'The Mother' was pervasive, either in terms of being a mother, as was the case for many of the nurses, or, thinking about becoming one, as was the case for the doctors. The 'mother' was often intertwined with an alternative orientation to time. Many of the women's life stories tended to be less linear than the men's – the 'career line' was less clearly drawn. In contrast, their past and future lives were constructed more as a patchwork of experiences, reflecting the interdependency of their involvements in both paid work and unpaid family responsibilities. Time in these narratives is thus less progressive – careers go forward and back, appear and disappear in importance as family and emotional commitments also ebb and flow.

This is by no means to argue that the women we talked to were less career minded or ambitious, but this was understood in terms of a different relationship with, and understanding of, time: other things had to be fitted in as well, time in life needed to be given to having children, raising them and enjoying them. This might mean that careers were put on hold, or that less popular shifts were worked, so that the jigsaw puzzles of lives could be worked out. Motherhood was also for many an epiphany in that it 'changed things' – before motherhood, time and life plans might have been constructed in similar terms to many of the men, but after, other factors come into play:

> *I think having children changed a lot – before then I could see how you could be sucked into everything involving your career and that...certainly having them meant stepping out a bit, and it has its place and I am not consumed by it. I mean it's important to me, but it is actually just a job, not a great career – it provides me with a bit of money, gives structure to my life – sounds very boring!* (Alice, an ex F Grade, now working part-time at D Grade)

The narratives of the nurses who were also mothers shared a remarkable similarity when they described that phase of combining their careers with motherhood. Some were still juggling, whilst others reflected back on their past selves as younger mothers with small children. The narratives have a pragmatic logic to them, as moves between hospitals, specialties or work times are rapidly explained through the discourse of 'children as priority'. Down-shifts in careers are mentioned almost without comment:

> *I worked in London in ENT in a big teaching hospital, then in the Special Baby Care Unit...then I gave up to have my first child...I didn't work, I had two very close together, and then went back after I had my second one...that was just doing nights in a General Practitioner unit...did that for a few years...then I came here doing nights as bank...then as the children got older I gradually did days, did my conversion and ended up here...*(Anne, Surgery nurse)

The emotional cost of trying to combine work and motherhood is still sharp in the memory of many nurses such as Maria:

> *I worked night duty at the time, because I had [young] children...then I got pregnant and found I couldn't cope with traveling to St Bernadette's , working the night, coming back, trying to sleep what you could, and then*

working again the following night...I already had two little ones as well...plus I missed my daughter, I just missed the whole thing, I used to go to work in tears, and thought this is not on...So I came to Lakeside and worked in the operating theatre – I wanted to stay in operating theatres, but I couldn't again because of the children, so I did night duty for quite a long time...and then one day I went and found myself a post on days....
(Maria, nurse, ENT)

Those with older children were no less wrapped up in them – the time commitments seeming to be no less or easier, just different. This is not to say that the choice between whether to prioritize motherhood or career was always an easy one, and interesting patterns of difference emerged. Whereas for Ruth, a sister in A and E with three children, career was always important:

I have asked myself why do so many women have children and come back with no ambition or motivation from a work point of view...I know I am different from that. I need something else. That is obviously why I am a Sister.

others knew this wouldn't work for them:

It's the way I've made it. I mean, I didn't have to make it. My ward sister here is full time with two the same age as my two, and she's managed to keep her career, whereas for me it didn't really come out, I couldn't do it...(Alice, D Grade)

For most of the mother/nurses, the future was something rather unpredictable, about which it is rather pointless to make cut and dried, hard and fast decisions. Few however, saw themselves throwing themselves back into the career model as fast as they could:

Even when the children are gone, I will never put myself in a position where I have to work full-time, because I simply do not want it

However, in general nursing was predominantly seen as a fairly family friendly career. The choices that the doctors felt they had to face were seen as tough ones however. Whilst past lives could be narrated according to a linear time perspective and clear sense of career, the future was seen as much less predictable. Some were already making the decision to become General Practitioners because they saw that this was a life which had the possibility of being able to combine career and motherhood. Some were still in the throws of decision making, whilst others were still avoiding thinking too specifically about the future:

> *There are so many things you can do as a woman, and I think you have to decide and change your main decisions to account for the fact that at one stage I will have kids and I will have a family and I am at this stage thinking maybe I shouldn't do a career where I will only have that career. It is important for me to have children and so I will choose a career where I can do that* (Sinead, Senior House Officer).

Concluding discussion

In this chapter we have discussed the importance of lifetimes as a resource in the negotiation and performance of gendered working selves. We have shown how broader social, professional and organizational contexts are used as framing devices to plan and shape lives, and how identities are narrated through conventional accounts of careers and rhetorical understandings of life rituals. Our identities are understood and negotiated through these framing devices, and the narratives of our doctors and nurses reveal the consequent opportunities and constraints. Differences exist within and between the ways which men and women have to narrate their lives. For many of the men, the key orientation to time is to look forwards: to plan for the future and gear their life and identity towards that. This was not only a masculine expectation, but also a middle class one, where maintenance of status, position and reward is a clear expectation. Social mobility was also revealed to be an important life plan for many of the male nurses, who saw this perhaps as part of the 'justification' for choosing a career which many understand as being feminized, and as such a non-traditional job for working class men. For others, perhaps especially the older female nurses, the primary orientation is to reflect backwards, to think with some regret about the ways in which the nursing profession has changed and the different discursive representations of working identities which were once important. These are identities which they once held and enjoyed, but which they are finding it increasingly difficult to negotiate in the present climate. Changes in professional and organizational discourses have thus had a clear impact on the availability of subject positions in nursing, and this impacts in key ways on the how people understand their lifetimes. Still others draw on time in an episodic way, through which they can construct and emphasize identities in particular ways. Keen to negotiate certain 'sorts' of identity for themselves, the narration of lives, and the stories of the careers and paths they have chosen, are seen as good resources through which to do this.

Gender, class, race, profession, organization and domestic life were all seen to be key contexts through which identities are negotiated. Changes in the medical and nursing professions as well as changes in the National Health Service were seen to interplay with people's lives and identities over their life course. People were bound up with the contexts in which they operated – and this was clear in the ways in which they recounted their lives and the ways in which they too felt they had changed. For some these changes, at both the contextual and the individual level were seen as beneficial, others mourned a time which was regarded as preferable to today.

The narratives of lifetimes once more reveals the complexity of time as a gendered resource. Whilst both women and men shared approaches to time, it was in the women's accounts that the simultaneity of time and its demands was most evident. Through the stories of their lives, the pressures of different conceptions of time were evident: juggling industrial, biological, domestic as well as individual time was a common factor for women. As Gergen (1992) also argued, the women's stories and identities are revealed to be built around the significant relationships in their lives. This was a factor which not only affects the contents of stories, but their formal structure as well, often being digressive and complex, and pointing less single-mindedly towards a pre-determined goal. This 'jumble' is clearly an important fact of many women's lives, and in the talk about their lifetimes, the importance of context is once more underscored. The where and when of work are clearly given a lot of thought, and life's events and decisions are explained through these. Indeed, the reason why many of the women have spent a large part of their working lives in one organization – whether that be Lakeside or Seaside – is because it fits with the routines and demands of their lives as the years go by. Clearly it is crucial that organizations have the ability to be flexible as people's lives change, accommodating the multiple demands which are placed on women in particular as they go through the days and years of their lives.

8
Negotiating Identities in Gendered Organizations

Introduction

The stories, vignettes and interpretations that we have presented so far in this book have opened up some of the intricate detail with which negotiations of gendered identities are made in everyday working lives. Focussing on just two of Britain's National Health Service hospitals, we have seen the distinctive organizational landscapes and timescapes that doctors and nurses inhabit. We have also seen that these are landscapes and timescapes that demand much from them, such that not only must they do the job for which they are paid-care for patients, but in doing so, they must negotiate complex and multiple expectations about *who they are* whilst they are at work. Performative demands are made on doctors and nurses from a vast array of sources, including National Health Service policy, hospital managers, professional bodies, specialities and wards, to name but a few. And these demands are ceaseless, fragmenting across the years of organizational and professional restructuring, between day and night and – sometimes – from one minute to the next. Arguably, there are few professions where the identities of the professionals are so looked at, moulded and judged as in medicine and nursing.

In this chapter, in order to move towards some assessment of the impact of this 'goldfish bowl' of identity-making on the men and women involved, we turn now to look more directly and explicitly at the issue of personal identity itself. So far in this book we have focussed our discussion on the complexity of ways in which gendered identities are made and re-made at work. However, what we have not yet considered in any explicit way are questions as to how these may affect conceptualizations of personal identity itself – that is, how people think about or view *themselves* as a result of the processes of identity-making and negotiation in which they are ever involved. We have, of course, outlined our theoretical understanding of identity in Chapter 1, and used this throughout the book. But we have yet to consider how the doctors and nurses themselves actually understand identity, or use the concept in thinking and talking about themselves. This is important, in some small part perhaps, because it is unusual for academic studies of identity to give voice to the more fundamental conceptualizations that their participants make. In itself this makes, we hope, for interesting reading. But, more importantly for our arguments in this book, we will show that gendered understandings of identity itself – as a concept – are also made from the gendered resources of work and everyday life.

Throughout the various chapters of this book one of our central arguments has been that the demands on doctors' and nurses' performances and identities are shot through with gender: the motherly nurse who smiles and holds her patient's hand, or the gruff but brilliant surgeon who can make life and death decisions in a flash. These gendered demands mean that for both doctors and nurses, for much of the time, whether you are a man or woman makes an enormous difference to who you can be and how you think and talk about yourself at work. In addition, we have argued that the different spaces, places and times that constitute the National Health Service are thoroughly gendered, and in multiple ways. Gender, and gender inequality, is played out differently in these different contexts, and the specific places, spaces and times of organizational life are crucial in the positioning of lives and the forging of gendered identities. To know the particularities of context thus gives us the detail of the range of specific opportunities – and constraints – through which men and women in an organization may craft themselves. But these contexts are never *only* gendered. We have for example also brought into our discussion ways in which they are also class-based, racialized and sexualized. This pluralistic approach demands a lot from us, as researchers, and you, as the reader. It demands that we see gender in the broader field of social relations, that we trace the ways that gender is woven in and out of the textured fabric of everyday working lives. This point has more than particular or local significance to this study. Many of *us* also work in gendered, racialized, class-based or ageist organizations, and questions as to who we are, or who we can be, and how we may operate at work, matter to all of us. A key aim of this book therefore has been to unravel organizational life to reveal the subtleties of gendering processes, to argue that (of course) gender is not only about unequal pay and opportunities, but that it affects the very ways we all have to be at work, and the very ways we have to think about our working selves.

In tracing the negotiation of gendered identities at work, this book has drawn on both theoretical and empirical resources. We began in Chapter 2 with an overview of the subjectivities that operate across medicine, nursing and management in the British National Health Service: the abstracted set of positions produced through professional and organizational discourses. In this account, we emphasized the gendered, yet at the same time multiple and contested nature of these subjectivities. In Chapter 3 we began the task of tracing the ways that these subjective possibilities are constituted and negotiated in everyday life. Our comparative methodology focussed on two very different hospitals and, in each case, employed documentary analysis, talk with doctors and nurses, observation of doctors and nurses at work, and our own engagement with hospital life. This multi-modal approach produced a wealth of data of some complexity. And at one level, it can be tempting to take analytical shelter (Knowles 2000) in this complexity. Our many stories offer us a collage of individual lives of some descriptive power. But these lives share too many things in common for them to be regarded merely at the level of fragmentation. We thus needed to move beyond the fascination of individual stories and consider what they tell us about work, and identity, and the relations between them. The lives we describe demand critical and analytical tools in order to trace the crafting of gender identities at work.

The point of any analysis is to open up a set of circumstances to political and social scrutiny. In this book, our research tools and theoretical approach have shown that gender and gender inequality are pervasive, and central to the negotiation of identities. In this final chapter we have three broad arguments that we would like to make about these empirically-based arguments. First, shared regimes of gendered organization and gendered profession remain influential in the negotiation of distinctive working identities for men and women albeit, *and our research shows that this is critical*, in contextually specific ways. Restructuring of the health service by successive governments, particularly since the 1980s; the introduction of new forms of managerialism; and the ascendancy of concepts such as 'efficiency', 'productivity and 'quality' as well as the use of tools such as 'clinical governance', 'audit', 'risk assessment' are widely associated with particular versions of masculinity, not only in theoretical sociology but in the routine accounts of everyday working lives. The gendering of managerialism and of management as an activity presents complex territories for negotiation as women and men, in management, nursing and medicine live out their working lives. For the women managers at Lakeside, their identities are carefully crafted from nursing backgrounds and feminized visions of management, yet the authority with which they carry this identity is uneven, they say, readily challenged by male dominated meetings or boardroom spaces. For male doctors, the challenge of an alternative masculinity invested in managerialism also raises tensions in the negotiation of working selves, but tensions that are reported more as irritants to be effectively managed, rather than sources of ontological doubt. Similarly, gendered professional regimes of nursing identity – themselves constituted unevenly over time and space – continue to be key in both doctors and nurses accounts of identity. Feminized accounts of the 'caring nurse' reached across all the places, spaces and times of our hospitals and were central to nurses' accounts of who they were, or were not. Masculine accounts of the rational, consumed professional continue to define medicine and especially surgery and, again, to be central resources in doctors' negotiation of identity.

Second, and arising from the previous point, these regimes were negotiated by women and men in ways that *reproduced* patterns of gender differentiation in working identities. In some cases this is simple. Most of the women nurses at Seaside say that male nurses simply cannot care in the way that women can. Meanwhile the surgeons at Lakeside define surgery in masculine terms and accept as a matter of fact that women cannot perform the package of skills and dispositions, according to the punishing schedules, as well as they can. Here then we see the reproduction of essentialist ideas about gender as gendered identities are made at work. But of course, we have seen far greater complexity than this. We have seen big differences between women, and between men, especially as we look across the different spatial and temporal contexts of our two hospitals. Compare Diana, the Accident and Emergency nurse at Lakeside, studying for her Management diplomas, with Anna, who moved to Seaside so that she could spend more time at the bedside. Or compare, Douglas who wants to be a 'hands on' and 'caring' nurse working with the elderly with Martin who prefers to deal only with dead people. These working identities are diverse and complex, but still they reproduce ideas about gender, about what women and men are, can be and should be. Douglas wants to be a caring nurse, but – and he is very clear about this – he wants to construct this position *as a man*. Indeed, he constructs his working identity directly against his representation of the 'bossy big arsed women' that dominate nursing. Similarly, Diana wants to go into management from the perspective of a woman, and a nurse to 'bring a bit of humanity to the wards'. Here we see the reproduction of gender difference in the negotiations of identity that these women and men, doctors and nurses are making in their everyday working lives. These differences are not singular or static. But difference remains central and it is in the repeated doing of difference that differences are made and alternatives are denied.

Third, and finally, there continue to be clear differences in the career trajectories that working women and men take, and the social circumstances surrounding their lives. These differences centre particularly on parenting identities and domestic responsibilities. For the male consultants, especially the surgical consultants at Lakeside, the consumed professional identity that has underpinned their career success has been enabled by a gender division of labour in their households. The cost of this absence from their own domestic lives is only sporadically visible to them, outweighed by the achievements, both professional and financial, that working 100 hours a week has brought. Meanwhile, the trajectory of women doctors out of hospital medicine (or, at least, out of the prestigious specialities) and into general practice continues as they ways of negotiating a mothering identity alongside a consultant identity continue to remain closed to them. Similarly, the number of nurses moving into part-time work, associated with childcare responsibilities, remains high. Nonetheless, we have seen that the opportunities for part-time and shift-work can offer the means with which to continue the negotiation of a professional and career led identity and that, for these nurses, provide part of a longer term career track. It is these sets of connected processes, brought together, that help to remind us how centrally inequality remains part of working lives and careers. But this depends on context: what is an option for (some of) the nurses at Lakeside barely registers on the radar of working opportunities for those at Seaside.

Our analysis in Chapters 4 to 7 has thus revealed how different hospitals are constructed as distinctive gendered contexts making them very different organizations in which working identities can be negotiated. Lakeside is felt by many of its employees to be a 'masculine' place – and as such the women have to negotiate themselves with care through and against this environment. In contrast, Seaside was felt by most if its staff to be a feminized place – and this was one of the specific reasons that many of them – but not all – enjoyed working there.

Space too was revealed to be highly gendered – affecting men and women's freedom to fabricate and use different areas of the hospital. Space is a way in which male privilege and power may be underscored, although space may also be used to challenge power. Time has also been revealed to be a key resource in the negotiation of gendered selves. Organizations and professions use time to demand total identities from their staff: they want these 'all the time'. Many of the men were found to fall into this positioning almost happily – their working identities were singular and wholly committed. Intensification of work was another way in which organization demands more and more from staff – particularly its nurses. There is certainly little time at Lakeside for many of the women nurses to do anything other than think, do and be 'nurse'. However, simultaneously, time is also used as a resource by many of these women. Yes, they *would* perform 'the nurse' while they were at work, but 'when' is something they can control. Shifts, nights, part-time work: these are all methods of fracturing the demand for total working identities from the organization. This diversity in the amount of time different people 'donated' to their working identities was re-emphasized in the ways in which women and men narrated their life stories. Whereas many of the men had constructed the whole of their lives towards the goal of 'being a doctor' – or being a 'resuscitation nurse specialist' and continued to look ahead and plan their lives and future identities in this way, the women were revealed to have a more fractured set of hopes, ambitions and reflections – and identities. They were more likely to have fallen into the career by accident, more likely to have a range of other identities besides work at play in their lives, and more uncertain as to the future, seeing a whole set of different alternatives presenting themselves.

What is 'identity'?

At the beginning of this book we asked the question: What are the relations between gender, identity and organization? We have explored some of the fine detail of this question, but we still have some unfinished business. Whilst we have looked at the *content* of gendered working identities, we have yet to look at the construction of identity *as a category in itself*. In this chapter we turn our attention directly to this point, exploring how doctors and nurses, women and men, talk about their identities. How doctors and nurses, women and men, account for the 'identity'. Does the constant business of 'doing gender' at work affect the very ways we have to understand ourselves? In more theoretical terms, we explore the ontological and epistemological frameworks that are used to understand and know 'identity'. In this way, the present chapter extends our account of negotiating gendered identities in context, considering 'what I am like' on a wider canvas and, beyond this, exploring 'what I am'. We examine not only how identities are made, but what identities are thought to be.

In exploring this we can only draw on the texts of our interviews with doctors and nurses. We could not observe them across the spaces and times of their everyday lives, however tempting that might be sociologically speaking! Our analysis of these texts for this chapter combines two different approaches. First, we analysed the full texts for accounts of identities in the different times and spaces of everyday life. These appeared in different parts of the text, brought into the narrative for diverse reasons, whether in relation to career choices, working lives, children or hobbies. Second, we used responses to a specific question posed by us about conceptualizations of identity. Towards the end of each interview we described different sociological accounts of identity to the people that we met, and we asked them what they thought. We were fully aware that this is regarded by some researchers as inappropriate (Chase 1995) on the grounds that non-sociologists should not be expected to see their lives in abstract theoretical terms. To us, this underestimates the interest that people have in thinking about many of the same sociological questions that engross those of us who make a living from the discipline; and the skill with which they are able to address these questions. Nonetheless, we will of course interpret their answers within our broader theoretical framework, a framework derived – in part – from our experience of discussing these matters with our doctors and nurses.

This framework insists that the self is processual: that identities only exist in the making. In this chapter we explore the understandings of 'identity' that this process produces. We look beyond work organizations to gendered lives, to explore how identities are understood across the places, spaces and times of everyday lives. Our attention to the on-going production of identity insists (along with most recent theoretical accounts of the identity as subjectivity) that there may be multiple and even competing identities as negotiation takes place in the different contexts of everyday lives. However, we suggest that this understanding of identity can also speak of stability and coherence, as well as fluidity and fragmentation. These outcomes are contingent. Whilst identities are constantly negotiated from the contextual resources on offer, repetition in particular contexts may produce the *effect* of a stable and coherent identity. Of course, as we show below, negotiations of identity may also produce other, less fixed understandings. In all cases, though, we show that negotiations of identity in the contexts of gendered organizations, and beyond, produce specific and gendered understandings of what identity is.

In what follows, we describe three broad perspectives on identity that were present in our doctors' and nurses' narratives: accounts of a singular coherent self; accounts of two or more separate identities co-ordinated by a central agency; and accounts of fragmented selves without conscious orchestration. What is especially striking is that, in each case, the account of identity offered is underpinned by gender. These different accounts of identity itself are made using gendered resources, indeed, they rely on gendered resources.

Coherent selves

In hospital medicine, less than a quarter of all consultants' posts are held by women (EOR 1998); as few as 17% in the medical specialties (EOR 2001); and fewer still in the most prestigious and/or lucrative specialties such as surgery and orthopaedics (ibid). In hierarchical career terms, men remain the most successful in hospital medicine. It is amongst these men that we find least reflection on any shifts or slips in negotiations of identity across the spaces and times of everyday life. Of all our doctors and nurses, the few who spoke of identity in seamless, coherent and stable terms were all doctors, and all consultants. These were the same individuals who spoke of medicine taking all their time (see Chapter 6) and described lives spent almost entirely within the organizational spaces of their workplaces. Negotiating working identities, repeatedly, in the landscapes and timescapes of their organizational and professional lives some of these doctors were almost incredulous that we might ask about 'other' identities. These doctors admit some subtle shifts *within* their medical identities. For example in the emphasis between professional and managerial selves (see Chapter 4; also Iedema et al 2004); or between the operating theatre and the hospital corridors (see Chapter 5). However, they deny larger scale shifts in the negotiation of identity as they move through the spaces and times of their everyday lives, offering a consistent account of identity, determined by a totalizing professionalism.

Andrew represented the extreme case of this identity. A highly successful specialist surgeon working at Lakeside, he is in no doubt about who he is:

I am a surgeon. That is who I am. That is who everybody knows me to be and I have very little existence outside of that ... It does consume most of my waking moments ... If I'm not here [in the hospital] doing it, I'm at home preparing to do it and preparing an article about it, or reading about it or talking about it

He explicitly denies any differentiation in his identity and – indeed – presents this coherence as an asset to medical practice

*I think I would function the same in any situation. In fact I tell my junior staff, if you can treat your patients, talk to them as if they were your child, your sibling or your parent, according to their age, you can't go far wrong ... I don't have a surgical persona **and** something else.*

The 'surgical persona' is all he needs, all he is and this has been consistent over many years;

I think there is no doubt that the thing that has first place in my life is being the surgeon, and [pause] family and other relationships take second place ... [pause] And as I said earlier on it's something I always wanted, it's something I can't imagine being different from

Andrew takes pleasure in this consistent and coherent identity. He has no regrets, despite the failure of his marriage, directly as a result of his career, which he presents as a sad fact rather than something that he might have been able to deal with any differently. Other consultants who speak of a totalizing identity, speak of a similar process whereby medicine has come to dominate their lives, has become the key or even only resource with which they negotiate their identities. However, there is a sense of helplessness in their lack of power to do things any differently, and a sense of loss in the cost that they have paid in other parts of their lives. Simon, a Care of the Elderly Consultant at Seaside describes his initial shock on realizing that he had taken on a medical identity, perceptible to others, even after a few years of medical training:

One of the worrying things that I once remember, I went on my elective, I mean this is before I qualified, I went on my elective and I had to catch a plane, in America this was ... and [I] sat next to this lady ... and we got nattering and she turned to me and she said 'you're a doctor aren't you?' and we hadn't talked about anything to do with medicine. So clearly my

> *behaviour was something to do with what she expected in a doctor, so clearly one does end up being like that ... So I suspect that, yes, I do end up being the doctor*

Now, in his late 40s, this medical identity dominates his identity, but this is a source of regret for him, and something he feels unable to control:

> *I'm afraid at the moment. I'd love to think that I really was, I don't know a father first and a husband, and perhaps, I don't know which should come first really, perhaps equally. But I don't, I think of myself as a doctor first.*
>
> **And has that always been the case do you feel?**
>
> *Yes, yeah, I think so. All the way since qualifying. Yes, I'm sure.*

Despite his regret, this dominating medical identity is underpinned by Simon's commitment to the concept of coherence when thinking about identity. To him it is a compliment, or an asset, to see identity as a fixed core – this is an understanding that he privileges. To be fragmented would be a flaw; it would be pretentious and inauthentic. Others may see this in him, but he hopes not. He strives to be a coherent person

> *The way that I am is the way I am ... I don't really think I'm that different in the different situations. I don't feel myself being different really ... I think there is an intrinsic person underneath it. Oh yes. I don't think we're just – that we just go like chameleons all the time.*

Beneath consultant level, the junior doctors at Lakeside (there were none at Seaside) know that this is what lies ahead for them, if they stay: the singular resources of an all encompassing surgical identity, sustained by a total time commitment and exclusion of the domestic. Men and women on the early rungs of the surgical career ladder position themselves distinctively in relation to this projected future. Whilst the men accept this outcome as inevitable, and even relish it, the women are more uncomfortable. This is strongly connected to family considerations, which raise competing demands for the women in a way that is far more limited for the men whom we met. Sinead, a young surgical Senior House Officer in her 30s, with an impressive career to date explains:

I think you have to decide and change your main decisions to account for the fact that at one stage I will have kids and I will have a family and I am at this stage thinking, no, maybe I shouldn't do a career where I will have to do only career ... I think you have to make decisions like that ... I think it is important to me to have children and so I will choose a career where I can do that

Does that mean being a General Practitioner?

I think if you are determined enough you can do it [surgery] even if you have a 100 children, you can still do it. But it is not just to do with doing it, it is to do with how much time and how much effort and how many sacrifices will I have to make and I think, yes, it is possible but am I the sort of person that would be happy making it possible or could I just do something else that would make me happier? ... I do think women think, no, career second, family life first. Its just inherent I think and if they don't they have got to sacrifice family life, often, unless they are real brainwaves, which not all of us are

Here, negotiating the demands of work and family life is not only seen in *practical* terms as is often represented in literature on women's careers. However improbable, Sinead is confident of managing practical concerns. Rather, it is a sense of different calls on identity that she finds too challenging and which, it seems, will ultimately lead her to choose either surgery; or motherhood combined with another form of medical practice. As she sees it now, it is from this (unwelcome) choice of gendered resources that her future identities will have to be negotiated. Perhaps not surprisingly, it is extremely unusual for women surgeons to have children and this is something that the young women doctors simply cannot see a way round. (See Chapter 6, for a specific discussion of this in relation to every day time). This is not something that the male surgeons feel they bear any responsibility for; it is simply the way surgery that is:

Surgery discriminates against women because it is a very long, hard training. And it is just not amenable particularly to doing part-time surgery, you know, part-time, flexible training. (Greg, SHO Surgery)

Surgery and consultancy more widely demand so much that they offer the resources for an understanding of identity as coherent. But this is not something that everyone is willing to give themselves over to. The women doctors that we met were never able to see this as the only choice, an inevitable progression. Whether or not some of these young women end up as surgical consultants is another question. It is entirely possible that they might. Then their negotiations of the gendered land-scapes and timescapes of surgery will continue, but – most likely – without the possibilities of alternative identities.

It is worth noting that, beyond our study, there is some evidence that male doctors too are leaving hospital medicine because of the totalizing identity that it demands. In a pilot study (not yet published), conducted with the British Medical Association, we found some dissat-isfaction amongst newly qualified male doctors, linked directly to shift-ing models of fatherhood etc and expressed in terms of their desires spend time with their children; to practise fatherhood in a way denied by (most specialities in) hospital medicine.

Talk of a singular coherent identity was unusual, and closely linked to the specific context of hospital medicine, the masculinized resources that this offers, and negotiations of identity within this context. Whilst selves were negotiated with the available contextual resources, these resources themselves privileged a dedicated and vocational model of medicine, underpinned by the notion of an authentic identity, to which Andrew and Simon were tied, albeit in rather different ways. However, we have suggested that junior doctors, especially women but also men, are making different negotiations with the gendered resources on offer in medicine, unwilling to abandon other potential identities and that – whether with pleasure or regret – they are seeking other con-texts, other resources to negotiate gendered identities at work.

Separate identities

Accounts which describe separate identities in the different spaces and times of everyday life were far more frequent than the singular coher-ent accounts offered above. Again, this understanding of identity itself was underpinned by gender. The ways that people described separate selves was done with the gendered resources that both positioned them, and with which they positioned themselves. We saw this operat-ing in two distinct ways.

First, were those doctors – all men – who described the deliberate construction of separate times and spaces which offered the resources to construct different identities. This is evidence of resistance to the totalizing identities of hospital medicine in doctors' narratives, but still depends on the notion of an authentic, 'real' identity-negotiating mul-tiple performances, much in the way that Goffman described (1959). Here, space and time offer key resources to negotiate other identities, distinct from those performed at work: to be someone else. For these doctors, this is bound with a rejection of the full package of privilege and power associated with traditional, masculine, consultant identities. Here we see the deliberate construction of boundaries between work and lives outside; the construction of separate social spaces in which the medical identity is denied. This construction of boundaries is used as a deliberate device to negotiate distinction from other consultants. For Bernard, a Care of the Elderly Consultant, the separation of identities in the different spaces of his life is a way of rejecting the stereotypical resources of masculinity on offer to male doctors (power, authority and superiority over nurses). Bernard describes his specialty as 'the feminine side' of hospital life, and claims to embraces this. Furthermore, describing his time off work, Bernard says:

> *If somebody asks me what I do when I'm outside the hospital, I say I work in a hospital. I don't say as what ... you know, you play different roles ... It's nice to be just the ordinary person. For instance, people I sit next to at the football match every week who don't know I'm a doctor, which is great, and we just talk about football and other aspects of life in general. They don't have that daft prejudice that you will instantly be stereotyped as, you know, wealthy, voting Conservative, all the things which are not necessarily true at all ... So it's nice to be able to escape from that and appear to be normal*

Similarly, Greg, a Surgical Senior House Office at Lakeside, described how he refused to identify as a doctor when moving into holiday time-space. He recounted with relish his *'great alter egos'* as a biscuit designer for McVities (a biscuit manufacturer) and as a nightclub bouncer. In part this is about his desire to really be 'on holiday' and not have to attend to minor illnesses and injuries (although in critical cases, as a surgeon, he would *'put my doctor cloak on'*). In the construction of these rather rigid and somewhat awkward boundaries it seems to us that these men are almost crying out for a way to manage the demands that being a male doctor, in particular, places on them. Like all junior doctors, and especially male doctors (women are exempted by virtue of their sex) they are expected to take on singular, goal driven medical identities that dominate in surgery especially, but in medicine too. This conceptualization of separate selves may be seen as a form of resistance.

In contrast, the youngest consultant that we met, rheumatology consultant Charles described a deliberate and strategic use of temporal and spatial boundaries to negotiate a rather different identity. Having moved into his specialty because of the regular working hours and opportunities for quick progression (see Chapter 6) Charles is actively marking the difference between vocation and career. For him, medicine is *not* a life but a rational means to an end: a good disposable income and a comfortable life. As we discussed in Chapter 6, this construction of medical identity is new, and something that many of the older doctors are highly critical of, associating it with a de-professionalization of medicine. In Charles' case, and in broader terms, we see a shift in the masculine resources being used to negotiate a powerful and desirable medical identity: a shift from professional power working through knowledge and vocation, to broader social values of wealth and individualism. Underlying this, Charles is certain that he can be the author of his identity

> *I think you are the person you are undoubtedly, but then you change it for the different situations ... I think you control the essential person that you are depending on the circumstances. But I do believe you have an inherent identity, and that's the person you genuinely are.*

For Charles this identity can orchestrate performances driven by clearly rationalized and articulated desires. Whilst Charles recounts this separation of identities as fully successful, the other male doctors that we have described above find this harder to achieve. In all cases, however, we are suggesting that this conceptualization of identity – as a deliberate device to manage the boundaries of work – is tied to the ways that men are positioned by gendered subjectivities in medicine, and their specifically gendered forms of resistance to this.

Our second instance of 'separate identities' – and the largest group of individuals across the study – was amongst parents, particularly mothers, and always nurses (since none of the women doctors had children). We may speculate two reasons for this. First, that nurses' confinement to the ward means that their 'work' identities are more containable than is the case for those – especially doctors – who feel that they are always on display wherever they are. Second, that the immediate and practical demands of parenthood, especially motherhood as it is constructed through family and social divisions of labour (women are far more likely to take primary responsibility for childcare, shopping and housework (Sullivan 2000)) relegate nursing identities to a secondary place when these parents are not on the wards: there is not the space or time to be writing a research paper once the demands of family life kick in.

This is clearly articulated by Alice, a surgical nurse at Lakeside:

I come into work and work is work. I walk back out into the car park to go back home and switch into children mode. I switch into 'what are we eating for tea tonight'. But I don't think about the children when I am at work, unless one of them is ill (Alice, Lakeside nurse)

Alice arranges her working hours so that she can start at 9 o'clock after dropping her children off at school, and pick them up again at the end of their school day. She enjoys the fact that she can be a nurse in the morning and still be at home for afternoon television and tea with the kids. If she is asked to work shifts, then this is more complicated: her husband does little round the house, expecting her work to be flexible and not to impact on the smooth running of his life.

However, it is possible that tendencies to this kind of separation are even stronger amongst male nurses. The difficulties of accommodating nursing work with masculine identity are always there – even at work – but can be negotiated using resources such as technology (see Douglas in Chapter 4) and trauma work. But performances of masculinity *outside* work may require a particularly strict separating off of the nursing identity, even denial. Martin, a resuscitation specialist nurse at Lakeside describes the boundaries with a similar starkness to Alice, but with an added dimension, the uniform:

*You walk in the door and I'm a nurse, and you walk out the door and leave it behind...I don't even wear (my uniform outside) ...my wife says 'pick up the kids' and I'll say I'll have to come home and get changed... she says why not? Other mothers do...I say I just don't feel comfortable walking around the streets if you like, going up to people in my nurse's uniform...**I guess that it's different for a man.*** (Our emphasis)

Amongst mothers who endorsed this model of 'separate selves' a wider point emerged too. This concerned their conceptualization of identity. In contrast with the male consultants discussed above, who articulated a 'real me' at the co-ordinating their separate selves, these nurses, specifically the women, were less sure. In their narratives they commonly described motherhood as a key transition point in their lives: a point at which previously understood selves had been disrupted and new selves had to be negotiated. For several this is recounted as an ontological crisis, as Sarah (Ward Sister, Seaside) explains:

*I've got three children. But I, when I was thirty I felt that I was the children's mum then and I was Paul's wife, and I didn't feel that I was **me*** (Emphasis in original).

For Sarah, as for at least half of the other mothers working as nurses, returning to work was described in terms of 'finding' myself again, providing other resources for the negotiation of another identity. This other identity is positioned against the mothering identity, as something separate, as Deidre, a staff nurse at Seaside, explained

I think my life at the moment's quite departmentalized, and I can feel that. I can feel that very much. But then I don't think that's a lack of identity really, I think that's just different expressions of your identity ... I wouldn't say you were a different person in those situations, it's just different aspects of you.

Nonetheless, for all that work is represented as a source of the 'real me' – a way forward from the ontological crisis provoked by motherhood – it seems that, for many, it has simply added another identity to the list without offering the resources for the negotiation of a sense of 'me'

I sort of feel [pause] it's like if you're somebody's mother and somebody's daughter, and somebody's everything, and when am I myself? (Deidre)

... the 15 seconds I have being me and not being anything else, not being a nurse, not being a wife and not being a mother. I'm not sure what I am when I'm not any of those other three things ... I would like to try to find out (Sandy)

So, we can see that the representation of separate identities is done in distinctly gendered ways. For the male consultants the idea of 'separate' identities is a conscious mode of coping, and a way to negotiated a desirable identity, in terms of masculinity as well as other components, for example politics or consumption practices. For nurses, specifically female nurses, endorsement of 'separate' selves is also a mode of coping with the gendered demands of family life: an effect of negotiating feminine subjectivities and practical demands. But here we see some profound doubt over whether this negotiation is co-ordinated by a 'real' me, or whether it is done in a less coherent and consciously reflexive way.

Multiple selves

From the accounts of the nurses, described in the previous section, we can see that whilst an assumed concept of identity is one of a conscious and coherent orchestrating agency, reflection on this provokes doubt. For a minority of people that we met, however, this lack of a core identity is far closer to the surface. In these accounts, gendered and other resources are negotiated both reflexively and un-reflexively in the production of multiple identities.

Amanda, a staff nurse at Seaside, illustrates this position fully. Across her narrative, she is constantly surprised, astonished even, at the course her life has taken. She describes her identity as fragmented and utterly contingent. Throughout, gender appears in contradictory ways. Ways that are sometimes accounted for as deliberate, whilst at other times they just seem to happen. Multiple constructions of gender are swirled throughout Amanda's account, fixing and unfixing themselves to her description of identity. In particular, she sharply differentiates her home identity from her work identity. She presents a slovenly and chaotic account of her home identity as antidote to the nursing subjectivities that she negotiates in the production of her working identity:

> *I mean my house is like a pig-hole, it's just disgusting. If I'm having someone round to eat the whole family has to clean the house, because I know they wouldn't eat if they saw what the kitchen was normally like. Things like that. Whereas here, I can't bear a messy desk, I can't bear a dirty kitchen. I just can't, whereas my house is a heap, and I don't care 'cause that's my slob area. But work, I can't stand it and I'll tidy up, I'll clean, I'll put things away.*

> *I've always been of the opinion that [...] this is how I am. I put this uniform on; I'm a completely different person. I take it off and I go home and I'm Amanda at home ... Uniform on, I'm a nurse. And at home it's forgotten about. Uniform off, I'm whoever I am when I'm out the building. I never, ever mix them. I take it off and I go home and I'm Carol at home. I don't think about work, I'm never one of those that takes work home, worrying about, 'Oh is this patient going to survive?' It doesn't. Uniform on, I'm a nurse and at home it's forgotten about. Uniform off, I'm whoever I am when I'm out the building*

In the movement between home and work, marked specifically by the uniform, Amanda describes distinctive and different gendered identities,

identities that hinge on her relation to dirt and cleanliness, caring and not caring at all. At times the differentiation is a deliberate construction, for example with patients' or relatives of patients

> *I'm just sort of grasping at straws really to explain, maybe a concept or something we're aiming for, I can look them in the eye and I can just tell them fact after fact: boom, boom, boom. Brilliant. And I'm just so convincing, I mean I'm a nurse, I know what I'm talking about. And they walk out the door and I think, 'Phew!'*

But, at other times the different identities are barely controlled

> *sometimes I worry the fact that I could say almost anything if I was that sort of a person and people would believe me. [pause] I mean, I could go up to patients and say, 'Take all your clothes off and stand at that window,' and they'd do it, they wouldn't even ask me why. Because I'm in uniform and I've told them to do it. [pause] But I find that worrying ... I mean, it's like a prison warden, I could do what I like, I could shut them all in or say, 'You're not getting up today,' or 'I'm not giving you your medication,'*

Combined with this reflexive understanding of fragmented identities, Amanda also articulates (initially) un-reflexive negotiations of identity, that she has only becomes aware of some time later

> *... it's bizarre; it comes out in even the way I walk.... I never walk the way I walk in this ridiculous dress. I don't do that at home. If I'm walking down the road ... I'm dragging my feet. I'm constantly in trainers, I just wander. Here, head up, and I walk straight, like a determined walk. You walk as if you're going somewhere, even if you're not, even if you're popping to the kitchen to make a drink, you'll walk in that manner. It's like policemen who say, 'Oh, I'm just the same.' They must be mad! They put that uniform on, they change. And I feel that really strongly.*

> *I mean even down to, my accent changes ... I've not been aware of it that long, but I'm aware that I do it now ... its like a telephone voice, only taking over wherever I go*

Arguably, this account of identity is more compatible with discourses of femininity than masculinity, where control, rationality and predictability preclude it. Already we have seen several of the male consultants interpreting multiple or fragmented identities as a weakness.

Conclusion

From the accounts of identity described above we can see that it is not only the resources and negotiations of identities that are gendered, but that the very conceptualization of identity itself is produced in gendered contexts and with gendered resources. However, throughout the previous section, and indeed throughout the book, we have emphasized the complexity of this gendering of 'identity', and identities. The negotiation of gendered identities, and gendered understandings of identity, is not essential, binary, stable or – necessarily – predictable. Framing this in terms of our original question about relations between gender, identity and organization, we can see that diversity of ways in which these connections are interwoven. This attention to diversity is important, because it helps to extend our understanding of relations between gendered organizations and working selves. It draws attention to the complexity of these relations, revealing on the one hand how the three categories are so thoroughly mutually implicated, but on the other how the balance of the relationship between them is continually dynamic, and in a state of flux.

We want to suggest that there we can get a handle on this complexity by thinking about three key aspects of relations between gender, identity and organization. The first aspect is degree of importance that *organization* plays in the narration of identity as a distinctive way of being in the world. Contrary to some of the argument rehearsed in Chapter 1, the material in this book has questioned the extent to which organizational and professional resources can exert power beyond the confines of working lives, such that we become wholly positioned by the discourses of our working lives (Rose 1989, du gay and Salaman 1992). Our material reveals that there is real difference in the 'take up' of this sort of coherent meta-identity. Those most likely to position themselves in this way were those people who might also be judged to be the most 'successful' and 'powerful' in career and economic terms: men at the top of the medical tree, or women nurses who have made it into the senior echelons of management Amongst many of the other men and women we talked to however, identities were negotiated through other resources of identity. Totalizing power relations from organization or profession to employee are resisted and alternative identities are fabricated, which draw on a range of other resources. These people did not want to position themselves through organizational resources alone, but negotiated themselves – sometimes in multiple ways – across and through the spaces of their everyday lives. Clearly, all these 'other', non-work spaces and times provide resources for the making of identities, and they may be imported – either literally or ideologically – to fracture identity from the power of the organization. Thus whilst some people – mainly women, but also some men – 'drop' the work identity as they leave the material space of the organization, and 'put it back on again' when they re-enter the next day, others may transport the resources of, for example, 'home' into their working lives and identities at work. Resources associated with domesticity do not only operate in homes, and workplace resources do not only operate in organizations. In this way, places spaces and times, or selves, are not clearly bounded, linear or singular. They are multiple and interwoven.

The second aspect is the pervasive, yet fragmented part that *gender* plays in narrations of identity. Whilst we are certainly not arguing in terms of universalized male domination and female subordination as determining features in all aspects of women's or men's lives, our research underscores the persistence of gender differentiation as a central discourse and resource which is drawn upon to produce and manage selves. As Bem has argued (1993: 2)

> it is thus not simply that women and men are seen to be different but that this male-female difference is superimposed on so many aspects of the social world that a cultural connection is thereby forged between sex and virtually every other aspect of human experience, including modes of dress and social roles and even ways of expressing emotion and experiencing sexual desire.

As well as being pervasive however, gender differentiation is plural and takes many different forms. Gender differentiation is not 'some kind of fixed, reified, monolithic entity, rather it is a shape-shifter, taking a multiplicity of forms and guises, and always open to contestation, reconfiguration, and redefinition' (Baxter 2003: 34). Clearly, as Baxter also goes on to argue, this is because discourses of gender differentiation do not act alone: they are drawn upon in specific contexts and in the process interwoven with other discourses and resources at play. We have seen this clearly in the ways in which gender is interpreted and understood in relation to the spaces, places and times of Lakeside, and how these differ from those at Seaside. The narration of gendered identities is, once again, clearly neither bounded, linear or singular. It takes multiple forms and is contextually interwoven. However, we cannot let our insights rest here. It must also be acknowledged that gender differentiation acts to constrain the ways in which identity may be narrated. In the ways in which the women position themselves in gendered terms, their minority status is frequently acknowledged or reinforced. Male nurses were often described as being promoted over women for no other reason than they were male. Even amongst those women who were on the face of it more successful in career terms, there was either an overt awareness of the necessity of game-playing (putting on a power suit for example) to attempt to 'counter-act' their gender – or a slippage into the appropriation of masculine management-speak in which to describe themselves. Many of the junior women doctors were already 'talking themselves' out of future hospital careers, accepting the male-defined norm of long hours being the only way to do the job. Gender discrimination was also evident in many of the ways the men narrated themselves. Male surgeons for example positioned themselves against women, who were seen as inappropriate or lacking in the necessary qualities for senior surgical careers. Douglas – the male nurse at Seaside – frequently revealed his scorn for women whom he regarded as overly-powerful and transgressing his views of how women should be: '*big-arsed, bossy women...*' It was true that women nurses did attempt to exercise power over their male colleagues: male nurses were derided as being lazy, sloppy, lacking in interest in the 'daily grind' side of the job. The real job of nursing, it was felt by many of them, should be done by women.

The third aspect is the operation of power and agency in negotiations of identities at work. Both the above aspects of relations between gender, identity and organization clearly involve power, but we want to make some more finely tuned comments about this. There is clearly fluidity in the degree to which individual doctors and nurses, women and men are able to negotiate the identities they want, and to control the effects of power. Selves are negotiated, and we exercise power in this process. Our arguments about both gender and organization show the ways in which selves are constrained however, and not always negotiated under conditions of our own choosing. Women in particular have been shown to be caught in complex gendered power relations in the places, spaces and times of their working lives, all of which constrain the sorts of gendered identities and performances they are able to negotiate. Men too of course are constrained in the range of identities they are able to negotiate, and we have seen some of the attempts made to minimize the impact of work on their sense of identity. Ironically those who have the most successful careers, in which they may exercise considerable power within their organization and over their colleagues, have also lost considerable power over their ability to negotiate other, non-work identities. The work identity has assumed precedence over all other identities, and in some of the narratives, regret was expressed about this loss. However what our discussion have also revealed, once again, is the unfixed and unbounded nature of power – it operates in circulatory and dynamic ways, as Foucault (1981) has insisted. The multiplicity and dynamism of context mean that opportunities are in a continual state of flux. In a moment, who is 'better placed' (Baxter 2003) may change, meaning that who is able to gain from the experience may also shift and change. We have seen this in some of the interactions between nurses and junior doctors: female nurses are able to control the (male) doctors' power by turning their back on them, glaring at them, making them wait for information. Power is obviously operating here at all sorts of levels – not only are there persistent gendered structural power relations at play between men and women, but there are also local power plays and relations. In this way it is possible for people to be located as *simultaneously* powerful and powerless (Baxter 2003).

An understanding of the mobility and fluidity of context is essential to this understanding of power and agency. Our discussions of context – place, space and time – have not been about illustrating already constituted processes or identities. Rather, we have seen that context is *integral to* those processes and identities, and as such that context is critical both theoretically and empirically. But these points about context are also important in terms of organizational change. The unbounded nature of place, space and time means that change is an ever present possibility. We suggested earlier that one of the aims of sociological research and analysis is to open up social situations to political scrutiny. In the inequalities which are revealed, the need for change is exposed. It is through acknowledgement of the importance of place, space and time that innovative and effective interventions may be made by individuals, managers and policy makers in the future.

References

Acker, J. (1990) 'Hierarchies, jobs, bodies: a theory of gendered organization', *Gender and Society* 5, pp. 390–407.

Acker, J. (1992) 'Gendering organizational theory' in Mills, A. and Tancred, P. (eds) *Gendering Organizational Analysis*, London: Sage, pp. 258–60.

Acker, J. (2000) 'Revisiting class: thinking from gender, race and organizations', *Social Politics* 7(2), pp. 192–214.

Ackroyd, S. (1996) 'Organization contra organizations: professional and organizational change in the United Kingdom', *Organization Studies* 17(4), pp. 599–621.

Adam, B. (1995) *Timewatch: the social analysis of time*. Oxford: Polity.

Allen, I. (1994) *Doctors and Their Careers: a new generation*, London: Policy Studies Institute.

Allen, D. (2001) *The changing shape of nursing practice: the role of nurses in the hospital division of labour*. London: Routledge.

Alvesson, M. and due Billing, Y. (1997) *Understanding Gender and Organizations*. London: Sage.

Antaki, C. and Widdicombe, S. (eds) (1998) *Identities in Talk*. London: Sage.

Augoyard, J. (1979) *Essai sur le cheminement quotidien en milieu urbain*. Paris: Seuil.

Barth, F. (1981) *Process and Form in Social Life: Selected Essays of Frederik Barth, Vol. 1*. London: Routledge and Kegan Paul.

Baxter, J. (2003) *Positioning Gender in Discourse: A Feminist Methodology*. Basingstoke: Palgrave Macmillan.

Bellaby, P. (1991) 'Histories of sickness: Making use of multiple accounts of the same process' in Dex, S. (ed.) (1991) *Life and Work History Analyses: Qualitative and Quantitative Developments*. London: Routledge.

Bem, S. (1993) *The Lenses of Gender: Transforming the Debate in Sexual Equality*. New Haven: Yale University Press.

Benhabib, S. (1992) *Situating the Self: gender, community and postmodernism in contemporary ethics*. Cambridge: Polity Press.

Bolton, S. (2004) 'A simple matter of control? NHS hospital nurses and new management', *Journal of Management Studies* 41(2), pp. 317–33.

Bourdieu, P. (1984) *Distinction: a social critique of the judgement of taste*. London: RKP.

Bradley, H. (1996) *Fractured Identities: changing patterns of inequality*. Cambridge: Polity Press.

British Medical Association (BMA) (2004) *Hospital Doctors – junior doctors hours*. Briefing Paper, May 2004, London: BMA.

Brooks and MacDonald (2000) '"Doing Life": gender relations in a night nursing sub-culture', *Gender, Work and Organization* 7(4), pp. 221–9.

Bryan, B., Dadzie, S. and Scafe, S. (1985) *Heart of the Race: black women's lives in Britain*. London: Virago.

Bryman, A. (2001) *Social Research Methods*. Buckingham: Open University Press.

Butler, J. (1990) *Gender Trouble: feminism and the subversion of identity*. London: Routledge.

Butler, J. (1993) *Bodies that Matter: on the discursive limits of sex*. London: Routledge.

Cameron, D. (1997) 'Theoretical debates in feminist linguistics: questions of sex and gender' in Wodak, R. (ed.) *Gender and Discourse*. London: Sage.

Cameron, D. (2001) *Working With Spoken Discourse*. London: Sage.

Campbell, J. and Harbord, J. (1999) 'Playing it again: citation, reiteration or circularity', *Theory, Culture and Society* 16(2), pp. 229–40.

Casey, C. (1995) *Work, Self and Society: after industrialism*. London: Routledge.

Chase, S. (1995) 'Taking narrative seriously' in Josselson, R. and Leiblich, A. (eds) *Interpreting Experience: the narrative study of lives*. Thousand Oaks: Sage, pp. 1–25.

Cheng, C. (ed.) (1997) *Masculinities in Organizations*. London: Sage.

Clinical Standards Advisory Group (CSAG) (1998) *Report on Clinical Effectiveness using stroke care as an example*. London: HMSO.

Cohen, S. and Taylor, L. (1976) *Escape Attempts: the theory and practice of resistance to everyday life*. London: Allen Lane.

Coleman, P. (1991) 'Ageing and life history: the meaning of reminiscence in late life' in Dex, S. (ed.) (1991) *Life and Work History Analyses: Qualitative and Quantitative Developments*. London: Routledge.

Collinson, D. and Hearn, J. (eds) (1996) *Men as Managers, Managers as Men: critical perspectives on men, masculinity and management*. London: Sage.

Conradson, D. (2003) 'Doing organizational space: practices of voluntary welfare in the city', *Environment and Planning A* 35, pp. 1975–92.

Collins, P. (1998) 'Negotiating selves: reflections on "unstructured interviewing"', *Sociological Research Online* 3(3) www.socresonline.org.uk/socresonline/3/3/2.html

Cook, L., Halford, S. and Leonard, P. (2003) *Racism in the Medical Profession: the experience of UK graduates*. London: British Medical Association.

Cortazzi, M. (2001) 'Narrative analysis in ethnography' in Atkinson, P., Coffey, A., Delamont, S. and Lofland, L. (eds) *Handbook of Ethnography*. London: Sage, pp. 384–94.

Cortazzi, M. (1993) *Narrative Analysis*. London: Falmer Press.

Crang, P. (1994) 'Its Showtime: on the workplace geographies of display in a restaurant in southeast England', *Environment and Planning D: Society and Space* 12, pp. 675–704.

Cresswell, T. (2004) *Place: a short introduction*. Oxford: Blackwell.

Crompton, R. (1989) 'Women in banking', *Work, Employment and Society* 3(2), pp. 141–56.

Crossley, N. (1994) *The Politics of Subjectivity*. Aldershot: Avebury.

Crouch, D. (2000) 'Spacing, performing and becoming: tangles in the mundane', *Environment and Planning A* 35, pp. 1945–60.

Deal, T. and Kennedy, A. (1982) *Corporate Cultures: the rites and rituals of corporate life*. Reading, MA: Addison-Wesley.

Davies, C. and Rosser, J. (1986) *Processes of Discrimination: a study of women working in the NHS*. London: Department of Health and Social Security.

Davies, C. (1995) *Gender and the Professional Predicament in Nursing*. Buckingham: Open University Press.

Davies, K. (1995) 'The tensions between process time and clock time in care work', *Time and Society* 3(3), pp. 277–303.

Davies, K. (2003) 'The body doing gender: the relations between doctors and nurses in medical work', *Sociology of Health and Illness* 25(7), pp. 720–42.

De Certeau, M. (1984) *The Practice of Everyday Life*. Berkeley: University of California Press.

Deleuze, G. (1991) *Empiricism and Subjectivity: an essay on Hume's theory of human nature*. New York: Columbia University Press.

Dent, M. (2003) 'Managing doctors and saving a hospital: irony, rhetoric and actor networks', *Organization* 10(1), pp. 107–27.

Denzin, N. (1989) *Interpretive Biography*. London: Sage.

Derrida, J. (1972) 'Structure, Sign and Play in the Discourse of the Human Sciences' in Macksey, R. and Donato, E. (eds) *The Structuralist Controversy: The Languages of Criticism and the Sciences of man*, Baltimore, MD: John Hopkins Press.

Dewsbury, J-D. (2003) 'Witnessing space: knowledge without contemplation', *Environment and Planning A* 35, pp. 1907–32.

Dex, S. (ed.) (1991) *Life and Work History Analyses: Qualitative and Quantitative Developments*. London: Routledge.

Doolin, B. (2002) 'Enterprise discourse, professional identity and the organizational control of hospital clinicians', *Organization Studies* 23(3), pp. 369–90.

du Gay, P. and Salaman, G. (1992) 'The Cult(ure) of the Consumer', *Journal of Management Studies* 29(5), pp. 615–33.

Duncan, N. (1996) '(Re)placings' in Duncan, N. (ed.) *Body Space*. London: Routledge.

Elston, M. (1991) 'The politics of professional power' in Gabe, J., Calnan, M. and Bury, M. (eds) *The Sociology of the Health Service*. London: Routledge.

Equal Opportunities Review (EOR) (1998) 'Equal Opportunities and Monitoring in the NHS', *Equal Opportunities Review* 82, pp. 25–7.

EOR (2000) 'Profile: Christine Hancock' *Equal Opportunities Review* 90, pp. 23–4.

EOR (2001) 'Gender bias deters female doctors', *Equal Opportunities Review* 99, p. 6.

Erben, M. (1998) 'Biography and Research Method', *Biography: A Reader*. London: Falmer Press.

Esmail, A. and Everington, S. (1993) 'Racial discrimination against doctors from ethnic minorities', *BMJ* 306, pp. 691–2.

Esmail, A. and Everington, S. (1997) 'Asian doctors are still being discriminated against', *BMJ* 314, p. 1619.

Essed, P. (1991) *Understanding Everyday Racism: an interdisciplinary theory*. Newbury Park, CA: Sage.

Exworthy, M. and Halford, S. (eds) (1999) *Professionals and Managers in the Public Sector*. Buckingham: Open University Press.

Ferguson, K. (1984) *The Feminist Case Against Bureaucracy*. Philadelphia, PA: Temple University Press.

Foucault, M. (1977) *Discipline and Punish: the birth of the prison*. London: Allen Lane.

Foucault, M. (1981) *The History of Sexuality Vol. 1*. Harmondsworth: Penguin.

Frankenberg, R. (1992) *Time, Health and Medicine* London, Sage.

Freeman, M. (1993) *Re-writing the Self: history, memory, narrative*. London: Routledge.

Friedson, E. (1994) *Professionalism Re-Born: theory, prophecy, policy*. Oxford: Polity Press.

Gatens, M. (1996) *Imaginary Bodies: ethics, power and corporeality* London: Routledge.

Geertz, C. (1973) *The Interpretation of Cultures*. London: Font.

Gergen, M. (1992) 'Life stories: pieces of a dream' in Rosenwald, G. and Ochbert, R. (eds) *Storied Lives*, New Haven, CT: Yale University Press, pp. 127–144.

Gergen, K and Gergen, M. (eds) (1984) *Historical social psychology*. Hillsdale, NJ: Erlbaum.

Glucksmann, M. (2000) *Cottons and Casuals: the gendered organization of labour in time and space*. Durham: Sociology Press.

Goffman, E. (1959) *The Presentation of Self in Everyday Life*. London: Penguin.

Gregson, N. and Rose, G. (2000) 'Taking Butler elsewhere: performativities, spatialities and subjectivities', *Environment and Planning D: Society and Space* 18, pp. 433–52.

Grosz, E. (1995) *Space, Time and Perversion: Essays on the Politics of Bodies*. New York: Routledge.

Hacking, I. (1986) 'Making Up People' in Heller, T., Sosna, M. and Wellbery, D. (eds) *Reconstructing Individualism: autonomy, individuality and the self in western thought*. Stanford, CA: Stanford University Press.

Halford, S. and Leonard, P. (2001) *Gender, Power and Organizations*. Basingstoke: Macmillan.

Halford, S., Savage, M. and Witz, A. (1997) *Gender, Careers and Organisations: current developments in banking, nursing and local government*. Basingstoke: Macmillan.

Halford, S. and Savage, M. (1997) 'Re-thinking re-structuring: agency, embodiment and identity' in Lee, R. and Wills, J. (eds) *Space, Place and Economy: states of the art in Economic Geography*. London: Edward Arnold.

Hall, S. (2000) 'Who needs identity?' in Hall, S. and du Gay, P. (eds) *Questions of Cultural Identity*. London: Sage, pp. 1–17.

Hallam, J. (2000) *Nursing the Image*. London: Routledge.

Ham, C., Kipping, R. and McLeod, H. (2003) 'Redesigning work processes in health care: lessons from the National Health Service', *The Milbank Quarterly* 81(3), pp. 415–39.

Hardy, C., Palmer, I. and Phillips, N. (2000) 'Discourse as a Strategic Resource', *Human Relations* 53(9), pp. 1227–48

Harrison, S. and Pollit, C. (1994) *Controlling Health Professionals*. Buckingham: Open University Press.

Harrison, P. (2000) 'Making sense: embodiments and the sensibilities of the everyday', *Environment and Planning D: Society and Space* 18, pp. 497–517.

Harvey, D. (1989) *The Condition of Postmodernity*. Oxford: Blackwell.

Hegelson, S. (1990) *The Female Advantage: Women's Ways of Leadership*. New York: Doubleday/Currency.

Hill-Collins, P. (1990) *Black Feminist Thought: knowledge, consciousness and the politics of empowerment*. New York: Routledge.

Holmes, K. (1995) *Spaces in Her Day: Australian women's diaries of the 1920s & 1930s*. Sydney: Allen & Unwin.

Holmes, M. (2002) 'Politicising time: temporal issues for second wave feminism' in Crow, Graham and Heath, Sue (eds) *Social Conceptions of Time*. Basingstoke: Palgrave.

hooks, B. (1990) *Yearning: race, gender and cultural politics*. Boston: South End Press.

HMSO (1997) *The New National Health Service: modern and dependable*. London: HMSO.

HMSO (2000) *The NHS Plan*. London: HMSO.

HMSO (2002) *Delivering the NHS Plan*. London: HMSO.

Hunter, K. (1988) 'Nurses: the satiric image and the translocated ideal' in Jones, A. (ed.) *Images of Nurses: perspectives from History, Art and Literature*. Philadelphia, PA: University of Philadelphia Press, pp. 113–27.

Iedema, R. and Wodak, R. (1999) 'Introduction: organizational discourses and practices', *Discourse and Society* 10(1), pp. 5–19.

Iedema, R., Degeling, P., Braithwaite, J. and White, L. (2004) 'It's an Interesting Conversation I'm hearing': The Doctor as Manager, *Organization Studies* 25(1), pp. 15–33.

Jenkins, R. (2004) *Social Identity*, 2nd edition. London: Routledge.

Jolley, M. (1995) 'The search for identity' in Jolley, M. and Brykczynska, G. (eds) *Nursing: beyond tradition and conflict*. London: Mosby, pp. 91–110.

Jones, A. (2001) 'Time to think: temporal considerations in nursing practice and research', *Journal of Advanced Nursing* 33(2), pp. 150–8.

Josselson, R. and Leiblich, A. (eds) (1995) *Interpreting Experience: the narrative study of lives*. Thousand Oaks: Sage.

Josselson, R. and Leiblich, A. (eds) (1999) *Making Meaning of Narratives*. Thousand Oaks: Sage.

Kanter, R. (1977) *Men and Women of the Corporation*. New York: Basic Books.

Keenoy, T. and Oswick, C. (2003) 'Organizing Textscapes', *Organization Studies* 25(1), pp. 135–42.

Keenoy, T., Oswick, C., Anthony, P., Grant, D. and Managham, I. (2002) 'Interpretive times: the timescape of managerial decision making' in Adam, Barbara, Whipp, Richard and Sabelis, Ida (eds) *Making Time: time and management in modern organizations*. Oxford: OUP, pp. 182–95.

Keith, M. and Pile, S. (1993) (eds) *Geographies of Resistance*. London: Routledge.

Kerfoot, D. and Knights, D. (1993) 'Management, Masculinity and Manipulation: from paternalism to corporate strategy in financial services in Britain', *Journal of Management Studies* 30(4), pp. 659–78.

Kerfoot, D. and Knights, D. (1996) 'The best is yet to come? The quest for embodiment in managerial work' in Collinson, D. and Hearn, J. (eds) *Men as Managers, Managers as Men: critical perspectives on men, masculinity and management*. London: Sage.

Knowles, C. (2000) *Bedlam on the Streets*. New York: Routledge.

Knowles, C. (2003) *Race and Social Analysis*. London: Sage.

Law, J. (ed.) (1986) *Power, Action and Belief: a new Sociology of knowledge?* London: RKP.

Law, J. (1992) 'Notes on the theory of actor-network: ordering, strategy and heterogeneity', *Systems Practice* 5, pp. 379–93.

Lefebvre, H. (1991) *The Production of Space*. Oxford: Blackwell.

Lefebvre, H. (1994) *Everyday Life in the Modern World*. New Brunswick: Transaction Publishers.

Lefebvre, H. (2004) *Rhythmyanalysis: space, time and everyday life*. London: Continuum.

LeGrand, J. (2002) 'The labour government and the NHS', *Oxford Review of Economic Policy* 18(2), pp. 137–52.

184   *References*

Leidner, R. (1993) *Fast Food, Fast Talk: Service Work and the Routinization of Everyday Life*. Berkeley and Los Angeles: University of California Press.

Leonard, P. (1998) 'Women behaving badly? Restructuring Gender and Identity in British Broadcasting Organizations', *Harvard International Journal of Press Politics* 3(1), pp. 9–25.

sLofland, J. and Lofland, L. (1995) Analyzing social settings: a guide to quantitative observation and analysis. Belmont, California: Wadsworth.

Lupton, D. (1997) 'Doctors on the medical profession', *Sociology of Health and Illness* 19(4), pp. 480–97.

Malpas, J. (1999) *Place and Experience: a philosophical topography*. Cambridge: Cambridge University Press.

Mandanipour, A. (1996) 'Urban design and dilemmas of space', *Environment and Planning D: Society and Space* 14, pp. 331–55.

Marshall, J. (1984) *Women Managers: travellers in a male world*. Chichester: Wiley.

Massey, D. (1994) 'Double articulation: a place in the world' in Bammer, A. (ed.) *Displacements: cultural identities in question*. Bloomington, IN: Indiana University Press.

Massey, D. (1997) 'Economic and non-economic' in Lee, R. and Wills, J. (eds) *Geographies of Economies*. London: Edward Arnold, pp. 27–36.

Massey, D. (2005) *for space* London, Sage.

Massey, D., Allen, J. and Sarre, P. (1999) (eds) *Human Geography Today*. Oxford: Polity.

McAdams, D. (1993) *The Stories We Live By: Personal Myths and the Making of the Self*. New York: The Guilford Press.

McDowell, L. (1997) *Capital Cultures: gender at work in the City*. Oxford: Blackwell.

McDowell, L. (1999) *Gender, Identity and Place: understanding feminist geographies*. Minneapolis, MN: University of Minnesota Press.

McMahon, B. (1994) 'The functions of space', *Journal of Advanced Nursing* 19, pp. 362–66.

McNay, L. (1999) 'Subject, psyche and agency: the work of Judith Butler', *Theory, Culture and Society* 16(2), pp. 175–94.

Mead, G. (1932) *The Philosophy of the Present*. La Salle, Il: Open Court.

Miller, R. (2000) *Researching Life Stories and Family Histories*. London: Sage.

Modjeska, D. (1990) *Poppy*. Melbourne: McPhee Gribble.

Naish, J. (1990) 'Hard-pressed Angels', *Nursing Standard* 4(42), p. 17.

Nash, C. (2000) 'Performativity in Practice: some recent work in cultural geography', *Progress in Human Geography* 24(4), pp. 653–64.

National Health Service (NHS) Confederation (2004) 'NHS management: exploding the myths' Factsheet, March.

Newton, T. (1999) 'Power, Subjectivity and British Industrial and Organisational Sociology: The Relevance of the Work of Norbert Elias', *Sociology* 33(2) pp. 411–40.

Noss, C. (2002) 'Taking time seriously: organizational change, flexibility and the present time in a new perspective' in Adam, Barbara, Whipp, Richard and Sabelis, Ida (eds) *Making Time: time and management in modern organizations*. Oxford: OUP, pp. 46–60.

Nursing and Midwifery Council (2002) *Statistical Analysis of the Register 1ˢᵗ April 2001–31 March 2002*. Nursing and Midwifery Council, London. http://www.nmc-uk.org/nmc/main/publications/Statistical_Analysis_2002.doc

Odih, P. (1999) 'Gendered time in the age of deconstruction', *Time and Society* 8(1), pp. 9–38.

Packwood, T. (1997) 'Analysing change in the nature of health service management in England', *Health Policy* 40, pp. 91–102.

Palmer, I. (1983) 'Nightingale Revisited', *Nursing Outlook* 31(4), pp. 229–33.

Passerini, L. (1990) 'Mythbiography in oral history' in Samuel, R. and Thompson, P. (eds) *The Myths We Live By*. London: Routledge.

Petras, J. (ed.) (1968) *George Herbert Mead: Essays on his Social Philosophy*. Columbia University, NY: Teachers College Press.

Pile, S. and Thrift, N. (eds) (1995) *Mapping the Subject: geographies of cultural transformation*. London: Routledge.

Plummer, K. (2001) 'The call of life stories in ethnographic research' in Atkinson, P., Coffey, A., Delamont, S. and Lofland, L. (eds) *Handbook of Ethnography*. London: Sage, pp. 395–406.

Portelli, A. (1998) 'What makes oral history different?' in Perks, R. and Thompson, A. (eds) *The Oral History Reader*. London: Routledge, pp. 63–74.

Porter, S. (1995) *Nursing's Relationship with Medicine*. Aldershot: Avebury.

Pringle, R. (1988) *Secretaries Talk: sexuality, power and work*. London, Verso.

Pringle, R. (1998) *Sex and Medicine: gender, power and authority in the medical profession*. Cambridge: Cambridge University Press.

Ricoeur, P. (1984, 1985, 1988) *Time and Narrative* 3 vols. Chicago Il: University of Chicago Press.

Roberts, B. (1999) 'Some thoughts on time perspectives and auto/biography', *Auto/Biography* VII(1/2), pp. 21–5.

Roberts, B. (2002) *Biographical Research*. Buckingham: Open University Press.

Roberts, B. (2004) 'Health Narratives, Time Perspectives and Self-Images', *Social Theory and Health* 2, pp. 170–83.

Roper, M. (1994) *Masculinity and the British Organizational Man since 1945*. Oxford: Oxford University Press.

Rorty, A. (1988) *Mind in Action*. Boston: Beacon Press.

Rose, G. (1999) 'Performing space' in Massey, D., Allen, J. and Sarre, P. (eds) *Human Geography Today*. Oxford: Polity, pp. 247–59.

Rose, G. (1993) *Feminism and Geography: The Limits of Geographical Knowledge*. Cambridge: Polity Press.

Rose, N. (1989) *Governing the Soul: The Shaping of the Private Self*. London: Free Association Books.

Rosener, J. (1990) 'Ways Women Lead'. *Harvard Business Review*, Nov–Dec, pp. 119–25.

Rosengren, W. and de Vault, S. (1963) 'The sociology of time and space on an obstetrical hospital' in Friedson, Eliot (ed.) *The Hospital in Modern Society*. New York: The Free Press, pp. 266–93.

Savage, J. (1987) *Nurses, Gender and Sexuality*. London: Heinemann.

Savage, M. and Witz, A. (1992) *Gender and Bureaucracy*. Oxford: Sociological Review Monograph.

Salvage, J. (1992) 'The new nursing: empowering patients, or empowering nurses?' in Robinson, J., Gray, A. and Elkan, R. (eds) *Policy Issues in Nursing*. Milton Keynes: Open University Press, pp. 9–23.

Schutz, A. (1971) *Collected Papers, I : The Problem of Social Reality*. M Natanson, The Hague: Martinus Nijhoff.

The Scotsman 11/04/05.

Seamon, D. (1979) *A Geography of the Lifeworld: movement, rest and encounter.* New York: St. Martins Press.

Segal, L. (1990) *Slow Motion: changing men, changing masculinities.* London: Virago.

Seidler, V. (1989) *Rediscovering Masculinity: reason, language and sexuality.* London: Routledge.

Sharpe, S. (1976) *Just Like a Girl: how girls learn to be women.* Harmondsworth: Penguin.

Sheller, M. and Urry, J. (2003) 'Mobile transformations of "public" and "private" life', *Theory, Culture and Society* 20(3), pp. 107–25.

Shilling, C. (1992) *The Body in Social Theory.* London: Sage.

Shotter, J. and Gergen, K. (1989) *Texts of Identity: Inquiries in Social Construction.* London: Sage.

Silva, E. (2002) 'Routine matters: narratives of everyday life in families' in Crow, Graham and Heath, Sue (eds) *Social Conceptions of Time.* Basingstoke: Palgrave, pp. 179–94.

Soja, E. (1996) *Thirdspace: journeys to Los Angeles and other real-and-imagined places.* Cambridge, MA: Blackwell.

Somers, M. and Gibson, G. (1994) 'Reclaiming the Epistemological "Other": Narrative and the Social Constitution of Identity' in C. Calhoun *Social Theory and the Politics of Identity.* Oxford: Blackwell.

Stanley, L. (1993) 'On Auto/Biography in Sociology', *Sociology* 27(1), pp. 41–52.

Starey, N. (2001) *What is Clinical Governance.* London: Hayward Medical Communications.

Steedman, C. (1992) *Past Tenses: Essays on writing, autobiography and history.* London: Rivers Oram Press.

Stein, L. (1967) 'The doctor-nurse game', *Archives of General Psychiatry* 16, pp. 699–703.

Strangleman, T. and Roberts, I. (1999) 'Looking through the window of opportunity: the cultural cleansing of workplace identity', *Sociology* 33(1), pp. 47–67.

Taylor, S. and Weatherell, M. (1999) 'A suitable time and place: speakers' use of "time" to do discursive work in narratives of nation and personal life', *Time and Society* 8(1), pp. 39–58.

Thomas, R. and Davies, A. (2002) 'Gender and new public management: reconstituting academic subjectivities', *Gender, Work and Organization* 9(4), pp. 372–97.

Thrift, N. (1996) *Spatial Formations.* Thousand Oaks, CA: Sage.

Thrift, N. (1997) 'The still point: resistance, expressive embodiment and dance' in Pile, S. and Keith, M. (eds) *Geographies of Resistance.* London: Routledge, pp. 124–51.

Thrift, N. (1999) 'Steps towards an ecology of place' in Massey, D., Allen, J. and Sarre, P. (eds) *Human Geography Today.* Oxford: Polity, pp. 295–322.

Thrift, N. (2003) 'Performance and ...', *Environment and Planning A* 35, pp. 2019–24.

Thrift, N. (2004) 'Intensities of feeling: towards a spatial politics of affect' *Geografiska Annaler* SLB, pp. 57–78.

Thrift, N. and Dewsbury, J-D. (2000) 'Dead geographies and how to make them live', *Environment and Planning D: Society and Space* 18, pp. 411–32.

Tuan, Y. (1977) *Space and Place: the perspectives of experience*. Minneapolis, MN: University of Minnesota Press.

Turkle, S. (1995) *Life on the Screen: identity in the age of the internet*. New York: Simon and Schuster.

Walby, S. and Greenwell, J. with Mackay, L. and Soothill, K. (1994) *Medicine and Nursing: professions in a changing health service*. London: Sage.

Wear, D. (1997) *Privilege in the Medical Academy: a feminist examines gender, race and power*. New York: Teachers College Press.

Weedon, C. (1997) *Feminist Practice and Poststructuralist Theory* (2nd edition). Oxford: Blackwell.

Whipp, R., Adam, B. and Sabelis, I. (eds) (2002) *Making Time: Time Management in Modern Organizations*. Oxford: Oxford University Press.

Whitehead, S. (2001) 'Woman as manager: a seductive ontology', *Gender, Work and Organization* 8(1), pp. 84–107.

Willis, P. (1977) *Learning to Labour: how working class kids get working class jobs*. Farnborough: Saxon House.

Witz, A., Warhurst, S. and Nickson, D. (2003) 'The labour of aesthetics and the aesthetics of organization', *Organization* 10(1), pp. 33–54.

Young, G. (1981) 'A woman in medicine: reflections from the inside' in Roberts, H. (ed.) *Women, Health and Reproduction*. London: RKP.

Zerubavel, E. (1979) *Patterns of Time in Hospital Life*. Chicago: University of Chicago Press.

Zimmeck, M. (1992) 'Marry in haste, repent at leisure: women, bureaucracy and at the post office' in Savage, M. and Witz, A. (eds) *Gender and Bureaucracy*. Oxford: Sociological Review Monograph.

Author Index

Subject Index